OLIVER GOLDSMITH
From a portrait by Sir Joshua Reynolds in the National Portrait Gallery

OLIVER GOLDSMITH

By

STEPHEN GWYNN

LONDON
Thornton Butterworth, Ltd.

First published 1935

CONTENTS

LIST OF ILLUSTRATIONS

PREFACE

EVERY student of Goldsmith must be first indebted to Forster, whose knowledge of the period is astonishing yet, to speak truth, a little bewildering. To borrow a phrase of Goldsmith's own, he has discharged such a load of learning on his subject that the essentials are sometimes buried. Cunningham's four-volume edition of the "Works" is also indispensable. These men, following Percy and Prior, supply nearly all the necessary material, but their work has been supplemented by Miss Balderstone's studies of Goldsmith's letters from the original manuscripts now in the British Museum. Dr. Kirkpatrick, Professor of the History of Medicine in Dublin University, has thrown useful light on Goldsmith's medical equipment by his paper in the "Irish Journal of Medical Science" for April, 1929—an offprint of which he kindly placed at my disposal.

Of the more recent biographers, Austin Dobson is chief; but in the very short "Life" by Richard Ashe King, which never had the attention it deserved, there will be found interpretation of Goldsmith by another Irishman familiar with the idiom of his mind. Local tradition is pleasantly available in the "Haunts of Oliver Goldsmith," by a Roman Catholic clergyman, the late Dean Kelly of Athlone.

For my illustrations, I owe to the National Portrait Gallery a version of the familiar Reynolds portrait of the poet, and also a Reynolds head of Johnson, by no means so generally known. The authorities of Westminster Abbey kindly provided a photograph of the memorial in Poets' Corner: it reveals much that is hard to see in the Abbey by most lights. Lord Astor has permitted me to reproduce the picture of the " Jessamy Bride," from a photograph supplied by Sir Robert Witt's invaluable collection. The print of Shuter and his companions in the original performance of " She Stoops to Conquer," comes from the Enthoven collection of theatrical records in the Victoria and Albert Museum : and here even more than elsewhere I owe gratitude for sympathetic assistance. The British Museum found me the Bunbury portrait which perhaps brings Goldsmith nearer to us than even the Reynolds—and not unkindly nearer. Foley's statue of the poet outside Trinity College has been specially photographed for this book ; and though it must be seen in its setting to be fully appreciated, I hope that even this suggestion may convey something of the character which a fine artist put into that formal monument. Mr. Clement Watson, of Youghal, kindly lent me the original design by his father, Mr. James Watson, for the memorial window in Forgney Church, a piece of work which deserves to be better known than it is, even in Goldsmith's own country.

I have also to thank the very old friend who has read the proofs of this book and given me the support of his taste and judgment.

CHAPTER I

THE SCHOOLBOY

OLIVER GOLDSMITH is the ugly duckling of English literature; and in one sense the analogy is complete. When the swan at last took the water in full plumage, all the world did homage; movement more stately and harmonious, whiteness more unsullied, had never been seen. But one thing, unhappily, limited the triumph. In the fairy-tale, based on sound natural history, there was metamorphosis; the duckling had vanished. In the world of literary life, when the swan paraded, there was the ugly duckling still splashing ungainly in its wake; and even admitted beauty was disparaged by this ignominious association. Indeed Goldsmith's reputation never began to receive full justice until the absurd little man himself was shovelled safely out of the way and replaced by an epitaph in Westminster Abbey. Someone asked Johnson once if Goldsmith had not been greatly assisted to success in literature by the prejudice of friends in his favour. "No, sir," the dictator retorted, "the prejudice of his friends was always against him."

It was a confession from the friend who could best afford to make it, since hardly any other but Johnson ever contributed in any way to the swan's avatar. But so long as Goldsmith lived—we have it plain enough on many evidences—even Johnson could never disengage his mind of its original prepossessions. It was always the ugly duckling that he bullied or was kind to, according as the humour took him.

As to the rest of the literary world, Horace Walpole tells us how once in a company where Garrick and Goldsmith were the chief notables, Garrick was detained at the theatre, and the hours till his arrival were spent, Walpole says, very tediously in the occupation of "playing off a butt" : the butt being already author of several admitted masterpieces.

For, if we are to rate men by achievement, hardly any writer of that century can be ranked so high as this one. "The Vicar of Wakefield" is at least as widely known as "Tom Jones," "Clarissa" or "Tristram Shandy"; outside Great Britain its fame has been more real. But in addition to this Goldsmith can show a comedy that holds the stage after nearly two centuries; no one else of that age but Sheridan can claim as much. Yet still we have not taken the poet into account; and, seriously, out of all the eighteenth century has to show, have any poems except Gray's "Elegy" meant so much to mankind as "The Traveller" and "The Deserted Village"? One must reckon also, among minor masterpieces it is true, but masterpieces none the less, his "Haunch of Venison" and "Retaliation." All this, too, accomplished within some fifteen years, alongside of uncountable journalism and hackwork. Why should such a man die, as he did die, feeling himself wretched, lonely and a failure?

Answer is given again and again through his writings, which abound in pathetic self-criticism. He suffered, and knew that he suffered, from faults which are in reality the excess of rare and lovely virtues, yet which in a hard world carry penalties much more surely than the ugliest vices. He knew they were faults, and directed satire against himself much more sharply than against any other creature; yet even in the satire there is always a note of condonation. In the last act, or the close of the chapter, some kind Christian arrives to deliver the over-generous or the over-credulous from the consequences of his folly. That is how it happens in the world of Goldsmith's making up. We find no such benignant intervention at the end of the actual story which this book is written to revive. He paid in full; he swallowed as much of life's bitterest potions as any man that ever wrote, and he died choked with the gall of them. Nobody can reach him now to offer the least penny-worth of reparation; but at least it is right that the profession which he adorned even in its lowest grades, and down to its very degradations, should pay tribute to his high example. When he wrote rapidly to order, the result was always something more than merely competent; when he wrote deliberately to express his inner thought, there was never a more meticulous artist, nor one who could so combine ease with finish. In short, no one ever did more to prove that a drudge of the publishers may be also a great writer. Yet it matters more perhaps that at a critical moment he established sharply the distinction between that which a professional writer may sell without dishonour, and that which he may not.

But, after all, the main purpose of this book is to follow a very lovable man through the ups and downs of a life in which his chief desire was to give pleasure—in his own phrase, to amuse. He found it a grim business, and his philosophy gradually took on graver airs than it set out with; but nothing, not even misery, ever altered his valiant faith that gentleness and cheerfulness marked the highest wisdom and the best courage.

Oddly enough, there is controversy both as to the exact time and place of his birth; and the only thing at all certain is that Johnson's epitaph has one of these details wrong; probably, it errs in both. Goldsmith was certainly born in 1728, not in 1731; however, this misstatement as to time occasions no jealous feeling. But place is serious. An inquirer will soon find that though nobody cares much whether his birthplace was in Westmeath, as the College register states, or in Longford, as Johnson places it, it is another matter when Roscommon on the other side of the Shannon sets up a claim. Connaughtmen and Leinstermen were never easily reconcilable. If reason had voice in such debates, I should say that Leinster might well afford to admit that he was actually born in Roscommon near

Elphin,[1] at Smith Hill, the home of his mother's father, the Rev. Oliver Jones. It would still be true that all that counted for most in Goldsmith's youth belonged to the fields and villages and little towns of Westmeath and Longford.

At all events, it is in county Longford that he is commemorated after a fashion which I believe to be unique : for surely no other English poet appears as the central figure in a stained-glass window. In the parish church of Forgney, near Ballymahon, where first Oliver Goldsmith's father, and then his brother, ministered so many years, this very attractive memorial to the poet was set up some forty years ago. The figure is no doubt represented as a clergyman : but it is the figure of Oliver Goldsmith.

The essential fact, however, is that he was Irish ; and a more serious handicap for a young man who must seek his fortune in England at that day could not be imagined. Those who wished to damage the greatest orator of his time always affected to call him " Mr. O'Bourke." Nobody needed to emphasize Goldsmith's place of origin ; the brogue which never left him did that more than sufficiently. But if we come to examine facts, these two great contemporaries, both Irish, both disadvantaged in life by being Irish, were Irish in different senses. Burke came of the great de Burgo stock, which of all the Norman houses became earliest and most completely Gaelicized ; and he had a historic sense about Ireland of which I find no trace in Goldsmith. And though Burke was a Protestant, his family had conformed to the pressure of the penal laws only a generation or two earlier. Goldsmith, on the other hand, was naturally by all his antecedents a part of the Anglo-Irish Protestant world. According to his biographer, Prior, one John Goldsmith held an office in Galway under Henry VIII ; and it must be remembered that the walled towns were much more English than the countryside about them. Dean Kelly of Athlone, in his little book on the " Early Haunts of Goldsmith," says that the descendants of this man were settled in Roscommon. One of them, Edward

---

[1] Pronounced El Finn.

INSCRIPTION

HE TRIED EACH ART, REPROVED EACH DULL DELAY,
ALLURED TO BRIGHTER WORLDS, HE LED THE WAY

Original Design for the Memorial Window in Forgney Parish
Church

By courtesy of Messrs. Watson, Youghal

Goldsmith, was Dean of Elphin in 1700, a generation before the poet was born. His son Isaac came to be Dean of Cloyne in county Cork, but was occasionally seen at his native place and comes into the story of Oliver.

In short, though they were not the richer class of gentry, some of the Goldsmiths owned land, and younger sons going into the Church had influence enough to attain modest preferment—bishoprics being then reserved for English importations. All of them, following the usage of the time, went for their university education to Trinity College, after some local schooling.

Goldsmith's grandfather was a landowner living at his house of Ballyoughter, near the little town of Elphin in Roscommon. It was no very spacious abode, but in the seventeenth century Irish gentry had not begun to spend so largely on stone and mortar as their successors did. Charles Goldsmith, second son of this well-to-do farm-house, went to school in Elphin, where he was instructed by the Rev. Oliver Jones, and then to Trinity, where he was an acquaintance of the poet Parnell and also of Swift's friend, the eccentric and talented Thomas Sheridan. Charles Goldsmith, like these two friends of his, took orders, and by 1718 at the age of twenty-eight he was curate of Forgney in county Longford, and husband of the daughter of his old schoolmaster, Mr. Oliver Jones. Forgney had no parsonage, so the curate lived at a cottage in Pallas near the little town of Ballymahon, and farmed some fields about it to eke out the modest forty pounds a year of his stipend. Yet even this was not misery; many an Irish curate even in my memory has been no better provided with a hundred and fifty instead of forty: and many a one also has brought up a large family on it. Within ten years Charles Goldsmith had five children, of whom Oliver, born in 1728, was the latest. Three more followed, and six out of the eight grew up—an unusually high proportion for that century. It was a healthy stock.

But they had every chance. Two years after Oliver's birth, Mr. Green, rector of Kilkenny West, died. It was by his influence that Charles Goldsmith got the curacy of Forgney, which was only a few miles distant from Kilkenny West, and the forty pounds a year had been increased by occasional fees for taking Mr. Green's duty. Now, on the death of this useful relation, Charles Goldsmith succeeded to the rectory and moved from his cottage at Pallas to a very decent house and farm at Lissoy. His income rose to nearly two hundred a year, which would be worth from six to eight hundred nowadays; and how pleasantly and safely he and his lived on it, may be known by anyone who reads the " Vicar of Wakefield." This is the countryside where Oliver Goldsmith grew up; here he had the only home he ever knew; his notions of the country life, which he always praised at the expense of every and any town, were formed in this peaceable prosperous region. Yet in his pictures of country life it would be hard to find any detail that is distinctively Irish; and more than one, as has been pointed out—the nightingale's song, for instance—is unknown in Ireland. But Goldsmith was never in the least degree what we should call either a realist or a romantic. When he spoke, as he spoke constantly, of " copying nature " he meant that a writer's true business was to seek after simplicity; to be easily intelligible to the greatest number. Search after the characteristic trait, which stamps individuality upon a landscape, and gives the local colour, was never his concern; if he described a country scene, he chose the most general features; and it so chanced that the Irish countryside in which he grew up was one of those the least unlike to England. It had its turf bogs, here and there; it had the great river Shannon spreading out above Athlone into a wide lake, Lough Ree, with flats yearly flooded, the haunt of wild fowl—most unlike to anything in the English home counties; but all this, in writing for his larger public, for the English world in which he lived, he instinctively dropped out, and dwelt only on the common familiar sights of a peaceful district where all was under tillage, remote from city influences. Dublin, seventy miles away, was at the end of two days' ride; the nearest approach to what could be called town life was in Athlone, where fortified barracks held the main crossing from Leinster into Connaught. But in that second quarter of the eighteenth century, Ireland had in it no stir of revolt; it is doubtful whether a garrison was maintained then in Athlone; the place grew quietly into a market town, with mills working. But above all, six long Irish miles separated Athlone from Lissoy. Anyone who grew up (like the writer of these lines) in old-fashioned Irish country knows that, even for those who had horse and carriage available, about three such miles was the radius limiting social intercourse. Mr. Charles Goldsmith had horses in his stable, but they were for the farm as well as for the road; they took the family to church on Sunday; but at other times the younger members of it depended on their legs for the range of their amusements; and doubtless they saw the little town of Ballymahon, three miles off, a score of times, for once they set eyes on Athlone. I speak the language of the country when I call it a town; for Ballymahon to-day is no more than a row of houses stretching perhaps three hundred yards along each side of the main road from Athlone to Longford. But as such towns or villages go in Ireland, it has an air of solidity and importance signifying that it ministers to a well-cultivated prosperous district; and probably many of its existing houses must have been familiar to Mr. Charles Goldsmith's ugly good-natured idle second son.

Oliver cannot have remembered anything earlier than the surroundings of Lissoy, for he was hardly out of long clothes when he came there. It seems pretty well established that, although in 1728 his father's home was at Pallas, the actual place of his birth was Smith Hill near Elphin, where Mrs. Jones, widow of the Rev. Oliver Jones, Charles Goldsmith's tutor and father-in-law, was still living. In 1807 the house was occupied by a certain Mr. Lloyd, whose grandmother was sister to Oliver Goldsmith's mother. According to him, Mrs. Goldsmith, when her confinement approached, went to lie in at her

mother's home. There is even a tradition that, she having
ridden pillion over from Pallas, the journey was too much
for her, and the birth came prematurely, at seven months.
I take leave to doubt, however, whether so notable a house-
keeper would have been willing to leave her family two
months before she expected the child. But as to the fact
of Goldsmith's birth at Smith Hill, Mr. Lloyd's statement
that his own mother, Mrs. Goldsmith's niece, often showed
him the very room and the spot where the bed had stood,
seems conclusive. On the other hand, he reports on the
same authority that the child was nursed and reared there
and got the early part of his education at the town of
Elphin. It is quite possible that the child may have been
left there ; three children already were tightly packed in the
cottage at Pallas, and the fact that Oliver was called after
his grandfather Oliver Jones, the original owner of Smith
Hill, is some corroboration of this story. But undoubtedly,
when promotion to Kilkenny West brought this family
into roomier quarters at Lissoy, Oliver was fetched home,
and his eldest sister, Mrs. Hodson, says in the notes which
she wrote for Bishop Percy, his biographer, that he was
his mother's favourite child.

This is easily believable, for Mrs. Hodson tells us also,
what has not been sufficiently noted, that he was born
" very unexpectedly " after an interval of seven years. An
eldest girl came first, but died young ; then Catherine,
born in 1721 ; then Henry and Jane, twins. All this early
brood were able to look after themselves to some extent
by 1728 ; what is more, they were well able to help their
mother with the care of the new baby. Under those conditions in a kindly affectionate household a child is sure to
be petted and noticed ; and, according to Mrs. Hodson,
this was a queer, ugly, engaging little imp : " subject to
particular humours for the most part, but when in gay
spirits, no one ever so agreeable as he." No doubt there
is memory of a later date mixed in here ; but she is clear
about one thing : " When he could scarcely write legibly,
he was always scribbling verse."

On the other hand, his first teacher was ready to testify that there "never was so dull a boy." This was Mrs. Elizabeth Delap, schoolmistress of Lissoy, who lived to boast twenty years after Goldsmith's death that she had taught a famous man his letters. He seemed, she said, "impenetrably stupid." [1] At six, however, he passed into other hands, and was entrusted to the schoolmaster Tom Byrne, who sat for one of the best-known portraits in all literature. Yet it must be reproduced here :

> A man severe he was, and stern to view,
> I knew him well, and every truant knew ;
> Well had the boding tremblers learn'd to trace
> The day's disasters in his morning face ;
> Full well they laughed with counterfeited glee
> At all his jokes, for many a joke had he ;
> Full well the busy whisper circling round,
> Convey'd the dismal tidings when he frown'd :
> Yet he was kind, or if severe in aught,
> The love he bore to learning was in fault ;
> The village all declar'd how much he knew,
> 'Twas certain he could write, and cypher too ;
> Lands he could measure, terms and tides presage,
> And even the story ran—that he could gauge :
> In arguing too, the parson own'd his skill,
> For even though vanquish'd, he could argue still ;
> While words of learned length, and thundering sound,
> Amaz'd the gazing rustics rang'd around ;
> And still they gaz'd, and still the wonder grew,
> That one small head could carry all he knew.

Once more it has to be observed that Goldsmith's knack of happy generalization (which gives us here at least one line that everyone knows by heart) sacrifices picturesque local colour. Tom Byrne was a soldier who had seen the

[1] "Because I had found it hard to attend to anything less interesting than my thoughts, I was difficult to teach. Several of my uncles and aunts had tried to teach me to read, and because they could not, and because I was much older than children who read easily, had come to think, as I have learnt since, that I had not all my faculties."—W. B. Yeats, "Reveries."

wars under Marlborough ; he had even been quartermaster-sergeant under Peterborough in Spain, and naturally had great stories to tell of his adventures. But that was by no means all : he was a native Irish speaker and had other stories of banshees, and of the Little People and of the Rapparee chiefs, like Galloping Hogan who guided Sarsfield's raid to destroy William's artillery on the road to Limerick, and Baldearg O'Donnell from whose red birthmark the " hidden Ireland " expected a deliverer.

How much of all this the rector's small boy took in and remembered, we cannot know ; but it has not always been understood that from his childhood he was in contact with an Ireland conscious of the Gaelic past ; and, as will be seen, till he left the country his associations were close with a student of this lore. His sister, however, thought that another aspect of Byrne's teaching had influenced him most—not the Irish stories, but the descriptions of foreign countries. They gave Oliver " that wandering and unsettled turn " which marked him through life.

But before he was done with the village school a misfortune befel him which made him fitter than ever for his predestined part of the Ugly Duckling. Smallpox caught him and left him dreadfully disfigured. Then at eight years old, he was sent off to a more ambitious school at Elphin, about a mile from Ballyoughter, the family place which had come to be owned by his father's elder brother, John Goldsmith. Here he lived during his Elphin schooldays, so that county Roscommon can claim a good share in him.

By all accounts, his schooldays were not agreeable. Mr. Griffin found his pupil as dull as Mrs. Delap had done ; and the marks of smallpox on his face fitted him more than ever to be a butt. There is a story that a visitor at his uncle's house asked the child, " Why, Noll, are you never going to get handsome again ? " and was answered, " I mean to get better, sir, when you do." If this is not apocryphal, Goldsmith was quicker with his tongue at ten than at forty. But his sister preserves another legend of the same time which tells how a dance was going on at

Ballyoughter when between two sets Oliver took the floor
alone for a hornpipe; and the fiddler, seeing the comic
little figure, cried out " Æsop." Thereupon the boy turned
on him and on the spur of the moment declaimed :

> " Heralds ! Proclaim aloud, all saying
> See Æsop dancing and his Monkey playing."

No wonder that at Ballyoughter they " thought him a
prodigy," as Mrs. Hodson writes. He can only have been
ten years old at most then; for when he was eleven his
father moved him to a more reputed school at Athlone,
where he must have been a boarder for a year or so, till
another change took him to the school at Edgeworthstown
kept by the Rev. Patrick Hughes.

This gentleman, who had Oliver under his charge for
three years, appears to have recognized something very
different from dullness; he made a friend of the awkward
ugly boy, and taught him to take pleasure in Ovid and
Horace, Livy and Tacitus. It seems also that here Oliver
began to be to the fore when any fun was going; for though
small, he was stocky and active and a great player of hand-
ball—then the national sport.

But there is nothing in his writings to suggest that he
looked back on any of his schooldays with pleasure. All
the happiness of his youth centred round his home. There
was a ball alley also in Ballymahon, and " Master Noll," as
the countryside knew him, was one of its regular fre-
quenters, long remembered by the court-keeper, who liked
to recall also one special occasion when Master Noll and a
band raided a neighbouring orchard. Yet if the " Vicar of
Wakefield " is a sure guide, Mr. Charles Goldsmith's household was its own best company, and Lissoy a centre of easy
hospitality. As was invariable in Ireland, the domestics
were part of the family : long after, when Oliver Goldsmith,
writing to his brother-in-law, looked back on all this, the old
maid, Peggy Golden, is at the centre of the picture :

If I go to the opera where Signora Columba pours out all
the mazes of melody; I sit and sigh for Lissoy fireside, and

Johnny Armstrong's Last Good Night from Peggy Golden. If I climb Hampstead Hill than where nature never exhibited a more magnificent prospect, I confess it fine; but then I had rather be placed on the little mount before Lissoy gate, and there take in, to me, the most pleasing horizon in nature.

It was no very wide horizon; Ireland has its mountains along the coast, and from the fertile districts of the western Midlands, little can be seen but gentle ups and downs— hardly anything much higher than the Hampstead which gave him the comparison. But its resources of beauty and pleasure afforded all that he cared about.

Lissoy parsonage, standing a couple of hundred yards back from the main road between Athlone and Ballymahon, faced down a drive between high hedges; the eight windows of its front gave a measure of its modest proportions, and no doubt the family was tight-packed according to modern notions. But no doubt also, according to Irish usage, room was found there, time and again, for casual guests.

About the house was the farm, and at haymaking or harvest everyone gave a hand; the rector himself had a general direction of operations. It is written in the " Advertisement " to " The Vicar of Wakefield " that " The hero of this piece unites in himself the three greatest characters upon earth; he is a priest, an husbandman, and the father of a family." One may be allowed to conjecture from the likeness so lovingly traced in the book that Mr. Charles Goldsmith was not notable as a farmer. His ministrations in the priesthood have left no mark, except indeed —and it is no small result—that his son, after long years struggling and starving or squandering as chance decided, in the worst slums of Bohemia, kept his highest and tenderest respect for the priestly office. But, as a father, Mr. Goldsmith has importance in the history of literature, and perhaps far beyond it. He made Oliver Goldsmith what he was; again and again Oliver stresses that responsibility for good, and also for what was at the very least unfortunate. Yet when the full and final portrait came to be drawn, the

son, knowing well, and having already expressed the knowledge, that his father's teaching had sent him out disabled
even for common prosperity, withheld in the picture every
touch of adverse criticism. He indicates indeed with a
smiling irony the failures in his hero's judgment and the
little foibles of vanity by which the vicar is misled; but
essentially he sets out his belief that goodness has a power
like sunlight to cleanse and invigorate and heal. In a word,
the rake and spendthrift, the rolling stone, the shiftless hack
of letters, so often abjectly indebted, preaches once and for
all his father's sermon; and it goes out into all lands and
is read in all languages by people not knowing they are
preached to.

Whatever the family life was, the father was at the centre
of it; mixed up in all their work and all their play, but
morning and evening asserting his priesthood in the household; drawing the moral from all that happened, teaching
both by example and precept the duty of being happy, of
imparting happiness, and of remedying pain.

There is, however, another side to this picture and it is set
out with an irony in which tenderness does not conceal censure. In his " Letters from a Citizen of the World " Goldsmith brings an imaginary traveller from China acquainted
with a certain " Man in Black "; the Man in Black tells his
story, which is indeed the author's:

My father, the younger son of a good family, was possessed
of a small living in the church. His education was above his
fortune, and his generosity greater than his education. Poor
as he was, he had his flatterers still poorer than himself; for
every dinner he gave them, they returned equivalent in praise;
and this was all he wanted. The same ambition that actuates
a monarch at the head of an army, influenced my father at the
head of his table; he told the story of the ivy-tree, and that was
laughed at; he repeated the jest of the two scholars and one
pair of breeches, and the company laughed at that; but the
story of Taffy and the sedan-chair was sure to set the table in
a roar. Thus his pleasure increased in proportion to the pleasure
he gave; he loved all the world, and he fancied all the world
loved him.

As his fortune was but small, he lived up to the very extent of it; he had no intention of leaving his children money, for that was dross; he was resolved that they should have learning; for learning, he used to observe, was better than silver or gold. For this purpose he undertook to instruct us himself; and took as much pains to form our morals, as to improve our understanding. We were told that universal benevolence was what first cemented society; we were taught to consider all the wants of mankind as our own; to regard the human face divine with affection and esteem; he wound us up to be mere machines of pity, and rendered us incapable of withstanding the slightest impulse made either by real or fictitious distress; in a word, we were perfectly instructed in the art of giving away thousands, before we were taught the more necessary qualifications of getting a farthing. I cannot avoid imagining that, thus refined by his lessons out of all my suspicion, and divested of even all the little cunning which nature had given me, I resembled, upon my first entrance into the busy and insidious world, one of those gladiators who were exposed without armour in the amphitheatres of Rome. My father, however, who had only seen the world on one side, seemed to triumph in my superior discernment; though my whole stock of wisdom consisted in being able to talk like himself upon subjects that once were useful, because they were then topics of the busy world; but that now were utterly useless, because connected with the busy world no longer.

In this retrospect, from which I shall have to quote again, Goldsmith plainly identifies his " first entrance into the busy and insidious world " with new experiences gathered or imposed when he became a student at Dublin University. For what the son suffered there—it is the only word—his father was in more ways than one responsible. Yet in fairness to the Reverend Charles Goldsmith it should be plainly set out that a great part of the student's troubles arose from characteristics that cannot be attributed to his father's teaching. He was ambitious; that was no fault; some instinct, rather than reason, prompted him to believe that in him lay a power to achieve real distinction; and heaven knows he made good that conviction through labour without limit,

But the worst handicap on his ambition was his vanity. Vaguely, he hoped to be a great man, to win fame ; as he went on, the object grew clearer ; and the fame which in the end he won was the fame which as a boy he would most have desired, that of a writer who can reach the reason through the heart. Yet this was terribly far off. As a collegian, for the moment, at every moment, he wanted desperately to cut a dash, and wanted it all the more because he knew painfully how ill he was equipped for the part. Ugly and awkward, he never forgot his ugliness and his awkwardness ; but the same strength of will which enabled him in spite of dreadful difficulties to bring to full lustre his shining qualities, here led him to a lifetime of petty defects. In one sense he was always striving to do what no one else could do so well ; in another, always attempting what any fool with a little money and good looks could do better. Naturally the defeats came daily from the first moment ; victories lay far ahead ; and even when the world knew that he was famous, his friends knew, and he knew, that he was absurd.

Nobody knew it so well as himself. In the opening sentence of his first paper, " The Bee," here is the avowal :

There is not perhaps a more whimsically dismal figure in nature than a man of real modesty who assumes an air of impudence.

Whether it be true or legendary, there is a story which suggests that Goldsmith as a growing boy was even more ridiculous than Goldsmith as a grown man. He himself, assuming the story to be true, had to modify and make more credible the adventure on which " She Stoops to Conquer " is based.

The story is that, leaving Lissoy for his last term under Mr. Hughes at Edgworthstown, on a borrowed horse and with a guinea in his pocket, he took a wrong turning and by nightfall found himself at Ardagh on the way to Longford. What was a shy boy of sixteen to do ? According to Goldsmith's philosophy, shyness may disguise itself in insolence, and the boy, meeting a passer-by, asked with great airs to be directed to " the best house in the town." Tradition, for the story lacks no detail, says that the passer-by was Mr. Cornelius Kelly, the local fencing master. (How the place came to own a fencing master is not easily explainable.) At all events Mr. Kelly had a sense of a joke and guessed at the situation ; for there was no likelihood of any choice of hostelries in Ardagh, and, bent on his joke, he volunteered to show the way, and stopping before an imposing gateway, said, " There, sir, you have the best house in town." The boy, still determined not to be taken for a novice, rode in, threw the bridle to a groom, and demanded supper. Mr. Featherston the squire, like Mr. Cornelius Kelly, had a sense of fun, and humoured the young gentleman up to the top of his bent. No doubt in the course of the evening he found out who his visitor was, and according to some authorities had been at college with the boy's father. At all events in the morning, when Oliver called for the reckoning, he was let know in a good-natured way that he had made a fool of himself, and saved his guinea at the expense of his gloriousness.

It may all be true : it was reported as true by the grandson of that Mr. Featherston ; it is still taken for gospel by the best authority on Goldsmith in the town of Athlone. But if it was true, what lessons life was likely to have in store for a young gentleman in whom the inferiority complex had such fantastic manifestations !

CHAPTER II

THE COLLEGIAN

ACCORDING to Mrs. Hodson, Charles Goldsmith had not originally intended to send his second boy to the university. His hopes were centred on Henry, who was clever and industrious, and who, being several years older than Oliver, was already at Trinity before Oliver had gone to Mr. Patrick Hughes. " The liberal education which he was then bestowing upon his eldest son bearing hard upon so small an income, he could only propose to bring Oliver up to some mercantile pursuit," we are told. But Mrs. Goldsmith protested. Three other boys had been added in succession in her nursery, but she still had a special interest in the one who had the chance to be the family pet. Henry, doing all that was expected of him, won a scholarship, and the omens were encouraging. But Henry, doing also the unexpected, was " unfortunately married at the age of nineteen which confined him to a curacy, and prevented his rising to preferment in the Church." So says Mrs. Hodson. But, if we can argue from the " Vicar," Mr. Goldsmith took the news like a Christian philosopher and welcomed the married son to a share in the duties of his parish, without altering the plans which at his wife's wish had been made for Oliver—who about this same time must have been sent to be fitted by Mr. Hughes for a university career.

Dublin University differs from Oxford and Cambridge in being a university of one college only ; but the discipline and ordinances of that college were modelled closely on the Trinity at Cambridge. As at Oxford and Cambridge, and as at no other European university, undergraduates lived within the academic precincts, each man having his own set of rooms (or, at Dublin, sharing them with a chum), waited on by a servant, and dining in the common hall, attended by the college servants. Theoretically, this implied a common standard of living ; in practice, through many generations it has been found to work out very agreeably for the well-to-do—much less so for the poor. Swift fifty years before Goldsmith resented his lack of money : it made his undergraduate days unhappy. But Swift learnt in them that fierce economy which ultimately, despite all his careful benevolence, grew into a miserly obsession. Moreover, Swift never really felt the pinch. Johnson at Oxford is more closely a case in point, and as all know, he suffered. " I was miserably poor," he said, " and I thought to fight my way by my literature and by wit ; so I disregarded all power and all authority." But Johnson, even as an undergraduate with feet bursting out through worn shoes, was a natural leader ; he was still the big lad who made his fellows carry him to school when he chose. Yet even he was unhappy. The young are less compassionate than their elders to the ill equipped, and the Latin tag which says that poverty's bitterest drop is that it makes men a laughing-stock holds even truer in the well-to-do British university life than elsewhere.

Oliver Goldsmith had a double dose of that sour potion. He was not only poor, he was ugly and insignificant, and though his gifts were far beyond what anyone suspected, they were not, like Johnson's, of a kind to assert themselves. To " fight his way by his literature and his wit " would have been wholly beyond his powers; for he was never equipped for intellectual battle, as Johnson was ; besides, there was nothing combative in his nature. He wanted greatly to be liked and to be admired, but just as a good companion, a leader in fun. Instead of that, from the first his fellow-undergraduates, if they noticed him at all, noticed him only to laugh at him. Scott tells of Leyden, the peasant lad who swept all before him at Edinburgh, that those who laughed at the ragged scholar never laughed twice :

Leyden was formidably pugnacious. Goldsmith had not that quality. He was no molly-coddle or mere bookworm; low-sized, but stout and active, it is on record that he won a competition for throwing the hammer at Ballymahon, a feat which implies not only strength but the knack of making strength tell. In our days he would have found his chance on the football field, and possibly, as a useful forward or half-back, achieved a reputation that would have salved all sores. But fisticuffs would never have been in his line. Shyness, and he was painfully shy, is a complete bar to pugnacity. A great many who probably never struck a man in anger found their place in the War as stretcher-bearers. One such I saw dead on the edge of a newly blown-up mine crater, fallen over the body of a comrade whose wound he was coolly bandaging when another shell splinter took him. Such courage as that, no one who has made himself familiar with Goldsmith's nature will doubt that he held within him. But it needs a different quality of endurance to make any man, but especially a young man, impervious to ridicule and to contempt. Goldsmith was drenched with both, by his equals and by his superiors.

The position in which he was placed at the university was painfully different from that of either Swift or Johnson. They were undergraduates short of money in varying degrees; but otherwise they were undergraduates like any-one else. Goldsmith's father had no doubt been a frugal student; his eldest son, Henry Goldsmith, whose college course had been completed before Oliver entered, probably was able to keep up a tolerable appearance, since his father in those years was living at Lissoy and had his full stipend. At all events, Henry was, as the father had been, an ordinary commoner. But before Oliver's turn came, the rector of Kilkenny West had been obliged to strain his resources to breaking-point. After the custom usual with those country clergy who had some tincture of scholarship, he had supple-mented his income by acting as tutor to a wealthy neigh-bour's son; and this young gentleman, Daniel Hodson, whose home was at St. John's on the Roscommon shores of

Lough Ree, presumably became an inmate of Lissoy, as the distance is too long for daily coming and going. So situated, he fell in love with his tutor's eldest daughter Catherine, a girl of three-and-twenty, and the pair got married, presumably by what Swift would have called a couple-beggar. Naturally enough Mr. Hodson of St. John's was angry and did not spare reproaches ; for the young woman must have been at least a year or two older than her lover. Remembering the " Vicar of Wakefield," I cannot but think that the rector's wife aided and abetted a love affair which was likely to give her daughter advancement to circles of the squirearchy ; neither can one doubt that the Reverend Charles Goldsmith was easily convicted of having lacked prudence. Country gentlemen in the eighteenth century, in Ireland and out of it, were not mealy-mouthed ; undoubtedly, Mr. Goldsmith had to hear words that stung him ; and even if he did not admit their justice, he proceeded to refute the charges by a practical demonstration. Having taught his children that " money was but dross, and a good name better than riches," he undertook to provide his daughter with a dowry much more suited to her new position than to his means, and entered into a bond to pay four hundred pounds—twice his total income—to Mr. Daniel Hodson of St. John's in county Roscommon. The sum was raised by a mortgage of his tithes and of the lease of his rented land. Mr. Goldsmith has been blamed for sacrificing his family's interests to a false pride ; but he was in a position of trust as regarded the young man ; his daughter had certainly behaved wrongly, possibly with her mother's connivance ; in the face of such a situation he did what any gentleman would have wished to do. Right or wrong, he would have been less the Vicar of Wakefield had he not done it. But it came hard on Oliver, then ready to go to the university. He was told that instead of entering as his father and his brother had done, he must read for a sizarship, which, if he won it, would reduce his fees to a minimum ; but in exchange he must render certain services. He must sweep the courts of a morning, carry dishes from the kitchen to the fellows' dining-table and wait in hall on the fellows. His position in the university would be marked by the red cap which servants wore, and by a sleeveless gown.

Oliver Goldsmith had opportunity to know from his brother what this meant and he showed what he thought of it by refusing for months to sit for the examination. He said he would sooner be apprenticed to a trade, as smith or carpenter, which was the only alternative—and heaven knows whether he would not have been happier in it. He was, however, talked over by his uncle Contarine, the widowed husband of Charles Goldsmith's sister, then rector of Oran near Roscommon. Oliver had always been welcome at the rector's house—welcome to his cousin Jane Contarine, and to the rector himself, a scholar who in his college days had made friends with Berkeley. Contarine had been a sizar ; and it is said that this argument prevailed. He alone of Oliver Goldsmith's kindred seems to have realized that the lad had in him something out of the common, and he knew how to represent the chances of university life in a way that would appeal to ambition.

At all events on June 11, 1745, Oliver was admitted sizar —last on a list of eight. The special knack of passing examinations was almost as foreign to him as that of quickness in retort. Undisturbed, in full possession of himself, he was one of the swiftest and easiest of workers : but no one was more readily flurried and disconcerted. In the college life, under such conditions as were imposed on him, experience only too fully confirmed his instinct. We have two utterances of his to judge by ; both written about ten years after he had left the university. The first is in his earliest published book, " An Enquiry into the Present State of Polite Learning in Europe," and it concludes the chapter which deals with universities :

Surely pride itself has dictated to the fellows of our colleges the absurd passion of being attended at meals, and on other public occasions, by those poor men who, willing to be scholars, come in upon some charitable foundation. It implies a contradiction, for men to be at once learning the *liberal* arts and at the same time treated as *slaves*; at once studying freedom and practising servitude.

The other is in a letter to his brother, then " rich on forty pounds a year," who proposed sending his son to Trinity.

If he be assiduous, and divested of strong passions (for passions in youth always lead to pleasure) he may do very well in your college; for it must be owned that the industrious poor have good encouragement there, perhaps better than in any other in Europe. But if he has ambition, strong passions, and an exquisite sensibility of contempt, do not send him there, unless you have no trade for him except your own.

He knew himself, and in these touches sets out the qualities which had made undergraduate life bitter to him : and there is nowhere any trace of a feeling that the ordeal had been profitable discipline. It is necessary to be clear what he resented. Probably half of the educated Frenchmen alive to-day have swept a barrack-room, and doubtless disliked the job; but it did not wound their sensibility. It was part of a soldier's duty and no man despised himself for being a soldier. For that matter, one of the finest aristocrats that ever lived, Ignatius Loyola, thought it desirable that every member of his chosen Company should have the experience of what are called menial duties; and there is no Jesuit who has not cleaned grates and washed out passages during his noviciate. Presumably the Founder's intention was to convey that every form of work is honourable in itself. No disparagement was inflicted because every novice, like every soldier, performed the same kind of duties. It was otherwise at the university. The sizar was an undergraduate on his way to the same university degree as the rest, but definitely marked with a menial badge and charged with menial duties. Oliver Goldsmith was specially unfitted to accept such a position. The lad knew nothing of the world, but he had been inspired with a love of philosophy; " and the first maxim among philosophers is that merit only makes distinction." Ten years later he wrote

34

these words in that passage of his " Enquiry " which asks why greater liberties should be given in the university to the son of the nobility than to those of a private man. At fifteen his faith would have been more ardent and his surprise the greater.

Evidently enough he could have made his life much easier by acceptance of facts, and slipped through college unnoticed. But his nature did not admit of this. He was ambitious and he had strong passions (" which in youth," as he said, " always lead to pleasure ") ; he was not content to be unobserved, and he wanted his share of whatever was going.

He was, of course, not without acquaintances. A lad called Beatty from the same school at Edgworthstown entered along with him, also as a sizar, and the two chummed in the front square at the top of a staircase near the library. Goldsmith scratched his name on the window-pane and it was still there in 1877 when Forster wrote. The block of buildings was renewed in 1880, and the pane, by that time a treasure, was placed in the Library where it is preserved.

Edward Mills, another contemporary, was a cousin ; so also in some degree was Robert Bryanton from Ballymahon, with whom he formed a friendship that lasted even some years after they had completely lost sight of each other. Others whom he encountered later in Grub Street may have seen something of the sizar ; but it is clear that Edmund Burke, for instance, did not, though he and one or two others who prospered in life agreed that they remembered him. Goldsmith was indeed enough of an oddity to be remembered. The college course had no attractions for this student. Formal logic had seemed futile to him, as it did to Swift, another master of clear statement. Mathematics bulked very large in it and he had no turn for mathematics. This was unfortunate as they were a speciality of the tutor under whom he had been entered and whose duty it was to take a special interest in his progress. The Reverend Theaker Wilder had been selected for the charge because he was a son of the house of Castle Wilder in county

Longford, only a few miles from Lissoy, and doubtless he promised Mr. Goldsmith that he would do his best. He had remarkable ability, for he was first Donegal Professor of Mathematics and later Regius Professor of Greek. But the man was a bully, physically and intellectually. When a passing cabman had flicked him accidentally with his whip, he jumped on to the box, and knocked the unlucky driver to the ground. At lectures it was his habit to gird at the slow-witted or slow of speech, and Oliver Goldsmith was both when it came to mathematics. To do Mr. Wilder justice, Goldsmith does not seem to have tried very hard. At all events, unfavourable reports went back to his father. Perhaps it increased Goldsmith's tenderness in retrospect that he knew how much disappointment he had caused to a very good man. But in 1760, when he wrote his " History of the Man in Black," the mood of criticism was uppermost. I have quoted already the passage which characterizes his father : here now is that which deals with the son, as collegian. It implies, and perhaps this is not strictly exact to the facts, that Mr. Goldsmith expected a good deal from his second son :

The first opportunity he had of finding his expectations disappointed, was at the very middling figure I made in the university : he had flattered himself that he should soon see me rising into the foremost rank in literary reputation, but was mortified to find me utterly unnoticed and unknown. His disappointment might have been partly ascribed to his having overrated my talents, and partly to my dislike of mathematical reasonings, at a time when my imagination and memory, yet unsatisfied, were more eager after new objects than desirous of reasoning upon those I knew. This did not, however, please my tutors, who observed indeed, that I was a little dull ; but at the same time allowed, that I seemed to be very good-natured, and had no harm in me.

Here for the first time comes a phrase (having the Irish accent on it strongly) which runs like a refrain through the phases of this " history." There " was no harm in him." Poverty combined with ambition did not make Goldsmith defiant as it made Johnson; he was never "mad and violent." The pain arising from "an exquisite sensibility to contempt" did not transform itself to rage: rather the result was despondency, a sense of defeat, from which his sweet and healthy nature recovered, thanks to its great "knack at hoping." But as often as this talent set him on his feet, the world knocked him down.

It was a knock-down blow when his father died, early in 1747, for that meant the break-up of his home. Chances of supply were worse than ever, for Henry Goldsmith with a curate's pay instead of a rector's was now the family's only support. Uncle Contarine, it seems, provided most of the money needed—perhaps he provided all that was, strictly speaking, necessary. But Oliver Goldsmith was never by any stretch of language to be called a good economist: he had all the ordinary temptations to part with money which he should have kept; but he had also one so unusual as to be extraordinary. Nearly all of us can without an effort see a beggar starving and yet retain our overcoats: Goldsmith lacked this self-protecting instinct, and he did not even stop at overcoats. Once his cousin Edward Mills went to look for him in his rooms and heard a voice calling for assistance: Goldsmith had got into the ticking of a mattress and was so wedged in that he could not escape. The reason for this was that the night before he saw a woman and her five children starving with the cold and carried out his blankets to cover them.

Such eccentricities of conduct will always be laughed at among the young, but even the young have some kind of respect for thoroughgoing sanctity. The trouble was that Oliver Goldsmith did not want to be a saint. He differed from other young men in a compassion that had the driving force of desire; but he had the ordinary desires also, and no wish to repress them. In addition to the common penalties for lateness at class or absence from it, which his idleness or laziness incurred, he came twice under severe censure from the authorities. The first occasion was not one to leave him with painful memories: on the contrary, he risked expulsion by taking part in a notable row, more or less of the town-and-gown character. College precincts were regarded as an Alsatia, a sanctuary against arrest; but bailiffs in defiance of this tradition slipped in and seized a student for debt. Thereupon the "college boys" (as Dublin still calls them) sallied forth, hunted for the offender, stripped him, carried him through the streets to the college pump and ducked him. If things had gone no further, it is probable that the university authorities would have been lenient; they might have even turned a Nelson eye; for the tradition had value for dons as well as undergraduates. But in all such enterprises the difficulty is to stop, and triumphant youth had the brilliant idea of a general jail delivery. They tried to rush the "Black Dog" prison; sympathetic townsmen joined the attack; but the warders opened fire, lives were lost and the whole affair turned out serious. Five students who had been ringleaders were struck off the college rolls; five others were publicly admonished for having aided and abetted disorder: and Oliver was one of the latter.

Surely such a censure must have gratified the young man who always wanted to distinguish himself and so seldom brought it off; at all events, in later life it must often have been a consolation for Oliver Goldsmith to remember that he once helped duck a bailiff. I cannot at all agree with Forster when he writes—"More galled by formal university admonition than by Wilder's insults, and anxious to wipe out a disgrace that seemed not undeserved, Goldsmith tried in the next month for a scholarship." On the contrary, I believe that it put heart into him to think that he had cut a dash; and in spite of his defect in mathematics, which put him out of the running for scholarship, he got on to the list of exhibitioners; not gloriously it is true, seventeenth out of nineteen awards, but still he got there; and thirty shillings, say five pounds of our money, were put into his unaccustomed hand.

Now, I do not suggest for a moment that Goldsmith, not yet out of his teens, stopped to reflect. But he was already, like Moses in the "Vicar of Wakefield," a philosopher, and he would no doubt, if challenged, have produced excellent reasons to show that such a sum was too small to be regarded as capital and should properly be used for the promotion of happiness. The way to do this was (speaking in current language) to throw a party; and he threw one. Subconsciously also, no doubt, it was another chance to cut a dash. But in fairness to all concerned, and especially to one who always figures as the villain of the piece, facts must be set out. He could have given a spree (Trinity never talked of "wines") and asked in Bob Bryanston, Ned Mills, Ned Purdon and so forth; and there would have been no more about it, unless possibly some of these young gentlemen had been noisy in the quad and made a bonfire. But it was not to be an undergraduate party. There were to be ladies. Now the discipline of Dublin University austerely forbade anything of the kind. If a woman were known to have been in an undergraduate's rooms, the presumption was that she was " an idle woman." Curran's answer, a generation or two later, when he also came under censure of the authorities, that he had never kept any woman idle in his rooms, sufficiently illustrates the meaning. Goldsmith did not get the chance to make any answer. Presumably some of the college porters reported to Mr. Wilder, who like all tutors was responsible for discipline in the precincts; and this gentleman, bursting suddenly into the middle of the party, knocked his pupil down, while the rest fled in confusion.

It is possible that Mr. Wilder thought this the best way to deal with the offence. He had a right to get Goldsmith sent down, and may have thought that this would deprive a poor student of his hope to qualify for a profession by taking a degree; so he knocked him down instead. Nevertheless, it was the action of a dirty bully, who used his physical superiority with assured impunity; for if brought before any available tribunal, the unlucky exhibitioner would have stood no more chance than would the careless cabman. Wilder was hitting a weaker man who had no possible redress ; and in both cases he inflicted and wished to inflict a physical humiliation. We know nothing about the cabman, but we know what the effect was on Oliver Goldsmith. The disgrace, dashed on him in his rare moment of triumph, was more than he could stand up to. Next morning he sold the few books he possessed for what they could fetch, and so mustered a few shillings. His one idea was flight. Biographers have fixed attention too strongly on a presumed wish to get away from the scene of his disgrace ; but they forget that in all probability the unlucky youth expected that he would not get the chance to stay on. Hotfoot on the jail riot came this new breach of discipline : and Goldsmith may well have thought that he would rather take his sentence in absence than attend on the Board to be expelled. But if he ran home, the prospect was no pleasanter. His family, his mother with whom he had no very strong sympathy, and the brother whom he loved, had every reason to reproach him for throwing away chances of education, procured for him at great sacrifice of their narrow means. And there was this story about the idle women which in such a household would shock and give pain. He hated to see pain. He would rather vanish : and now for the first time we find him moving instinctively, in obedience to a vagrant instinct, towards unknown lands and skies. Already America began to hold out a vague promise to the young in Ireland, and already Cork harbour was the way to America. He thought of Cork.

But though Oliver Goldsmith came to be in time stouthearted after his own fashion, time had to do the toughening ; and at best, practical resolution was never one of his qualities. Instead of acting, he hung about Dublin—if the truth were known, probably seeking consolation from some of the women who were at the disastrous party ; and so the few shillings became fewer till only one was left. So at least he remembered the story and told it in the friendliest company he ever knew, at the house of Joshua Reynolds. For three days he tramped it, and made his first experience of actual hunger—so sharp that (he had eaten nothing for twenty-four hours) when he found a wake going on in a cottage by the road, he entered and begged. Food was no plentier then than a hundred years later, when bread was a great rarity in Irish cottages : potatoes probably were not so universal : but a girl gave him a handful of grey peas and he remembered it as the most delicious meal he ever tasted.

Then he gave up Cork and headed back for Lissoy. He sent word from a neighbouring town to his brother, who met him on the road, took him home, and finally brought him back to Trinity, where peace was made with the authorities. He had to spend two years more in Trinity before, on February 27, 1749, he graduated Bachelor of Arts.

To judge by what we know, experience had taught him nothing, except how to make shift by borrowing and by the pawnshop. But at some time in his college career, he had opened, or scratched, the mine which lay within him. Ballad-singers did an active trade in the Ireland of that day ; it is not quite dead yet ; but the ballad in those days took the place of the news-sheet. Swift used it to supplement his pamphleteering ; and the Reindeer shop in Mountrath Street kept a store from which the singers renewed their repertory. Goldsmith wrote ballads and got five shillings apiece for them. He got also the pleasure of hearing them sung in the streets.

As to academic culture proper, I cannot think that Goldsmith acquired much at Trinity that was of value to him. There is a passage in one of the essays often included in his works (though Cunningham, I think rightly, prints it in the category of the wrongly attributed) which has at least a bearing on his case, as well as on that of Swift, which the essayist has been discussing.

" When a youth appears dull of apprehension, and seems to derive no advantage from study and instruction, the tutor must exercise his sagacity in discovering whether the soil be absolutely barren, or sown with seed repugnant to its nature, or of such a quality as requires repeated culture and length of time to set its juices into fermentation."

This is true whoever wrote it; and in Swift's case, St. John Ashe, a tutor, at least exercised sagacity so far as to make friends with his pupil. Goldsmith had nothing of the kind to look back on, and his "Enquiry into the State of Polite Learning" is severe on the use to which universities in Great Britain apply their "magnificent endowments." These "at best more frequently enrich the prudent than reward the ingenious." There follows a judgment which is also an admission:

A lad whose passions are not strong enough in youth to mislead him from that path of science which his tutors, and not his inclinations, have chalked out, by four or five years perseverance may probably obtain every advantage and honour his college can bestow. I forget whether the simile has been used before but I would compare the man whose youth has been thus passed in the tranquillity of dispassionate prudence, to liquors which never ferment, and consequently continue always muddy. Passions may raise a commotion in the youthful breast, but they disturb only to refine it. However this may be, mean talents are often rewarded in colleges with an easy subsistence. The candidates for preferments of this kind often regard their admission as a patent for future indolence; so that a life begun in studious labour, is often continued in luxurious laziness.

One cannot mistake the autobiographic note in such a passage; and it means plainly that Goldsmith attributes his lack of success at college to lack of application caused by his "passions." And to that word one must give the very simplest meaning.

In all Goldsmith's writings there is very little about what nowadays we call "sex": there is no analysis of the particular attraction exercised by a particular man on a particular woman, or by a particular woman on a particular man. In a sense he is no more interested in this phenomenon than in the daily recurrence of hunger; but certainly this is not because Goldsmith underrated the urgency of these desires. In his "Animated Nature" he sets it down quite simply as a fact of nature that adult man is more ruled by this appetite than by all others.

While the animal is yet forming, hunger excites it to that supply which is necessary for its growth; when it is completely formed, a different appetite takes place that unites it to an animate existence. These two desires *take up the whole attention at different periods*, but are very seldom found to prevail strongly together in the same age; one pleasure ever serving to repress the other : and if we find a person of full age placing a principal part of his happiness in the nature and quality of his food, we have strong reason to suspect, that with respect to his other appetites he still retains a part of the imbecility of his childhood.

So far as we can judge, Goldsmith always gave this appetite whatever satisfaction he could procure ; and, as he writes in " The Life of Nash " : " A mind strongly turned to pleasure is first seen at the university; there the youth first finds himself freed from the restraint of tutors, and being treated by his friends in some measure as a man, assumes the passions and desires of riper age, and discovers in the boy what are likely to be the affections of his maturity." In days " of his maturity," when he was famous, his friends counted him " a rake," and some were hilarious about it. Johnson, who admitted it, deplored it, but said that he thought he was making an effort to improve.

It is an odd thing to say about one of the most delicate and refined of English writers, but I think that Goldsmith came back from the university (which was, more than it would have been at Oxford or Cambridge, a first experience of city life) coarsened. He had let himself go more than is usual for young men coming as he came from a devout household, with generations of clean-living people behind them, because he had, in his own words, " strong passions." Yet there is more than that to take into account. The best preservative of clean living for such a young man as Goldsmith was is to idealize some young woman. He was sentimentally starved, because lack of money, lack of looks, lack of address, lack of everything that can make up for lack of money, decided that no young woman whom he could idealize would waste attention on him. Except for his cousin Jenny Contarine, several years his elder, no female creature of his own degree appears to have been decently civil to him. He cannot have been a pleasing lad in his teens; but the passions were there and they got their way, in such squalid contacts as were possible. The result was to exaggerate in the grown man what had been the boy's shyness. So at least I construe this piece of psychology in "She Stoops to Conquer" when the hero Marlow is misled into an adventure like that which befel Goldsmith on his way to school. Hastings the confidant is rating him for lack of "a requisite share of assurance."

Mar. But tell me, George, where could I have learned that assurance you talk of? My life has been chiefly spent in a college or an inn, in seclusion from that lovely part of the creation that chiefly teach men confidence. I don't know that I was ever familiarly acquainted with a single modest woman—except my mother—— But among females of another class, you know——

Hast. Ay, among them you are impudent enough of all conscience.

Mar. They are of *us*, you know.

Hast. But in the company of women of reputation I never saw such an idiot, such a trembler; you look for all the word as if you wanted an opportunity of stealing out of the room.

Mar. Why, man, that's because I *do* want to steal out of the room. Faith, I have often formed a resolution to break the ice, and rattle away at any rate. But I don't know how, a single glance from a pair of fine eyes has totally overset my resolution. An impudent fellow may counterfeit modesty; but I'll be hanged if a modest man can ever counterfeit impudence.

Hast. If you could but say half the fine things to them that I have heard you lavish upon the barmaid of an inn, or even a college bed-maker——

Mar. Why, George, I can't say fine things to them; they freeze, they petrify me. They may talk of a comet, or a burning mountain, or some such bagatelle; but to me, a modest woman, drest out in all her finery, is the most tremendous object of the whole creation.

44

At all events, nowhere in Goldsmith's writings is there any trace that he knew modest women except as fussy housewives or marriageable young persons whose sole thought was to get married. There is not even the trace of a tradition that he was ever in love with one. Steele was not a discreet or decorous liver, but he had learnt enough to write of a woman : " To love her is a liberal education." That is the education which Goldsmith lacked : yet no man was by nature ever more fitted to receive it. For through all the sordid contagion of such a life as he led, his nature retained its essential cleanness. It is not by avoidance of such topics as Fielding handled with a lusty grossness and Sterne with smirking awareness that he remains the most modest of authors. He too handles them, but with a delicacy that is hard to match.

On the common theme of seduction and its consequences he never dwelt voluptuously, like the virtuous Richardson ; and his well-known verses expressed his sincere feeling. No woman, I am sure, ever " stooped to folly " for his pleasure ; and his conscience with all its country-parson antecedents would scarcely have accepted a *liaison*, such as even Wordsworth formed. In short, he had enough sentiment to prevent him from giving to his strong passions any but the most unsentimental satisfaction ; and the price he paid was heavy. No woman ever helped him to find himself ; no woman ever lightened his hardships by sharing them, even for a while.

CHAPTER III

IN SEARCH OF A PROFESSION

AFTER having taken his degree, early in 1749, Goldsmith came home to his mother who was now living in a cottage in the village of Ballymahon. Lissoy had been taken over by her daughter's husband, Daniel Hodson : Henry Goldsmith was at Forgney in his father's old cure. Thus the family, though scattered, were still in the same neighbourhood and Uncle Contarine was a day's ride away at Emlaghmore.

All these folk were of opinion that Oliver had best follow the family tradition and seek a living by taking orders. From his own point of view, this had the advantage of postponing work for a couple of years, since he could not be ordained till he was three-and-twenty ; and so he settled down to enjoy himself in what was probably the happiest period of his life. He certainly thought so when, just turned of thirty, he first began to express himself freely as an essayist. In the second number of " The Bee " he wrote :

When I reflect on the unambitious retirement in which I passed the earlier part of my life in the country, I cannot avoid feeling some pain in thinking that those happy days are never to return. In that retreat all nature seemed capable of affording pleasure ; I then made no refinements on happiness, but could be pleased with the most awkward efforts of rustic mirth ; thought cross-purposes the highest stretch of human wit, and questions and commands the most rational amusement for spending the evening. Happy could so charming an illusion still continue ! I find that age and knowledge only contribute to sour our dispositions. My present enjoyments may be more refined, but they are infinitely less pleasing. The pleasure Garrick gives can no way compare to that I had received from a country wag, who imitated a Quaker's sermon. The music of Mattei is dissonance to what I felt when our old dairy-maid sung me into tears with Johnny Armstrong's Last Good Night, or the Cruelty of Barbara Allen.

Of course, it was not all so idyllic. There was a convenient public-house kept by one George Conway in Ballymahon; it had not attained to the ostentation (rare in Ireland) of a sign, but the landlord had ambitions that way. "Has George Conway put up a sign yet?" Oliver writes from Edinburgh to his friend Bob Bryanton, one of the circle which regularly assembled at Conway's and played whist ("I preside in fancy over your cards and am displeased with your bad play when the rubber goes against you, though not with all that agony of soul as when I was once your partner"). There was no doubt a good deal of drinking: Bryanton drank too much. Goldsmith happily did not; at this point an element of balance in him prevented him from going completely under in the mire through which he had to plough. But cards were to be one of the usual means by which he rid himself of money when he got it.

Here at Ballymahon, however, one may be sure that the stakes were not serious. All were poor together; and there was no one to look down on anybody else. Goldsmith came to the front because he had more talent for fun than any of them; he could sing a good song, tell a good story, and nothing checked his high animal spirits. Very likely there was not as yet much wit mingled with the fun; but he learnt to have confidence in himself as a fun-maker, and to be sure, in spite of fashion, what sort of fun would please. Those years were the best medicine his mind ever had and he turned back to them again and again with painful longing.

Of course, what he looked back on was not only the tavern; we can learn from his "Animated Nature" a good deal as to how this country-bred youth spent his time. Evidently he lived in the middle of a farming community without taking the least interest in farming, because, when

translating Buffon's observations on the cow, he sets
down without raising an eyelid Buffon's surprising statement that cattle shed their horns at the third year. But
when it comes to the otter's habits, we find a very different
Goldsmith : he refuses to accept the tradition recorded in
" British Zoology," according to which the otter's holt is
always entered from under water and is ventilated at top
by a narrow blowhole.

I have never observed any such contrivance. The otter
generally brings forth her young under the hollow banks of
some river or lake upon a bed of rushes, flags or such weeds
as the place affords. But the young are always found at the
edge of the water, and if under the protection of the dam she
teaches them instantly to plunge among the rushes and weeds
that fringe the shore.

Disputing against Buffon also, who says that they breed
in March, Goldsmith affirms that they " are never found
with us until the latter end of summer and I have frequently
as a boy discovered their retreats and pursued them at that
season."

Another note concerning bats sets down that he found
five young ones in a hole together—whether of one brood
or not. In short, if he was not to be called a field naturalist,
he had a country-bred eye and had noticed, in solitary explor-
ations, much that many of the country lads never see. Fish
had no interest for him ; he was never an angler ; but he
knew well all the bird life which haunted the Inny, a considerable river running from Ballymahon to Lough Ree,
and all the great stretches of reed-swamp about the Shannon.
There is no evidence that he ever shot or rode to hounds,
though in most of Ireland anyone who rides well and understands horseflesh can generally get a mount. But certainly
he was often out on foot with harriers or greyhounds ; a
long passage devoted to the hare shows close familiarity, as
even a few sentences of it will show :

The first doubling a hare makes is generally a key to all its
future attempts of that kind, the latter being exactly like the

former. A buck hare is known by its choosing to run upon hard highways, feeding further from the woodsides and making its doublings of a greater compass than the female. The male, having made a turn or two about its form, frequently leads the hounds four or six miles on a stretch; but the female keeps close by some coverts, turns, crosses and winds away among the bushes like a rabbit and seldom runs directly forward.

Much wisdom of this kind was no doubt exchanged of an evening at George Conway's after the young men had followed the course. Nobody who assisted then could have guessed that there was growing up in one of those " vacant minds " an image of pity that should take shape in the central passage of one of the best-known English poems.

So the months slipped by, and the time came when Goldsmith had to present himself as a candidate for ordination in the diocese of Elphin. It seems that his friends were surprised when he was rejected : but the Bishop did a service to the Church and to the candidate. It is plain enough from all accounts, but chiefly from his own, that Goldsmith simply drifted towards a profession for which he had not the least vocation, because it was the readiest way to get a living out of the university degree—his only visible asset. Why he was rejected does not matter : it may be, as some have asserted, that his tutor Wilder, a native of that diocese, sent in an unfavourable report ; in any case, some reference must have been made to the College authorities and they could hardly have been enthusiastic as to his fitness. A picturesque legend says that he presented himself in scarlet breeches and that this was his undoing. One might easily construct a theory to show that this was done deliberately, either to court rejection or to make a last use of liberty ; but unfortunately I cannot believe that the elders who pushed the youth on to this examination would not have seen him suitably turned out. At all events two things are certain ; first, that his family were disappointed and angry, finding themselves with Oliver still on their hands, and secondly, that Oliver himself was by no means sorry to fail and had made no effort to succeed. When he is writing the story of the " Man in Black," he simplifies matters by representing it as a deliberate rejection :

In order to settle in life my friends advised (for they always advise when they begin to despise us), they advised me, I say, to go into orders.

To be obliged to wear a long wig when I liked a short one, or a black coat when I generally dressed in brown, I thought was such a restraint upon my liberty, that I absolutely rejected the proposal. A priest in England is not the same mortified creature with a bonze in China : with us, not he that fasts best, but eats best, is reckoned the best liver; yet I rejected a life of luxury, indolence, and ease, from no other consideration but that boyish one of dress. So that my friends were now perfectly satisfied I was undone ; and yet they thought it a pity for one who had not then the least harm in him, and was so very good-natured.

The recurring refrain " had not the least harm in me " tells us what rang in Oliver Goldsmith's ears as he thought back to those days when reproaches of his indolence or feebleness were met even by indulgent friends with excuses of this kind, which have more contempt in them than sympathy. But when he tells us that what he disliked was the colour of the coat, we must not take him literally. Swift who went into Orders deliberately at a mature age accepted fully the consequences of his decision. But it was part of Swift's view that a clergyman should be allowed to dress like any other gentleman ; he disliked and resented being stamped as of a class apart—and of a class which the world somewhat looked down on. Goldsmith, whose conception of the priestly duties differed greatly from Swift's, agreed in this dislike, but I think from a different cause. A parson wore a black coat as a sign of sobriety, as a reminder that he must preach by example. Now Goldsmith with a pen in hand was never unwilling to write what might do good, but he had not the least desire to set an example of strict living. What he wanted of all things was to show his neighbours how to be a jolly fellow—and to be admired for it.

It may be well to consider his own stylized and symbolic account of what came next in the series of failures. This is how he represents it through the story of the "Man in Black":

Poverty naturally begets dependence, and I was admitted as flatterer to a great man. At first I was surprised, that the situation of a flatterer at a great man's table could be thought disagreeable; there was no great trouble in listening attentively when his lordship spoke, and laughing when he looked round for applause. This even good manners might have obliged me to perform. I found, however, too soon, that his lordship was a greater dunce than myself; and from that very moment my power of flattery was at an end. I now rather aimed at setting him right, than at receiving his absurdities with submission: to flatter those we do not know is an easy task; but to flatter our intimate acquaintances, all whose foibles are strongly in our eye, is drudgery insupportable. Every time I now opened my lips in praise, my falsehood went to my conscience; his lordship soon perceived me to be unfit for service; I was therefore discharged; my patron at the same time being graciously pleased to observe, that he believed I was tolerably good-natured, and had not the least harm in me.

From this point on, correspondence between the actual story and the imaginary one ceases to exist in detail: and even here already there is considerable divergence. What happened was that Mr. Contarine, always kind, looked about him and found a certain Mr. Flynn in county Roscommon wanting a tutor for his family. Goldsmith stayed there a year and came back with thirty pounds in his pocket, mounted on a decent horse of his own; he only left because he had quarrelled with the family after accusing one of them of cheating at cards. Taking the two accounts together, I cannot feel that Goldsmith's lovers need have any grudge against Mr. Flynn; and I think there might have been no quarrel if this young man had not seen his way to gratify the roving impulse.

Having reported himself at home, and doubtless been told that he had no right to quarrel with good bread and butter, he and the horse and the thirty pounds set out for

Cork—with the same vague notion of America. At the end of six weeks he was back again with empty pockets, riding a beast to which he had given the descriptive name of Fiddleback.

About this episode there is abundant detail, resting at least in part on his own authority. We know the story that he told his mother, as it was remembered by his sister. We have also a complete literary version of the saga, taking the form of a letter to his mother, and for several reasons this must be given in full.

MY DEAR MOTHER,—If you will sit down and calmly listen to what I say, you shall be fully resolved in every one of those many questions you have asked me. I went to Cork and converted my horse, which you prize so much higher than Fiddleback, into cash, took my passage in a ship bound for America, and, at the same time, paid the captain for my freight and all the other expenses of my voyage. But it so happened that the wind did not answer for three weeks ; and you know, mother, that I could not command the elements. My misfortune was that when the wind served I happened to be with a party in the country, and my friend the captain never inquired after me, but set sail with as much indifference as if I had been on board. The remainder of my time I employed in the city and its environs, viewing everything curious ; and you know no one can starve while he has money in his pocket.

Reduced, however, to my last two guineas, I began to think of my dear mother and friends whom I had left behind me, and so bought that generous beast Fiddleback, and made adieu to Cork with only five shillings in my pocket. This to be sure was but a scanty allowance for man and horse towards a journey of above a hundred miles ; but I did not despair, for I knew I must find friends on the road.

I recollected particularly an old and faithful acquaintance I made at college, who had often and earnestly pressed me to spend a summer with him, and he lived but eight miles from Cork. This circumstance of vicinity he would expatiate on to me with peculiar emphasis. " We shall," says he, " enjoy the delights of both city and country, and you shall command my stable and my purse."

However, upon the way I met a poor woman all in tears,

who told me her husband had been arrested for a debt he was not able to pay, and that his eight children must now starve, bereaved as they were of his industry, which had been their only support. I thought myself at home, being not far from my good friend's house, and therefore parted with a moiety of all my store; and pray, mother, ought I not to have given her the other half-crown, for what she got would be of little use to her?—However I soon arrived at the mansion of my affectionate friend, guarded by the vigilance of a huge mastiff, who flew at me, and would have torn me to pieces but for the assistance of a woman, whose countenance was not less grim than that of the dog; yet she with great humanity relieved me from the jaws of this Cerberus, and was prevailed on to carry up my name to her master.

Without suffering me to wait long, my old friend, who was then recovering from a severe fit of sickness, came down in his night-cap, night-gown, and slippers, and embraced me with the most cordial welcome, showed me in, and, after giving me a history of his indisposition, assured me that he considered himself peculiarly fortunate in having under his roof the man he most loved on earth, and whose stay with him must, above all things, contribute to his perfect recovery. I now repented sorely I had not given the poor woman the other half-crown, as I thought all my bills of humanity would be punctually answered by this worthy man. I revealed to him my whole soul; I opened to him all my distresses; and freely owned that I had but one half-crown in my pocket; but that now, like a ship after weathering out the storm, I considered myself secure in a safe and hospitable harbour. He made no answer, but walked about the room rubbing his hands as one in deep study. This I imputed to the sympathetic feelings of a tender heart, which increased my esteem for him, and as that increased, I gave the most favourable interpretation to his silence. I construed it into delicacy of sentiment, as if he dreaded to wound my pride by expressing his commiseration in words, leaving his generous conduct to speak for itself.

It now approached six o'clock in the evening, and as I had eaten no breakfast, and as my spirits were raised, my appetite for dinner grew uncommonly keen. At length the old woman came into the room with two plates, one spoon, and a dirty cloth which she laid upon the table. This appearance, without in-

creasing my spirits, did not diminish my appetite. My protec-
tress soon returned with a small bowl of sago, a small porringer
of sour milk, a loaf of stale brown bread and the heel of an old
cheese all over crawling with mites. My friend apologized that
his illness obliged him to live on slops, and that better fare was not
in the house ; observing, at the same time, that a milk diet was
certainly the most healthful ; and at eight o'clock he again
recommended a regular life, declaring that for his part he would
lie down with the lamb and rise with the lark. My hunger was at
this time so exceedingly sharp that I wished for another slice
of the loaf, but was obliged to go to bed without even that
refreshment.

This lenten entertainment I had received made me resolve
to depart as soon as possible ; accordingly next morning, when
I spoke of going, he did not oppose my resolution ; he rather
commended my design, adding some very sage counsel upon the
occasion. "To be sure," said he, "the longer you stay from
your mother the more you will grieve her and your other friends ;
and possibly they are already afflicted at hearing of this foolish
expedition you have made." Notwithstanding all this, and
without any hope of softening such a sordid heart, I again
renewed the tale of my distress, and asking "how he thought I
could travel above a hundred miles upon one half-crown?" I
begged to borrow a single guinea, which I assured him should
be repaid with thanks. "And you know, sir," said I, "it is
no more than I have often done for you." To which he firmly
answered, "Why, look you, Mr. Goldsmith, that is neither here
nor there. I have paid you all you ever lent me, and this sickness
of mine has left me bare of cash. But I have bethought myself
of a conveyance for you ; sell your horse and I will furnish you
with a much better one to ride on." I readily grasped at his
proposal, and begged to see the nag ; on which he led me to
his bedchamber, and from under the bed he pulled out a stout
oak stick. "Here he is," said he ; "take this in your hand, and
it will carry you to your mother's with more safety than such a
horse as you ride." I was in doubt, when I got it into my hand,
whether I should not, in the first place, apply it to his pate ;
but a rap at the street-door made the wretch fly to it, and when
I returned to the parlour, he introduced me, as if nothing of
the kind had happened, to the gentleman who entered, as Mr.
Goldsmith, his most ingenious and worthy friend, of whom he

had so often heard him speak with rapture. I could scarcely compose myself; and must have betrayed indignation in my mien to the stranger, who was a counsellor at law in the neighbourhood, a man of engaging aspect and polite address.

After spending an hour, he asked my friend and me to dine with him at his house. This I declined at first, as I wished to have no further communication with my hospitable friend; but at the solicitation of both I at last consented, determined as I was by two motives; one, that I was prejudiced in favour of the looks and manner of the counsellor: and the other, that I stood in need of a comfortable dinner. And there indeed I found everything I could wish, abundance without profusion, and elegance without affectation. In the evening, when my old friend, who had eaten very plentifully at his neighbour's table, but talked again of lying down with the lamb, made a motion to me for retiring, our generous host requested I should take a bed with him, upon which I plainly told my old friend that he might go home and take care of the horse he had given me, but that I should never re-enter his doors. He went away with a laugh, leaving me to add this to the other little things the counsellor already knew of his plausible neighbour.

And now, my dear mother, I found sufficient to reconcile me to all my follies; for here I spent three whole days. The counsellor had two sweet girls to his daughters, who played enchantingly on the harpsichord; and yet it was but a melancholy pleasure I felt the first time I heard them; for that being the first time also that either of them had touched the instrument since their mother's death, I saw the tears in silence trickle down their father's cheeks. I every day endeavoured to go away, but every day was pressed and obliged to stay. On my going, the counsellor offered me his purse, with a horse and servant to convey me home; but the latter I declined, and only took a guinea to bear my necessary expenses on the road.

Now first of all, nobody should be asked to credit a word of this, beyond believing that Goldsmith got so far as Cork, which I think probable though not proven. At all events he got somewhere where he found company, masculine or feminine, which helped him to make away with the guineas and the well-fed horse. Returning home, the fact which mattered, which had to be faced, was that he was back on his mother's hands, and back penniless. It seems clear that he thought it the best way to make a joke of the ugly situation, and invented a story which might set them all arguing and in the end perhaps laughing. However foolish he may have been, he had not the kind of foolishness which could expect such a story to be swallowed; and his sister's account makes it plain that he did not seriously pretend it to be true.

The story was therefore in the first place a piece of impertinence, and, if one is to be severe, of heartless impertinence, remembering what his follies had inflicted on his family. But spendthrift young men are often heartless, and Goldsmith never at any time in his life attained to a reasonable sense of responsibility where money was concerned. What is more, it was impertinence to his mother.—We have to recognize that whatever she deserved, Mrs. Goldsmith inspired no tenderness in her famous son. "The Vicar of Wakefield" is perhaps the most moving tribute ever paid by a writer to his father; but Mrs. Primrose is a character regarded at the best with indulgence. Mrs. Hodson in her account says that Oliver had been her favourite child, but it seems clear that this special affection did not stand the strain which he put on it. As I read it, when he faced homeward, he made ready to meet, not such a rebuke as the Vicar of Wakefield might have delivered, but a scolding the like of which had often rung about his ears. When the scene was over, or when it had been renewed for the third or fourth time—when he had been catechized by the Hodsons and by his younger brothers and sisters about the amazing yarn—I think that he decided at least to show his family how clever a fellow he was, and wrote out the story as an exercise in wit. He would certainly not have the least intention of showing it to his mother, but possibly might hope to avert the wrath of Mr. Contarine in his vicarage. Possibly, again, it had no other purpose than to furnish an evening's entertainment in George Conway's tap-room; and there is at least this to be said for it: Goldsmith did not deceive himself when he thought that his composition might be good enough to earn indulgence.

It is the first piece of his writing that we have of any kind ; and I agree with Miss Balderstone that it is not like the rest of his Letters, which she has edited with so much scholarship.   But I cannot agree that it is not like what Goldsmith wrote in his Essays.   If it is a forgery, it must be among the most skilful in existence.   It has the personal inflexion which Goldsmith manages to impart to a sentence that seems academic ; nothing could be more characteristic than the first paragraph : " You know, mother, that I could not command the elements. . . .   You know no one can starve while he has money in his pocket."   How he conveys, without appearing to depart from the most matter-of-fact tone, laughter bubbling inside !   And if anyone compares the end of the second paragraph with that already quoted from " The Man in Black," precisely the same cadence will be noted and the same irony—though without its note of bitterness.

In short, Oliver Goldsmith, by the time he was four-and-twenty, several years before he thought of literature as a livelihood, had made himself master of a prose style which, simple as it is, is too personal to be called a model.   Unlike Addison or Steele, far unlike Johnson, but resembling Swift in this—and in nothing else—he gave to English prose a peculiar accent which is his own and no one else's.   It is possible that this early *jeu d'esprit*—for it is nothing else— may have served its purpose.   It may have convinced Contarine, the one relative who persistently had hopes of the young man, that there was in him a real talent to develop.

At all events, though there was estrangement between Oliver and his mother, Contarine's house, as well as Henry Goldsmith's, remained open to the prodigal.   Not only that, but he was equipped again for a new venture.   The Church having failed, law was thought of ; and they started Oliver off for London to enter himself at the Inns of Court, having fifty pounds in his pocket.

They might as well have put water in a sieve.   The intending or intended barrister met an acquaintance in Dublin who set him down at a card-table ; and very soon he had to write back to his uncle that this money too had gone. We have not that letter. If we had, it would certainly have resembled others that have been preserved, in its abject contrition. But Contarine took him in again to the shelter of a household which deserves to be remembered with special kindness wherever literature is loved.

Lyric poets have often learnt to utter their feeling with perfection before the first flush of exaltation is gone ; whereas in prose, apprenticeship to literature is often, though not always, a long one : Congreve, half a century earlier than Goldsmith, was doing some of his best work at an age when Goldsmith perhaps never thought seriously of writing. Yet Goldsmith like Congreve had, as has been seen, an early and easy mastery of the medium he must use. He could say what he had to say : the question was what had he to say ? In the last resort what gives Oliver Goldsmith his place among the really great writers is not only nor chiefly his exquisite style. It is his philosophy of life ; and that philosophy had to be a philosophy of the heart. A young man may succeed as Congreve did by glittering epigrams ; but that was not where Goldsmith's gift lay. He was never to discover new veins of thought, but rather to rediscover old ones and give them fresh life. Such a philosophy, if it is to carry conviction, must be distilled from experience ; it must be both thought out and felt out ; thought must have been tested and proven before it can attain the sincerity which pierces. Life had to show Oliver Goldsmith its most ungracious aspect, it had to drench him with bitterness and squalor, before he could be what he became, able to set aside these appearances of reality, and affirm his belief that kindness, gentleness, compassion and gaiety were the lasting truths in life. It is not believable that he would have come through the ordeal but that he had deep in him the knowledge of people who were kind, gentle and compassionate, and were at the same time, like the Vicar, " great lovers of happy faces." Nothing that the world could do to him—even with the assistance of his own follies—ever blotted out the memory of his father, his brother and this other relation, who had been, and who deserved to be, the friend of Berkeley.

Contarine was not just the ordinary country parson, full of the affairs of his parish and his tithes. He was a scholar, and one of those who in that day showed an interest in the native language and literature of Ireland. Charles O'Conor of Belanagare, a leader in these studies, though a Catholic, was often at his parsonage: Contarine's nephew had a chance to acquire knowledge which was not common in that age. Unfortunately, there is no indication that Oliver Goldsmith interested himself either in the native language or the history of Ireland. Dean Kelly and some others have suggested that he knew Gaelic, and he must certainly have heard it spoken, if only by his schoolmaster Tom Byrne. But when we find him noting (in No. iv of " The Bee ") as instances of popular traditions " handed down among the vulgar, . . . the bravery of Johnny Armstrong among the English, of Kaul Dereg among the Irish and Creichton among the Scots," an Irish reader at once gets a check : for Kaul Dereg is the barbarous transformation of " Ball Dearg " (Red Spot) O'Donnell, a famous guerrilla leader in the Williamite wars. It is not possible that anyone who knew even a little of the language should have so distorted the well-known name.

On the other hand, there is the Essay on " Carolan, the Last Irish Bard," contributed to the " British Magazine " in 1760, at the beginning of Goldsmith's literary career. Yet it has no ring of first-hand knowledge. If Goldsmith ever met Carolan, who died in 1738, it can only have been when he was a child. But the bard had certainly been at Contarine's house, and what we read here in Goldsmith no doubt represents Contarine's account of his poems. When he is writing about " several parts of that country " where the " ancient language, dress, furniture and superstitions " were still to be found unchanged, he writes only from report : his acquaintance with Ireland does not go beyond the midlands, where English was at least everywhere understood. But he had certainly acquired familiarity with the best of Carolan's art; for music speaks a common tongue. In the next stage of his wanderings we find him confidently recognizing a distinction between the Highland music, which was "Irish" and sung to "Irish words" and the Lowland, English in character, and sung to English.

The next stage was decided at Contarine's house by the remark of a visitor. Dean Goldsmith of Cloyne, coming to visit his relations in county Longford, saw Oliver and having heard him talk, suggested that he had the makings of a good medical man. Once more the question of funds had to be faced, and Mr. Contarine had to provide them. But Mrs. Hodson tells us what promises were exacted, and what entreaties were necessary, before Oliver Goldsmith was once more sent on his way with a few pounds in his pocket. This time, however, he did not miscarry, but reached Edinburgh safely; and here began a period of his education in which he really learnt something from his teachers. He had good words for Edinburgh. It is worth while to set down the conclusions which this "wandering scholar" reached concerning a subject of which he had a singularly wide experience. At the close of his "Essay on the Present State of Polite Learning in Europe," he wrote:

The universities of Europe may be divided into three classes. Those upon the old scholastic establishment, where the pupils are immured, talk nothing but Latin, and support every day syllogistical disputations in school philosophy. Would not one be apt to imagine this was the proper education to make a man a fool? Such are the universities of Prague, Louvain, and Padua. The second is, where the pupils are under few restrictions, where all scholastic jargon is banished, where they take a degree when they think proper, and live not in the college but the city. Such are Edinburgh, Leyden, Gottingen, Geneva. The third is a mixture of the two former, where the pupils are restrained but not confined; where many, though not all, of the absurdities of scholastic philosophy are suppressed, and where the first degree is taken after four years' matriculation. Such are Oxford, Cambridge, and Dublin.

As for the first class, their absurdities are too apparent to admit of a parallel. It is disputed which of the two last are more conducive to a national improvement.

Skill in the professions is acquired more by practice than study; two or three years may be sufficient for learning their rudiments. The universities of Edinburgh, &c., grant a licence for practising them when the student thinks proper, which our universities refuse till after a residence of several years.

The dignity of the professions may be supported by this dilatory proceeding; but many men of learning are thus too long excluded from the lucrative advantages which superior skill has a right to expect. . . .

The man who has studied a profession for three years and practised it for nine more, will certainly know more of his business than he who has only studied it for twelve.

The universities of Edinburgh, &c., must certainly be most proper for the study of those professions in which men choose to turn their learning to profit as soon as possible. The universities of Oxford, &c., are improper for this, since they keep the student from the world, which, after a certain time, is the only true school of improvement. . . .

Teaching by lecture, as at Edinburgh, may make men scholars, if they think proper; but instructing by examination, as at Oxford, will make them so, often against their inclination.

Edinburgh only disposes the student to receive learning; Oxford often makes him actually learned.

In a word, were I poor, I should send my son to Leyden or Edinburgh, though the annual expense in each, particularly in the first, is very great. Were I rich, I would send him to one of our own universities. By an education received in the first, he has the best likelihood of living; by that received in the latter, he has the best chance of becoming great.

But we must consider in another chapter what intimate experiences were gathered during this period in which Oliver Goldsmith the writer was being slowly formed, while Oliver Goldsmith, medical student, was seeking acccess, impatiently, to " the lucrative advantages which superior skill has a right to expect."

CHAPTER IV

THE YEARS OF TRAVEL

IT was early in 1752 that Goldsmith, twenty-four years old, left Ireland, presumably sailing from Dublin to Glasgow. But whatever port he sailed from was the last he ever saw of Irish soil. Ireland he never shook off. It hung about him in the brogue, anything but a passport to employment; it assured him the company of men even more impecunious than himself; it was a lasting handicap in life, and at the same time a melancholy, ineffectual longing, never strong enough to effect its own fulfilment, yet inveterate as a disease.

I cannot myself feel that he had a distinctive love of Ireland as Ireland—any Irish patriotism. But love of home he had, and home meant Ireland: it was only in Ireland that this home-lover ever had the experience of a home. Yet the wandering instinct that in the Middle Ages drew the *vagantes* from Ireland to Europe in shoals as salmon are drawn to the sea, and in modern times went far to people North America, has always been more potent than the other impulse which draws the wanderer back. I make no doubt but that Oliver Goldsmith went off with a light heart. When he reached Edinburgh, he was so eager to see the town that when the caddy had brought his luggage to a lodging-house, he set off at once without noting either house or street, and could not find them until at last providentially he encountered the same porter. We have the story from his sister, so no doubt he wrote it home: and it is fully in character. But now we have first-hand material to go on in his own letters.

It seems that he reached Edinburgh in the autumn and

put in the session from October to March. At all events, on May 8, 1753, he wrote to Contarine, and the opening words tell us a good deal of the relation between uncle and nephew:

My dear Uncle,—In your letter (the only one I received from Kilmore), you call me the philosopher who carries all his goods about him. Yet how can such a character fit me, who have left behind in Ireland everything I think worth possessing—friends that I loved, and a society that pleased while it instructed?

In reading Goldsmith, or in reading about him, we never get away from one word. Nobody ever was less of a sage; nobody ever more determined to be a " philosopher." His friends saw from the first that such philosophy is likely to travel light, and he himself had no fear of physical privations. But he suffered always from lack of congenial company:

Who but must regret his absence from Kilmore, that ever knew it as I did? Here, as recluse as the Turkish Spy at Paris, I am almost unknown to everybody, except some few who attend the professors of physic as I do.

He goes on then to sketch the professors, with high praise for the teacher of anatomy and little good to say for the rest:

Munro is the only great man among them; so that I intend to hear him another winter, and go then to hear Albinus, the great professor at Leyden. I read (with satisfaction) a science the most pleasing in nature, so that my labours are but a relaxation, and, I may truly say, the only thing here that gives me pleasure. How I enjoy the pleasing hope of returning with skill, and to find my friends stand in no need of my assistance!

His project, then, at this time was to qualify abroad and return to practise in Ireland. Contarine was financing him —on a very modest scale, as the postscript shows:

I draw this time for 6*l*., and will draw next October but for 4*l*., as I was obliged to buy everything since I came to Scotland, shirts not even excepted. I am a little more early the first year

63

than I shall be for the future, for I absolutely will not trouble you before the time hereafter.

It looks as if he were hoping to subsist on five pounds a quarter, which would certainly be a tight fit; and a page from an old tailor's account, unearthed for Forster, shows the strain. In January, 1753, "Mr. Oliver Goldsmith student," introduced by Mr. Honner, ordered and received two and a half yards of rich 'Sky-Blew sattin' at twelve shillings a yard; one and a half of 'white Allapeen,' 1¼ of white Fustian, four yards of 'Blew Durant' and three-quarters of 'fine Sky-Blew Shalloon.' In February he ordered material and trimmings for a suit of "fine Priest's grey cloth," and in November he paid for the whole— "£3.15.9¾." Having paid, he profited by his solvency to order "a sfine small Hatt," with "silver Hatt-Lace" and another suiting of "best sfine high Clarett-colour'd Cloth" (this time at 19s. the yard), with accompaniment as before of white shalloon—and a pair of "sfine Best Blk worsed hose."

These adornments were not designed merely to impress "some few who attended the professors of physic" along with him. He had considerably exaggerated to Contarine his lack of society; and a letter to Bob Bryanton, dated September 26, 1753, puts it beyond a doubt that he was seeking company in Scotland. He had no admiration for the country itself, "where I must lead you over their hills all brown with heath or their vallies scarce able to feed a rabbit" (this impression was derived from a month spent in the Highlands, about which he had written to Contarine); but none the less a Scotchman, he found, was "one of the proudest things alive."

From their pride and poverty, as I take it, results one advantage this country enjoys, namely, the gentlemen here are much better bred than amongst us. No such characters here as our fox-hunters; and they have expressed great surprise when I informed them that some men in Ireland of 1000 l. a-year spend their whole lives in running after a hare, drinking to be drunk, and getting every girl that will let them with child.

They were, however, much given to dancing. "Balls are very frequent here"; but these were gloomy entertainments where "there is no more intercourse between the sexes than there is between two countries at war. . . . They dance much and say nothing, and so concludes our assembly." He is severe on the accent of the Scotch ladies, and thinks them ridiculously censorious of the beautiful Gunning, Duchess of Hamilton ("that fair who sacrificed her beauty to ambition and her inward peace to a title and gilt equipage").—In short, we find the young gentleman practising his pen at something in the manner of Steele's "Tatler"; but then the tone drops and we have the authentic Oliver Goldsmith speaking:

But how ill, my Bob, does it become me to ridicule women with whom I have scarce any correspondence! There are, 'tis certain, handsome women here; and 'tis as certain there are handsome men to keep them company. An ugly and a poor man is society for himself; and such society the world lets me enjoy in great abundance.

Yet according to himself, in another couple of months he could if he chose have bragged of friendship with the handsomest of all handsome women then living. Writing to Contarine about the close of that year, he says:

I have spent more than a fortnight every second day at the Duke of Hamilton's, but it seems they like me more as a *jester* than as a companion; so I disdained so servile an employment: 'twas unworthy my calling as a physician.

This is a very odd story, and it would be hardly believable, were it not that the beautiful Duchess came from the county Roscommon, and if she met Goldsmith, would have probably taken pleasure (for she was a very well-natured woman) in showing hospitality to anyone who came from the county she grew up in. This would be all the more possible if, as some accounts suggest, Oliver had earned repute as an amusing companion and a singer of Irish songs. Yet I remain slightly in doubt whether this should not be classed along with the adventures encountered on the way

E

back from Cork. Until Goldsmith had more than his belly-ful of real adventures, he was, I incline to think, continually making up imaginary ones : but never at any time in his life had he the least part of Defoe's instinct, or Swift's, for verisimilitude in fiction.

Yet there is this to be noted. Sketching in summary out-line the phases of his own career (under the thinnest of dis-guises), he attributes, as we have seen in the last chapter, this particular experience to his " Man in Black."

Goldsmith may be combining two episodes and mixing up Mr. Flynn of county Roscommon with the Duke of Hamil-ton. At all events, so far as this, and no further, the imaginary biography corresponds closely with incidents that we know to have occurred in Goldsmith's actual life.

His period of study in Edinburgh covered two winter sessions. It did not terminate with graduation, but Dr. Kirkpatrick observes that it was then the exception rather than the rule at Edinburgh University for students to pro-ceed to a degree either in Arts or Medicine. Goldsmith himself says in his " Essay on Polite Learning " that a licence for practising the profession was granted at Edin-burgh, " when a student thinks proper ", and that in his opinion " two or three years may be sufficient for learning the rudiments." It does not appear, however, that he applied for this licence or got it, and the second letter to his uncle makes it plain that he did not consider his studies com-plete, and proposed to pursue them on the Continent. He writes :

MY DEAR UNCLE,—After having spent two winters in Edin-burgh, I now prepare to go to France the 10th of next February. I have seen all that this country can exhibit in the medical way, and therefore intend to visit Paris, where the great Mr. Farhein, Petit, and Du Hammel de Monceau instruct their pupils in all the branches of medicine. They speak French, and conse-quently I shall have much the advantage of most of my country-men, as I am perfectly acquainted with that language, and few who leave Ireland are so.

Probably this means no more than that he could read

French easily. But there was at this period a considerable body of French Huguenots in Dublin, and they had the right to hold a service weekly in one of the chapels of St. Patrick's Cathedral; Swift speaks of " gabbling French " with their clergy. Goldsmith may have learnt to speak it; at all events, wherever he got it, the knowledge of French was invaluable to Oliver Goldsmith; his mind was formed by French literature more than by English.—The same letter sets out his plans, his finances, and his state of mind.

I shall spend this spring and summer in Paris, and the beginning of next winter go to Leyden. The great Albinus is still alive there, and 'twill be proper to go, though only to have it said that we have studied in so famous a university.

As I shall not have another opportunity of receiving money from your bounty till my return to Ireland, so I have drawn for the last sum that I hope I shall ever trouble you for; 'tis 20*l*. And now, dear sir, let me here acknowledge the humility of the station in which you found me; let me tell how I was despised by most, and hateful to myself. Poverty, hopeless poverty, was my lot, and Melancholy was beginning to make me her own. When you—but I stop here, to inquire how your health goes on. How does my dear cousin Jenny, and has she recovered her late complaint? How does my poor Jack Goldsmith? I fear his disorder is of such a nature as he won't easily recover. I wish, my dear sir, you would make me happy by another letter before I go abroad, for there I shall hardly hear from you. I shall carry just 33*l*. to France, with good store of clothes, shirts, &c., &c., and that with economy will serve.

" Jenny " was Mrs. Lawder, Contarine's daughter; and "poor Jack Goldsmith," Oliver's youngest brother, who in fact did not recover from a sickly boyhood. The plans, sketched here, miscarried; and as to the economy, it is possible that Mr. Contarine read the proclamation of it with a mixture of resignation and amusement. But another letter takes up the story:

LEYDEN (*April* or *May*, 1754).

DEAR SIR,—I suppose by this time I am accused of either neglect or ingratitude, and my silence imputed to my usual slowness of writing. But believe me, sir, when I say, that till now I had not an opportunity of sitting down with that ease of mind which writing required. You may see by the top of the letter that I am at Leyden; but of my journey hither you must be informed. Sometime after the receipt of your last, I embarked for Bordeaux, on board a Scotch ship called the *St. Andrews*, Capt. John Wall, master. The ship made a tolerable appearance, and, as another inducement, I was let to know that six agreeable passengers were to be my company. Well, we were but two days at sea when a storm drove us into a city of England called Newcastle-upon-Tyne. We all went ashore to refresh us after the fatigue of our voyage. Seven men and I were one day on shore, and on the following evening as we were all very merry, the room door bursts open, enters a serjeant and twelve grenadiers with their bayonets screwed, and puts us all under the King's arrest. It seems my company were Scotchmen in the French service, and had been in Scotland to enlist soldiers for the French army. I endeavoured all I could to prove my innocence; however, I remained in prison with the rest a fortnight, and with difficulty got off even then. Dear sir, keep this all a secret, or at least say it was for debt; for if it were once known at the university, I should hardly get a degree. But hear how Providence interposed in my favour: the ship was gone on to Bordeaux before I got from prison, and was wrecked at the mouth of the Garonne, and every one of the crew were drowned. It happened in the last great storm. There was a ship at that time ready for Holland: I embarked, and in nine days, thank my God, I arrived safe at Rotterdam; whence I travelled to Leyden; and whence I now write.

Now this was certainly a very remarkable adventure; and, to be frank, I am not very sure that it ever happened. After reading Mrs. Hodson's account of the Fiddleback saga, no one will think to disparage Goldsmith's veracity by treating as apocryphal what was never meant to deceive: and it seems to me remarkable that nothing like this episode is to be found either in the " Adventures of the Man in Black " or in the wanderings of Mr. Primrose's son, which so closely resemble those of Oliver Goldsmith. On the other hand, we meet in the latter of these narratives the case of a young gentleman who went to Holland hoping to support himself by teaching English, and omitted to remember that before he could succeed in this purpose he must first know Dutch. We have also a statement repeated by two doctors, Fenn Sleigh and Lachlan McLean, that Goldsmith backed a bill for a friend in Edinburgh and narrowly escaped being put in jail when his friend defaulted.

My own inclination is to believe that the Newcastle adventure never happened at all ; that the subsequent loss of the vessel with all hands is a fancy touch added to complete the marvel ; that in reality the thirty-three pounds which were to be carried to France melted out of sight (very possibly into a friend's pocket) ; that some chance offered a cheap passage to Holland and that Goldsmith jumped at it, very probably telling himself and his friends that he could easily earn a living by giving English lessons.

This may be over-sceptical. But on the face of it, the letter is written to break to his provider of funds the fact that instead of carrying out his plans as announced, he had landed up in Leyden. Moreover, the letter is written to amuse. Now, F. S. Oliver points out in the last volume of his " Endless Adventure " that letters are often misleading because we who read are unaware of a tacit convention which exists between the correspondents. Very often a phrase may be intended to be taken in a sense opposite to its literal meaning : and it may quite well be that Contarine was well used to receiving some entirely fantastic story to account for an unexpected result. I am certain that he read and laughed over the Fiddleback narration ; and I incline to regard this letter as meaning no more than to say : " Here I am where you did not expect to find me : but before you disapprove, listen to the surprising series of adventures which I have for your ear." From them, the epistle slides into a characterization of the Dutch which was certainly calculated to put Contarine into a lenient humour, and is a foretaste of many passages in the " Cities of the World."

Most significantly, there is no mention whatever of money. Is it believable that if any part of the January £33 was left, Goldsmith would not have enlarged upon his economy ? It is certainly not by any means believable that the traveller did not want more funds. The only part of this very long epistle which has a business aspect comes at the end :

Physic is by no means here taught so well as in Edinburgh ; and in all Leyden there are but four British students, owing to all necessaries being so extremely dear and the professors so very lazy (the chemical professor excepted) that we don't much care to come hither. I am not certain how long my stay here may be ; however, I expect to have the happiness of seeing you at Kilmore if I can, next March.

We know nothing of his life for the next four years, except by vague report. Part of it comes from one of the four British students to whom his letter refers. Dr. Kirk-patrick has found their names entered in the " Album Studiosorum " for 1754: George Lennox, brother of the Duke of Richmond, Guy Carleton, afterwards first Lord Dorchester, and Andreas MacLachlan—a group who came together. The fourth was Thomas Ellis an Irishman. Goldsmith's name does not appear. It will be remembered that he notes the annual expense in Leyden as being " very great "—greater even than in Edinburgh ; and one may fairly infer that he could not pay his fees. Ellis says that he was usually short of money, often because he had lost at play ; but he has also one charming and entirely character-istic story. Goldsmith had made up his mind to quit Leyden and went to Ellis for a loan of money, which he got. Returning to his lodgings, he passed a shop where choice tulips were on sale. These flowers were then much talked of and Contarine was gardener enough to have often ex-pressed a wish for them ; so his nephew, reflecting that the combination of chances which brought tulips on sale when money was in his pocket might never recur, bought a con-signment of bulbs and dispatched them to Kilmore. Next day, as Forster says, he left Leyden with a guinea in his pocket, one shirt to his back, and a flute in his hand.

This was in February, 1755. Within the next twelve months he had travelled through Flanders, into France through Normandy (he wrote, he says, from Rouen), reached Paris, stayed there some time ; then made his way into Switzerland, and across the Alps to Italy. Then he set his face for England, probably returning by Germany. We have no means to trace his route, though stray allusions, or passages of description in what he wrote later, indicate some of the points of his slow passage from " lazy Scheldt " to " wandering Po." But two problems can be resolved summarily.—How did he travel? The answer is, He walked. How did he support himself? He lived by his wits. There could not have been a more formative experience for a philosophic writer whose philosophy was to be based on knowledge of life.

Some obscure instinct pushed him on ; for he does not seem to have clearly formed yet his purpose of writing ; it was that restless desire for new contacts, a curiosity of the mind far more than that lust for seeing which is nowadays the main inducement to what the agencies call " travel "— though ordinary men and women more aptly speak of it as " going abroad." But Goldsmith, if he was to accomplish his desire, had no choice but to be a traveller in good earnest. Necessity imposed an ascetic discipline on him, and there is no pretence that he liked it. Significantly, his thoughts on travel are put at the beginning of his chapter " On Universities " in the " Enquiry " :

We seem divided, whether an education formed by travelling or by a sedentary life be preferable. We see more of the world by travel, but more of human nature by remaining at home ; as in an infirmary, the student who only attends to the disorders of a few patients is more likely to understand his profession than he who indiscriminately examines them all.

A youth just landed at the Brille resembles a clown at a puppet-show ; carries his amazement from one miracle to another ; from this cabinet of curiosities to that collection of pictures : but wondering is not the way to grow wise.

Whatever resolutions we set ourselves, not to keep company with our countrymen abroad, we shall find them broken when once we leave home. Among strangers we consider ourselves in a solitude, and it is but natural to desire society.

In all the great towns of Europe there are to be found Englishmen residing either from interest or choice. These generally lead a life of continued debauchery. Such are the countrymen a traveller is likely to meet with.

This may be the reason why Englishmen are all thought to be mad or melancholy by the vulgar abroad. Their money is giddily and merrily spent among sharpers of their own country ; and when that is gone, of all nations the English bear worst that disorder called the *maladie de poche*.

Countries wear very different appearances to travellers of different circumstances. A man who is whirled through Europe in a post-chaise, and the pilgrim who walks the grand tour on foot, will form very different conclusions. *Haud inexpertus loquor*.

To see Europe with advantage, a man should appear in various circumstances of fortune ; but the experiment would be too dangerous for young men.

There are many things relative to other countries which can be learned to more advantage at home ; their laws and policies are among the number.

The greatest advantages which result to youth from travel, are an easy address, the shaking off national prejudices, and the finding nothing ridiculous in national peculiarities.

The time spent in these acquisitions could have been more usefully employed at home. An education in college seems therefore preferable.

He had, in short, to travel slowly and laboriously when a chaise would have been pleasant : alone, when he would have liked company : finding strange bedfellows, but not agreeable ones : always conscious that he was not seeing Europe ' to advantage.' It was not in human nature that he should be thankful for the chance which threw him for the first time in his life entirely back upon himself and on his own thoughts. " Remote, unfriended, melancholy, slow " : the first line of his " Traveller " makes a gloomy impression.

When another member of the Literary Club asked Goldsmith what he meant by " slow "—" Did he mean tardiness

of locomotion " ?—Goldsmith answered " Yes."   Johnson
was sitting by and said : " No, sir, you do not mean tardiness of locomotion ; you mean that sluggishness of mind
which comes upon a man in solitude."

It is a famous and admirable example of literary exposition ; and essentially Johnson was right.   But he lacked
something which Goldsmith possessed strongly, the pic-
torial mind ; he lacked also the vagabond experience.   One
may be certain that when Goldsmith shaped that line, with
its powerful emphasis on the last word, there was before
him a physical image : the lonely traveller trudging in solitude who saw and envied young gentlemen whisked past in
their chaises, chatting agreeably to their companions, ex-
hilarated by the clatter and jingle of trotting horses.   It is a
fine thing when you have the price of a fare in your pocket
to despise effeminate persons who get themselves conveyed :
but the Merediths and Leslie Stephens, lyrical over stout
walking and deep draughts of clean air, certainly do not
interpret the habitual feelings of a man who walks because
he cannot get a lift.   There is a tediousness of the road
known only by those who have tried it, and Johnson was
not one of them.   What Johnson did know and feel acutely,
was the depression of solitude.   On the other hand, Goldsmith knew quite well what solitude was worth to him as a
discipline.   Here is the opening to his essay on Beau Tibbs :

Though naturally pensive, yet I am fond of gay company,
and take every opportunity of thus dismissing the mind from
duty.   From this motive I am often found in the centre of a
crowd ; and wherever pleasure is to be sold, am always a purchaser.   A mind thus sunk for awhile below its natural standard,
is qualified for stronger flights.

It would never have occurred to Johnson, for it would
never have been true, that his mind went off duty when he
was in company.   On the contrary, it then did its true work ;
his best writings are like his own talk remembered.   But
when Goldsmith was with friends, his sole wish was to be
merry and idle—to save himself all trouble of thinking.
Thought and the shaping of thought had to be done in

solitude : and well he knew that when there was society to be had, he would never avoid it. Only when necessity denied to his weakness the power to idle, when he could no longer be a purchaser of pleasure, could the master-impulses of his mind get play.

Chief among these was the desire for a richer experience ; that pushed him on the road. Nothing could be more truly autobiographic than this piece of self-study in one of his first published essays (in " The Bee ") which tells us, not where he actually travelled, but the mood he travelled in—

CRACOW, *Aug.* 2, 1758.

You see, by the date of my letter, that I am arrived in Poland. When will my wanderings be at an end ? When will my restless disposition give me leave to enjoy the present hour ? When at Lyons, I thought all happiness lay beyond the Alps ; when in Italy, I found myself still in want of something, and expected to leave solicitude behind me by going into Romelia ; and now you find me turning back, still expecting ease everywhere but where I am. It is now seven years since I saw the face of a single creature who cared a farthing whether I was dead or alive. Secluded from all the comforts of confidence, friendship, or society, I feel the solitude of a hermit, but not his ease.

Yet we can examine further this self-revealing witness. Two motives urge him, or rather, two aspects of one motive. He neglects his ease and his affections in the pursuit of a higher happiness, vague and elusive ; but also he is the seeker after knowledge. The " philosophic vagabond " wanders because he is a poet and because he is a philosopher ; and in separate passages we find each facet of his mind displayed. It is the poet who first sketches in " The Traveller " the remembered happiness of his early home—" Blest that abode where want and pain repair, and every stranger finds a ready chair"—and then draws the contrast :

> But me, not destin'd such delights to share,
> My prime of life in wandering spent and care,
> Impell'd, with steps unceasing, to pursue
> Some fleeting good, that mocks me with the view,

74

That, like the circle bounding earth and skies,
Allures from far, yet, as I follow, flies,
My fortune leads to traverse realms alone,
And find no spot of all the world my own.

All here belongs to the domain of feeling. It is the imaginary Chinaman, his " Citizen of the World," who sets out the philosophic side of Oliver Goldsmith's impulse to travel :

Let European travellers cross seas and deserts merely to measure the height of a mountain, to describe the cataract of a river, or tell the commodities which every country may produce : merchants or geographers, perhaps, may find profit by such discoveries ; but what advantage can accrue to a philosopher from such accounts, who is desirous of understanding the human heart, who seeks to know the *men* of every country, who desires to discover those differences which result from climate, religion, education, prejudice and partiality ?

It is even extraordinary how indifferent the actual travel-ler, Mr. Oliver Goldsmith, " citizen of the world," could show himself to cataracts, mountains, and such-like. As will be seen, he had early formed the opinion that a modern writer could best imitate the classics by " copying nature." Here he was now, at seven-and-twenty, already working on the masterpiece by which he first achieved fame, (for part of " The Traveller," he says to his brother, " was formerly written to you from Switzerland ") ; and he was among scenes that fifteen years earlier had left another English poet " astonished even beyond expression." Gray, travelling in Horace Walpole's company writes : " In our little journey up the Grande Chartreuse I do not remember to have gone ten paces without any exclamation that there was no restraining." In the same letter (for it was a joint epistle to their poetic friend West), listen to Horace Walpole :

But the road, West, the road ! winding round a prodigious mountain, and surrounded with others, all shagged with hanging woods, obscured with pines, or lost in clouds. Below, a torrent

75

breaking through cliffs and tumbling through fragments of rocks. Sheets of cascades forcing their silver speed down channelled precipices and hasting into the roughened river at the bottom. Now and then an old footbridge, with a broken rail, a leaning cross, or cottage, or the ruins of an hermitage. This sounds too bombast and romantic to one that has not seen it, too cold for one that has. If I could send you by letter post between two lovely tempests that echoed each other's wrath, you might have some idea of this noble roaring scene.

Not a word of all this romanticism in " The Traveller " : no " lovely tempests," no sense even of the austere beauty. What the poet fastens on is man's victory over nature—but here indeed, the philosopher gets somewhat the better of the poet. Let us look at it. He has been stigmatizing the Italians, Rome's degenerate heirs :

> My soul, turn from them, turn we to survey
> Where rougher climes a nobler race display;
> Where the bleak Swiss their stormy mansion tread,
> And force a churlish soil for scanty bread.
> No product here the barren hills afford,
> But man and steel, the soldier and his sword :
> No vernal blooms their torpid rocks array,
> But winter lingering chills the lap of May :
> No Zephyr fondly sues the mountain's breast,
> But meteors glare, and stormy glooms invest.

Your poet nowadays, whether he wrote in prose or verse, would have a quick eye to notice the blue gentians coming out like jewels when the snow was hardly gone ; Goldsmith thinks it his business to generalize, to stylize, and he suppresses the gentians and their company to give the impression—which is a true one—of barrenness. But nobody need suppose that he went through the Alps with eyes that saw nothing. After nearly twenty years, he wrote in " Animated Nature " :

It need scarce be said that, with respect to height, there are many sizes of mountains, from the gently rising upland, to the tall craggy precipice. The appearance is in general different in those of different magnitudes. The first are clothed with

verdure to their very tops, and only seem to ascend to improve
our prospects, or supply us with purer air ; but the lofty mountains of the other class have a very different aspect.   At a distance
their tops are seen, in wavy ridges, of the very colour of the
clouds, and only to be distinguished from them by their figure,
which, as I have said, resembles the billows of the sea.   As we
approach, the mountain assumes a deeper colour ; it gathers
upon the sky, and seems to hide half the horizon behind it.   Its
summits also are become more distinct, and appear with a broken
and perpendicular line.   What at first seemed a single hill, is
now found to be a chain of continued mountains, whose tops,
running along in ridges, are embosomed in each other ; so that
the curvatures of one are fitted to the prominences of the opposite
side, and form a winding valley between, often of several miles
in extent ; and all the way continuing nearly of the same breadth.

Here again is a passage which tells charmingly with what
pleasure he saw the continued reality of what, reading the
classics, he had believed to be poetic invention :

In many parts of the Alps and even some provinces of France
the shepherd and his pipe are still continued, with true antique
simplicity.   The flock is regularly penned every evening, to
preserve them from the wolf ; and the shepherd returns homeward at sunset with his sheep following him, and seemingly
pleased with the sound of the pipe which is blown with a reed
and resembles the chanter of a bagpipe.   In this manner in those
countries that still continue poor, the Arcadian life is preserved
in all its former purity ; but in countries where a greater in-
equality of conditions prevails, the shepherd is generally some
poor wretch who attends a flock from which he is to derive no
benefits.

Other detailed descriptions could be given ; for instance,
of a cave near Maestricht with astonishing stalagmites, or of
beehives allowed to float down Italian rivers.   Or we find
him noting a simple fact, for instance, that he flushed wood-
cock on the Jura in June or July.   But every single one of
these records of visual observation comes out of a work in
the main borrowed from the French : they were side notes
on what he found in Buffon—and a work done at the end of
his career as a bread-winning task.   All that he selected at

first, when drawing on the gathered experience of his philosophic vagabondage, was concerned with the manners of men. The first runnings of his genius, whether in prose or verse, came out of what he had gathered through the mind and not through the eyes. Intellectual contacts alone to him were of important significance.

Such, then, were the fruits of the two years spent in continental travel. No one from these islands did " the grand tour " more intensively, more intimately, than Oliver Goldsmith ; and certainly no one else did it at so little expense. For his year at Leyden he was to some degree at all events financed from home, yet even then his scanty resources were eked out by borrowing : and through the whole of his journey he pursued the same method. " There is hardly a kingdom in Europe in which I am not a debtor," he wrote to his brother-in-law, Hodson, after his return to England—and Forster comments on " that strange indifference to what was implied in such obligations, which is not the agreeable side of his character." The trait was Irish, of course, and Goldsmith must have known that a great proportion of the Irish gentry borrowed as much and paid as little as they could ; he was a proud landlord who could say that his tenants had thrown a process-server into the nearest boghole. Yet I do not think that Goldsmith's " strange indifference to such obligations " was a result of the example set by hard-riding, hard-living fox-hunters. He had two countries, and though the roots of his heart were in Ireland, his spiritual home was Bohemia. In that frontierless community which has its Alsatia in every great city of Europe, and a raggle-taggle of its citizens scattered along every great road, the rule of life is that when you can lend, you lend, and when you can borrow, you borrow. From the standpoint of other communities, there are objections to this plan of finance, because the citizens of Bohemia have always sought to apply it beyond their own freemasonry—and Goldsmith was no exception. But if he is to be judged by the standards of his tribe, few could emerge with more credit. Certainly for a long period he was habitually a borrower ; but

when he could lend, no one was ever more lavish. As
between Bohemian and Bohemian, the end of his short
life certainly found more owing to him than he ever
owed.

But it is useless to deny that shiftlessness in money matters
tarnished his name while he was living ; and death has not
quite effaced the stain of contempt. Magnificent plungers
like Charles James Fox wear their list of unpaid borrowings
as a Red Indian wore scalps. Some, indeed, have been severe
judges of Fox since his day ; but nobody blames Mr. Pitt—
because Mr. Pitt had to be so busy saving his country that
he could not attend to private affairs. It was right that his
friends should finance him—though probably not all did so
willingly. Well, those who contributed to Goldsmith's
support in this period of preparation paid their share, willingly or unwillingly, to the making of a poet. If they had
not their money, they had " The Traveller " to show for it ;
and, from the standpoint of Bohemia, that is a fair and
sufficient answer.

There is this to be said further. If Goldsmith allowed
himself to be dependent on his friends for support till the
age of twenty-eight, while he pursued what could scarcely
be called anything so definite as a purpose, at least he made
his own large contribution : paying in person so far as he
could, when there was nothing in his pocket. His two
stout legs carried his hardy body from one stage to the next,
and then his wits were employed to earn a welcome, in a
fashion that caused him no shame. It was not Bohemia but
Lissoy that taught him to think a request for food and
shelter the most natural thing in the world. At Lissoy
" every stranger found a ready chair " ; and even to-day in
any outlying part of Ireland, every stranger can count on at
least some welcome as a bringer of news. Oliver Goldsmith never doubted of his power to entertain simple
people, and when this was cramped by imperfect knowledge
of a foreign tongue, he had the common language in his
pocket ; out came his flute. What he gave had no great
cash value, but neither had the lodging nor the fare ; he

could go on his way feeling that he left a pleasant memory ; entertainment paid for entertainment.

I met within the last few years in Kerry a man of over eighty who had never had a fixed lodging or owned anything but his fiddle, on which he had, in truth, no great skill ; but for the sake of his talk and his music, he had free quarters on half a barony. There is therefore nothing remarkable in Goldsmith's achievement, especially as it was in an age without newspapers. What is remarkable is that he should have had the enterprise to attempt it : though he did not lack an example to imitate. Forster is assuredly right in thinking that the impulse came from the career of a scholar who died while Goldsmith was at Leyden and must therefore have been the subject of talk there. A long passage in Goldsmith's first published book not only indicates where the prompting came from but also suggests what aspirations may have been in the Irish student's mind when he set out to imitate " the late famous Baron Holberg."

This was perhaps, one of the most extraordinary personages that has done honour to the present century. His being the son of a private sentinel did not abate the ardour of his ambition, for he learned to read though without a master. Upon the death of his father, being left entirely destitute, he was involved in all that distress which is common among the poor, and of which the great have scarcely any idea. However, though only a boy of nine years old, he still persisted in his studies, travelled about from school to school, and begged his learning and his bread. When at the age of seventeen, instead of applying himself to any of the lower occupations, which seem best adapted to such circumstances, he was resolved to travel for improvement from Norway, the place of his birth, to Copenhagen, the capital city of Denmark. He lived there by teaching French, at the same time avoiding no opportunity of improvement that his scanty funds could permit. But his ambition was not to be restrained, or his thirst of knowledge satisfied, until he had seen the world. Without money, recommendations, or friends, he undertook to set out upon his travels, and make the tour of Europe on foot. A good voice, and a trifling skill in music, were the only finances he had to support an undertaking so

extensive ; so he travelled by day, and at night sung at the doors
of peasants' houses to get himself a lodging. In this manner,
while yet very young, Holberg passed through France, Germany,
and Holland ; and coming over to England, took up his residence
for two years in the university of Oxford. Here he subsisted
by teaching French and music, and wrote his Universal History,
his earliest but worst performance. Furnished with all the
learning of Europe, he at last thought proper to return to Copenhagen, where his ingenious productions quickly gained him that
favour he deserved. He composed not less than eighteen
comedies. Those in his own language are said to excel, and
those which are translated into French have peculiar merit. He
was honoured with nobility, and enriched by the bounty of the
king ; so that a life begun in contempt and penury ended in
opulence and esteem.

Perhaps the hope of some such an ending supported
Goldsmith on his pilgrimage ; but it is certain that his
notion of the flute came from there. He never had the
least false shame about these experiences. Cooke, one of
his friends, writes : " He frequently used to talk of his
distresses on the continent, such as living on the hospitalities
of the friars at convents, sleeping in barns, and picking up a
kind of mendicant livelihood by the German flute with
great pleasantry." For that matter, he made public avowal
of them in passages where it was evident to all his friends
that he drew from his own life. The first of these does not
indeed suggest the search of " a mendicant livelihood " but
merely the ready welcome which he found in France.

> Gay sprightly land of mirth and social ease,
> Pleas'd with thyself, whom all the world can please,
> How often have I led thy sportive choir,
> With tuneless pipe, beside the murmuring Loire ?
> Where shading elms along the margin grew,
> And, freshen'd from the wave, the Zephyr flew ;
> And haply, though my harsh touch, faltering still,
> But mock'd all tune, and marr'd the dancer's skill ;
> Yet would the village praise my wondrous power.
> And dance, forgetful of the noon-tide hour.

But elsewhere there is no concealment of the beggary.

When in "The Vicar of Wakefield" Mr. Primrose has re-discovered on the boards of a strolling company his long-lost son, there is a gathering at a friendly house and the prodigal tells his tale—significantly described in the chapter heading as "The History of a Philosophic Vagabond pursuing Novelty but losing Content." Now, beyond yea or nay, Oliver Goldsmith's personal experiences furnished the groundwork on which young Primrose's adventures are built up, though the sequence of them is altered. It is comparatively late in his career that Primrose finds himself in Holland, proposing to live by teaching English, and disappointed by the discovery that it was impossible for him and his would-be pupils to make themselves mutually understood. The next stage is suggested by "an Irish student who was returning from Louvain" and reported "that there were not two men in the whole university who understood Greek." "Instantly," says young Primrose, "I resolved to travel to Louvain and there live by teaching Greek; and in this design I was heartened by my brother student who threw out some hints that a fortune might be got by it."

I cannot but wonder whether Oliver Goldsmith had any such purpose when he headed for Louvain. His Greek was competent if not remarkable, and a sentence which he put into the mouth of young Primrose was entirely applicable to himself. "No person ever had a better knack at hoping than I." There is, too, a strong atmosphere of reminiscence about the following sentence. "Every day lessened the burden of my moveables, like Æsop and his basket of bread; for I paid them for my lodgings to the Dutch as I travelled on." At all events, I believe that Goldsmith, like young Primrose, only bethought him of music after he left Louvain behind him; and we may be certain that Goldsmith's experience is described exactly when the Philosophic Vagabond says:

I was now too far from home to think of returning; so I resolved to go forward. I had some knowledge of music, with a tolerable voice, and now turned what was once my amusement into a present means of subsistence. I passed among the harmless peasants of Flanders, and among such of the French as were poor enough to be very merry ; for I ever found them sprightly in proportion to their wants. Whenever I approached a peasant's house towards night-fall, I played one of my most merry tunes, and that procured me not only a lodging, but subsistence for the next day. I once or twice attempted to play for people of fashion ; but they always thought my performance odious, and never rewarded me even with a trifle. This was to me the more extraordinary, as whenever I used in better days to play for company, when playing was my amusement, my music never failed to throw them into raptures, and the ladies especially ; but as it was now my only means, it was received with contempt ; a proof how ready the world is to underrate those talents by which a man is supported.

He was bound to learn by experience that if you must beg, it should be at a poor man's door. But he acquired so completely the strolling fiddler's philosophy as to look on hospitality as a right, as much in cottages as in convents ; and because for once he was refused shelter on a bleak night, he has left a stigma on the Tyrol :

> Where the rude Carinthian boor
> Against the houseless stranger shuts the door.

This experience must, I think, have come after he had turned his face for home and left Italy where undoubtedly he passed some considerable time ; and we meet record of this period in the philosophic vagabond's history.

My skill in music could avail me nothing in a country where every peasant was a better musician than I ; but by this time I had acquired another talent which answered my purpose as well, and this was a skill in disputation. In all the foreign universities and convents there are upon certain days philosophical theses maintained against every adventitious disputant ; for which, if the champion opposes with any dexterity, he can claim a gratuity in money, a dinner, and a bed for one night. In this manner therefore I fought my way towards England.

We have no information as to the route he took, but passages in the " Polite Learning " show an intimate acquaintance with the German universities—and a well-nourished distaste for the German mind. My own conception of his route would make him foot it from Louvain to Rouen and thence to Paris; from Paris probably to Dijon, and thence taking the shortest line to Geneva, which lies over the heights of the Jura; for I do not believe that the philosophic vagabond ever climbed a mountain unless it was on his way. Tramps do not do such things. Then from Switzerland by the St. Gothard to Mantua. (If he had taken the Mont Cenis route, he would certainly have seen the Grande Chartreuse, and probably mentioned it somewhere.) Milan, Mantua and Padua he certainly knew; and my belief is that he left Italy by the way that led into Austria and thence to Germany. All this travel was accomplished by his own resources, for the first letter of his which we have after his return to England makes it clear that no subsidy reached him from home.

There is indeed a story that at one point in his travels he got the chance to act as bear-leader to a rich young man; and the philosophic vagabond describes such an experience, which, it may be observed, begins in Paris, brings him to Leghorn and drops him there. Now certainly it was not under such conditions that Goldsmith learnt how the French esteemed his merry tunes: though it has to be noted that in the philosophic vagabond's account, all the fluting was done on the way to Paris. On the whole, I incline to regard this episode as imaginary, or rather to believe that here Goldsmith assigns to his vagrant an experience which had been described to him by some other Bohemian; for we do not often find in him any but the most obvious invention, and it would have been ingenious to think of a rich youngster whose chief anxiety was to save money. What is like his method, is to have put into concrete shape wayside fancies of things that might happen when he reached Paris on foot with nothing in his pockets.

I had much sooner take this supposition than believe him simply to have chosen the easiest rhyme when he wrote:

How often have I led thy sportive choir,
With tuneless pipe beside the murmuring Loire?

The next couplet for all its conventional phrasing has a touch of nature : he remembered that shade and that fresh-ness on one of France's dusty roads ; and it is no great stretch of fancy to suppose that instead of taking the line of the Seine and Yonne, he struck south to Orleans, and so along the great river towards Nevers on his way to Dijon. This would fit in with a detailed story that he picked up the unpleasant young man in Geneva, after having got so far unaided. But the same story brings them to Marseilles where they parted company. I find no trace of this.

However, it all comes down to this.—After a year spent in the universities of the Low Countries, he spent another year on the roads of Europe, and soaked himself in the life of the peoples through whose lands he travelled, until, like Ulysses, he had seen the cities of many men and known their spirit; until he could say, like his philosophic vagabond, "I now was left once more upon the world at large ; but then it was a thing I was used to." Life made him resourceful : Boswell's phrase that " he disputed his way across Europe " is grossly inadequate : he fluted it, disputed it, begged it and borrowed it. Unfortunately, if the life of a rolling stone teaches courage, it has never been a school for prudence ; but it puts no damper on gaiety : " the merry heart goes all the way, the sad tires in a mile-o ! " No doubt it was of himself he thought when he sketched " Dick Wildgoose " in the " Bee " : " Whenever Dick fell into any misery, he usually called it *seeing life*." He did not find Tirnanoge, the Land of Heart's Desire, " some spot to real happiness con-signed " : but then, had his philosophy ever expected to find it ? He might be disappointed as a philosopher : but as a man and a young man, surely he had had fun out of it all. The road had been a peripatetic academy, kinder to him than Dublin or Edinburgh or Leyden. Now, quitting vagabondage, and settling down, he was to come to grips with life ; and this he found a grim business.

CHAPTER V

THE APPROACH TO GRUB STREET

WE do not know for certain in what circumstances Goldsmith landed on the English shore at the beginning of February, 1756; but probably Forster is not far from actual truth in saying that he had not a farthing in his pocket. On the other hand, I believe that he put into the mouth of the philosophic vagabond what he remembered of his own feeling:

Being now at the bottom of fortune's wheel, every new revolution might lift, but could not depress me. I proceeded therefore, towards London, on a fine morning, no way uneasy about tomorrow, but cheerful as the birds that carolled by the road, and comforted myself with reflecting that London was the mart where abilities of every kind were sure of meeting distinction and reward.

His only stock-in-trade was some knowledge of medicine, and the possession of a degree in arts—which has always been taken as a qualification to teach schoolboys. But he preferred to rely on medicine, and made application first to the apothecaries for a job in dispensing. For several days, possibly for weeks, he existed as he could. " When I lived with the beggars in Axe Lane," was a phrase that he used in days when actual beggary was among the bygones. Finally, a chemist named Jacob took him into his shop, somewhere near Billingsgate, and set him mixing and pounding. It was natural that with a chemist he should hear news of practitioners whom he had known at Edinburgh, and one of these was Dr. Fenn Sleigh. On him he called. "But, notwithstanding it was Sunday and it was to be supposed I

Mr. Bunbury delint.   J. Bretherton fecit.

DR. GOLDSMITH.

From the British Museum

was in my best clothes, Sleigh did not know me. Such is the tax the unfortunate pay to poverty." So Goldsmith said when he was telling the story to Percy. Only two years before he and Sleigh had been fellow-students at Edinburgh. But Sleigh, who was a Quaker, behaved in a manner worthy of the Friends—as indeed he continued to do through a long and distinguished life. Once the recognition was effected " I found his heart as warm as ever," Goldsmith says, " and he shared his purse and friendship with me during his continuance in London." The practical result was to fit out Goldsmith so far decently that he could set up in Southwark as a physician among the poor.

According to Dr. Kirkpatrick, at that period " the want of a medical qualification was no hindrance, and the want of any previous study was far from being an absolute bar to the practice of medicine." Goldsmith certainly could claim previous study and at some period he acquired a degree— though Dr. Kirkpatrick thinks that this official status came later. But practise he did for some brief period, and according to tradition attended a patient who worked as a journeyman printer in Samuel Richardson's establishment. Forster's reading of the story makes this printer take compassion on a doctor manifestly out at elbows, and suggest that his employer had often been kind to clever men. My opinion is that when Goldsmith heard what was his patient's trade, and for whom he worked, there was sudden opening for his " knack at hoping." A young man who had already written some part of " The Traveller " was, by the very nature of things, a young man who desired to see himself in print, and who could not meet a printer without at least some movements of curiosity. But when the printer proved to be working for the most admired writer of that moment (" Sir Charles Grandison " was held to have even added to the glory won by " Clarissa Harlowe "), it was impossible that the would-be literary man should not have jumped at any means to establish a contact. Quite possibly the workman did tell him, as Forster suggests, that Richardson had before now befriended clever men, and had even visited Mr. Johnson when he was in durance for debt. At all events, contact was made and the smug, obese, prosperous little tradesman of genius took on the starving medico as proof-reader.

The job did not last. Though Goldsmith earned a little of Richardson's money, Richardson earned none of Goldsmith's gratitude : he did not even manage to win Johnson's, though Johnson admired his novels fervently. But the creator of Clarissa and Lovelace had no gift for friendship with men ; rich and married, with an imagination perpetually in chase of sexual adventures, he remained in daily life an old maid, and the untidy thriftless young Irishman was in no way fitted to gain his approval. How it ended, we do not know. But under Richardson's auspices Goldsmith made his first acquaintance with proof-sheets : moreover, Richardson was the first literary authority to whom he submitted specimens of his own work.

One of his Edinburgh fellow-students, Dr. Farr, was at this time attending the hospitals in London and has left an account of the renewal of their acquaintance. Goldsmith called one morning, Farr says, " dressed in a rusty full trimmed black suit, with his pockets full of papers, which instantly reminded me of the poet in Garrick's farce of Lethe." After breakfast, out came the papers—"part of a tragedy which he said he had brought for my correction ; in vain I pleaded inability when he began to read, and every part on which I expressed a doubt as to the propriety was instantly blotted out." Then the unwilling critic pressed his friend to try better-qualified judges : "on which he told me he had submitted his production, so far as he had written, to Mr. Richardson the author of Clarissa." Thereupon Fenn declined further audience. The whole of his story is touched with that unlenient contempt which it was Goldsmith's lot to evoke : and no doubt Richardson felt the same emotions, though perhaps less complacently. But I do not see how Forster, after printing this story, continued to believe that Goldsmith only conceived the idea of literature as his profession when all else had failed. It was certainly the main purpose of his life to be "a poet"—though he was always easily diverted from it by any project that offered a new adventure and hopes of money to spend.

Fenn refers to one of these:

In this visit I remember his relating a strange Quixotic scheme he had in contemplation of going to decipher the inscriptions on the *written mountains*, though he was altogether ignorant of Arabic, or the language in which they might be supposed to be written. The salary of 300*l.* per annum, which had been left for the purpose, was the temptation !

And a very natural one. After all, Goldsmith, now nine-and-twenty, had for five years been living from hand to mouth, and finding the hand too often empty. Things were desperate again, when he met another Edinburgh fellow-student, whose father, Dr. Milner, directed the Peckham Academy. There was a vacancy in the school for an assistant, and Goldsmith now became an usher.

Some reminiscences of him were written down by Dr. Milner's daughter, when she was a very old lady and Goldsmith had been dead and famous a matter of thirty years. One concerns a reply, made to herself when she asked him at the table of her father (a Presbyterian controversialist) what commentary on the Bible he would recommend. Goldsmith answered, and it is like him, that in his opinion common sense was the best interpreter of Scripture. Other recollections recall the detail of two practical jokes played by the usher on the household's factotum, which show his taste for broad farce. But one of her notes is significant. Whatever little salary he earned was generally spent in advance, and for the most part went to beggars, or in sweets for the small boys ; and Mrs. Milner used to say to him, "Mr. Goldsmith, you had better let me keep your money for you as I do for some of the young gentlemen." To this he would reply, "In truth, madam, there is equal need."

That story has a pleasant kindly ring : there was no trace of Mr. and Mrs. Squeers in the Peckham establishment. But boys are little beasts, and one of Milner's scholars preserved another story of a very different tone. The usher had been amusing his boys with his flute and encouraging them to acquire what he said was " a gentlemanlike accomplishment," when one of them interrupted with the genial observation, " Why, surely you do not consider yourself a gentleman ? " No ingenuity of insult could have hit the young man more sharply on the raw than this crude impertinence. It drove home the penalties of poverty, of which he was no doubt unduly conscious, because he lacked that defensive pride which strengthened men like Johnson or Carlyle. Yet the instinct to give pleasure, to be liked for good humour and fun, was strong in him, and it exposed him to rebuffs which he expected no more than a friendly dog does. There are advantages in being a cross dog, and boys will torment a kind one.

At all events, we cannot doubt that Goldsmith was unhappy in his new trade. Cooke, who was intimate with him during the last ten years of his life, says that the circumstance of having been an usher was the only era of his life " that he was vain enough to be ashamed of."

He frequently used to talk of his distresses on the continent such as living on the hospitality of the friars in convents, sleeping in barns and picking up a kind of mendicant livelihood by the German flute, with great pleasantry ; but the *little story of Peckham School* he always carefully avoided ; and when an old friend one day made use of the common phrase " Oh that's all a holiday at Peckham," he reddened with great indignation and asked him whether he meant to affront him.

His own writings bear this out fully. Among his first essays in " The Bee " the case is seriously argued :

I would make the business of a school-master every way more respectable, by increasing their salaries, and admitting only men of proper abilities.

There are already school-masters appointed, and they have some small salaries ; but where at present there is but one school-master appointed, there should at least be two ; and wherever the salary is at present twenty pounds, it should be an hundred. Do we give immoderate benefices to those who instruct ourselves, and shall we deny even subsistence to those who instruct our children? Every member of society should be paid in proportion as he is necessary; and I will be bold enough to say, that school-masters in a state are more necessary than clergymen, as children stand in more need of instruction than their parents.

But instead of this, as I have already observed, we send them to board in the country to the most ignorant set of men that can be imagined. But, lest the ignorance of the master be not sufficient, the child is generally consigned to the usher. This is generally some poor needy animal, little superior to a footman either in learning or spirit, invited to his place by an advertisement, and kept there merely from his being of a complying disposition, and making the children fond of him. " You give your child to be educated to a slave," says a philosopher to a rich man; " instead of one slave you will then have two."

It were well, however, if parents, upon fixing their children in one of these houses, would examine the abilities of the usher as well as the master; for, whatever they are told to the contrary, the usher is generally the person most employed in their education. If then, a gentleman, upon putting out his son to one of these houses, sees the usher disregarded by the master, he may depend upon it, that he is equally disregarded by the boys: the truth is, in spite of all their endeavours to please, they are generally the laughing-stock of the school. Every trick is played upon the usher; the oddity of his manners, his dress, or his language, are a fund of eternal ridicule; the master himself now and then cannot avoid joining in the laugh, and the poor wretch, eternally resenting this ill-usage, seems to live in a state of war with all the family. This is a very proper person, is it not, to give children a relish for learning?

One must allow that Goldsmith's own lack of fitness for the profession added to his troubles. There should be something of the sergeant-major in a good schoolmaster—or at least of the company officer; and Oliver Goldsmith was never a natural-born disciplinarian; we may be sure that he suffered for the lack of this faculty. The most temperamental expression of his dislike is to be found when, in " The Vicar of Wakefield ", an acquaintance warns the Philosophic Vagabond:

I have been an usher at a boarding-school myself, and may I die by an anodyne necklace, but I had rather be an under-turnkey in Newgate. I was up early and late; I was browbeat by the master, hated for my ugly face by the mistress, worried by the boys within, and never permitted to stir out to meet civility abroad.

That same passage, however, preserves a link in Goldsmith's career. The imaginary vagabond gave up ushering for a project of commencing author : and, in fact, it was at Dr. Milner's table that the road opened to the real one. Griffiths, a bookseller who, after the usage of that time, both published and edited the " Monthly Review," dined one day with Dr. Milner who occasionally wrote for him. Goldsmith, being present, took his part in the conversation, and if proof were needed, we have proof here that he did not always " talk like poor Poll " ; for after they left the table Griffiths drew him aside and asked him to submit " a few specimens of criticism." They were submitted, and the result was an offer that Goldsmith should bind himself for a year's work on the " Monthly Review " in return for board and lodging and a small salary. Forster says, " The sorrowful road seemed the last that was left to him ; and he entered it." I think there is a much truer account of the matter given in Goldsmith's own words through the person of the Philosophic Vagabond :

Finding that there was no degree of gentility affixed to the character of an usher, I resolved to accept his proposal, and having the highest respect for literature, hailed the *antiqua mater* of Grub Street with reverence. I thought it my glory to pursue a track which Dryden and Otway trod before me. I considered the goddess of this region as the parent of excellence, and however an intercourse with the world might give us good sense, the poverty she granted, I supposed to be the nurse of genius.

But this apprenticeship to literature for a livelihood was not made agreeable by Mr. Griffiths and by his spouse, who shared with him the task of editing. That an author should live, move and have his being for ever under the taskmaster's eye was an unusual and galling arrangement: Goldsmith only stood it for six months, and it seems to me that what he wrote shows all the marks of flagging interest.

We can trace the contributions, because Griffiths kept a file copy in which authorship was indicated : though, of course, this does not tell us what the editorial pen struck out or what it put in. However, they are worth examining ; and they begin with the specimen submitted for approval which is headed : " Mythology and Poetry of the Celtes." A note adds : " The following paper was sent us by the gentleman who signs D, and who we hope will excuse our striking out a few paragraphs for the sake of brevity."

Irish readers, hoping to find trace of Goldsmith's interest in his country shown by this choice of a subject, will be disappointed. The " Celtes " are the Scandinavian people who wrote the " Edda "—in Iceland. If Contarine had taught his nephew anything about the mythology of those " Celtes " who lived in Ireland, we find no trace of it here. Nor, and this is more important, do we find here any touch of the manner which was to make Oliver Goldsmith. Writing for the first time for print, he is affected, like all beginners, with a self-conscious stiffness : witness the opening :

If all the brilliancy of sentiment which so dry a subject may require to its support, and all the laborious assiduity which may be necessary in the solution of its intricacies, demand applause, Professor Mallet must deserve it, who has so happily united both. The learned on this side the Alps have long laboured at the antiquities of Greece and Rome, but almost totally neglected their own ; like conquerors who, while they have made inroads into the territories of their neighbours, have left their own natural dominions to desolation.

But in the next number, when the new hand reviews Home's " Douglas," we begin to find our author. Goldsmith, it should be admitted at once, was never a good critic, but in this instance his judgment of a piece about which London had gone crazy is not far from the estimate to which opinion has settled down. He is writing of what keenly interested him, the contemporary theatre ; and he speaks now with his own voice, even though the structure of his sentences is more laborious than he allowed it to be when his hand was in. For instance, after laying down that a play must be judged by its total effect, and not by the purple patches, he condemns alike " the unfolding a material part of the plot in soliloquy ; and the preposterous distress of a married lady for a former husband, who had been dead near twenty years."

Next comes laudation of the " Connoisseur," a defunct weekly paper which had attained glorious resurrection in a successful reprint. Bonnell Thornton and the elder Colman were the joint authors, but wrote as ' Mr. Town,' and Goldsmith praises them as one :

The writer may be styled the friend of Society, in the most agreeable acceptation of the term ; for he rather converses with all the ease of a cheerful companion, than dictates, as other writers in this class have done, with the affected superiority of an author. He is the first writer since Bickerstaff, who has been perfectly satirical yet perfectly good-natured ; and who never, for the sake of declamation, represents simple folly as absolutely criminal.

Then follow these significant remarks on style :

The dread of falling into what they are pleased to call colloquial barbarisms, has induced some skilful writers to swell their bloated diction with uncouth phrases and the affected jargon of pedants. For my own part, I never go out of the common way of expression, merely for the purpose of introducing a more sounding word with a Latin termination ; the English language is sufficiently copious, without any further addition of new terms ; and the native words seem to me to have far more force than any foreign auxiliaries, however purposely ushered in—as British soldiers fight our battles better than the troops taken into our pay.

Goldsmith had not " commenced author " until he was past thirty : his literary judgment was mature, he had his formed opinions as to how writing should be done : and this is only the first of many occasions when he declares for simplicity and the accent of living speech.

The next example of his work shows the craftsman rather than the artist. His job was to summarize and popularize Edmund Burke's " Essay on the Sublime and Beautiful," and it is a masterly piece of fluent easy exposition. Criticism is given in detached footnotes " to prevent any interruption of the author's choice of reasoning," and very acute criticism it is. We can argue confidently from the " Vicar of Wakefield " (and from many other passages) that Goldsmith grew up in a circle where disputation was encouraged as man's finest accomplishment ; in short, as the training for philosophy. It is the philosopher who speaks here— perhaps also the disputant who in many continental universities had argued a way to his dinner. One should observe also, in taking stock of the man's equipment, how he deals with Burke's thesis that darkness which by general consent is terrible, and " therefore an element in the sublime", may have become terrible because of pain resulting from " too great a dilatation of the pupil of the eye." The footnote reads :

The muscles of the uvea act in the contraction, but are relaxed in the dilatation of the ciliary circle. Therefore, when the pupil dilates, they are in a state of relaxation, and the relaxed state of a muscle is its state of rest. In an amaurosis, where these muscles are never employed, the pupil is always dilated. Hence darkness is a state of rest to the visual organ, and consequently the obscurity which the author justly remarks to be often the cause of the sublime is often caused by a relaxation of the muscles, as well as by a tension.

Every kind of information is useful to the general practitioner in letters. Goldsmith may not have been a very serviceable doctor, but his acquaintance with anatomy helped him again and again in the breadwinning task of popularizing knowledge.

Of course, this paper has another and different interest for Goldsmith's biography. Burke and he had been at Trinity together ; later, in London, they were to be closely associated in Johnson's circle ; but it is certain that at this time the early acquaintance had not been renewed. In Goldsmith's review, though it is critical of research into a subject where " doubts instead of knowledge must terminate the enquiry," the desire to praise is unmistakable. Probably Burke saw the review and wished to know who had dealt so competently and so courteously with his book ; but years had to go by before the Grub Street critic emerged into any region of which Burke had cognizance.   In the next of his efforts, however, Goldsmith again sat in judgment on a man of mark, but one who had close touch with the *antiqua mater* of Grub Street.   He reviewed Smollett's " History of England."   Unfortunately, we cannot count on it that the review as published gives us fully what Goldsmith wrote ; for Smollett was editing the " Critical Review," a rival to Griffiths' " Monthly," and the two editors were as cat and dog.   Clearly, however, it is Goldsmith who lays emphasis on the necessity that a historian should authenticate his narration by reference to the original sources ; it is he who blames Smollett for leaving his reader to rely solely " on the veracity of the relation " ; it is he also who praises the style, " clear, nervous and flowing." But then comes a gap, and where the printed sentence reads " we forbear to enlarge," I cannot but think that Goldsmith had enlarged considerably, whereas Griffiths preferred to fill up several pages with titbits from the book under discussion.   This method of reviewing is one for which the author is seldom grateful ; it is however extensively practised in all the three papers which Goldsmith contributed to the July number, on Cardinal de Polignac's " Anti-Lucretius," on Hanway's " Eight Days' Journey," and on the " Memoirs of Madame de Maintenon " ; and even more extensively in those devoted (in August) to Voltaire's " Universal History," and to Wilkie's " Epigoniad " in September.   Frankly, one perceives that the reviewer's chief concern was to fill the space which he had to fill, and fill it with the least exertion to himself.   But it is another story when, also in September, he reviews Gray's Odes— " On the Progress of Poesy " and " The Bard."

These had just appeared in July, published in quarto by Horace Walpole at Strawberry Hill as " the first-fruits of my press; " and the review's opening more than hints dislike for this esoteric way of approach.   " As this publication seems designed for those who formed their taste by the models of antiquity, the generality of readers cannot be supposed adequate to judge of its merit." But Goldsmith, who held as an article of faith that writers should "follow the ancients" and imitate their excellencies, had arrived at a very clear idea how this should, and should not, be done :

We cannot behold this rising poet seeking fame among the learned, without hinting to him the same advice that Isocrates used to give his scholars, *study the people*. Pindar himself, of whom our modern lyrist is an imitator, appears entirely guided by it. He adapted his works exactly to the dispositions of his countrymen. . . . He chose the most popular subjects, and all his allusions are to customs well known, in his days, to the meanest person.

His English imitator wants these advantages. He speaks to a people not easily impressed with new ideas ; extremely tenacious of the old ; with difficulty warmed ; and as slowly cooling again. How unsuited then to our national character is that species of poetry which rises upon us with unexpected flights ! where we must hastily catch the thought, or it flies from us ; and, in short, where the reader must largely partake of the poet's enthusiasm, in order to taste his beauties.

Criticism passes then into an attack on the use of irregularly distributed rhyme, and here modern taste has to part company with Goldsmith. But the essential is to find out where he seems right. To him Gray had reached his highest point in the " Elegy "—a poem that made no sharp break with current standards. Admitting the merit of the Odes, the reviewer says :

We would only intimate that an English poet,—one whom the Muse has " *marked for her own*," could produce a more luxuriant bloom of flowers by cultivating such as are natives of the soil, than by endeavouring to force the exotics of another climate : or, to speak without a metaphor, such a genius as Mr. Gray might give greater pleasure, and acquire a larger portion of fame, if, instead of being an imitator, he did justice to his talents, and ventured to be more original.

G

Then, in a sentence which has both judgment and beauty, he finds this phrase for the Odes :

They are in some measure a representation of what Pindar now appears to be, though perhaps not what he appeared to the states of Greece, when they rivalled each other in his applause, and when Pan himself was seen dancing to his melody.

That was, for a while, Goldsmith's last contribution to the " Monthly " : he broke away from his bond. Drudge to literature he could be, but not a domestic drudge. Griffiths tried to keep him to office hours, and said he shirked them ; Goldsmith said that Mrs. Griffiths starved him, and that Griffiths mauled his articles. Probably both parties could justify their accusations ; at all events, the arrangement ended and once more Goldsmith was left upon the world at large—but then " It was a thing he was used to." He is said to have got lodgings in a garret near Salisbury Square and his letters were addressed to the Temple Exchange Coffee House near Temple Bar.

And now at last we begin to get direct personal contact with the struggling author.

Since the earliest stages of his continental wandering, Goldsmith had ceased to write to his people in Ireland ; and even before he left Leyden, either they had ceased to write to him, or the letters miscarried. But he had now been nearly two years in London and, for the best part of one, settled in Paternoster Row ; the Exchange Coffee House probably knew him well. News spreads. News spread even to Ballymahon that the vagrant Oliver was now well established as a literary man in London. A younger brother, Charles, kicking his heels in county Longford, decided to push out into the world and thought that Oliver might help to launch him. So after inquiries at the Temple Coffee House, this lad of twenty made his way up the stairs near Salisbury Square, and was grievously disillusioned. Long afterwards he told Malone the story and how Oliver put a good face on it :

" All in good time, my dear boy," cried Oliver joyfully, to

check the bitterness of despair; " all in good time : I shall be richer by and by. Besides, you see, I am not in positive want. Addison, let me tell you, wrote his poem of the Campaign in a garret in the Haymarket, three stories high ; and you see I am not come to that yet, for I have only got to the second story."

Charles naturally told Oliver all the news from home : how their mother was going blind, how Mr. Contarine was in his dotage, how the younger sister Jenny had married a poor farmer. He told also how their prosperous brother-in-law Daniel Hodson had busied himself to get up a subscription to subsidize the traveller—a piece of news which does not seem to have pleased Goldsmith, though perhaps the funds, if they had arrived, would have reconciled him to the humiliation of such an appeal.

Within a few days Charles was gone for good out of his brother's life. Deciding that London prospects were not promising, he managed to get passage to Jamaica, and did not see England again till some twenty years after Oliver was dead. But his coming and going set up a stir of old cravings in Oliver's mind, and at long last the " cold chain of silence " was broken. The man whom he loved best was certainly his brother Henry, to whom his unfinished " Traveller " was already addressed. Yet I cannot but think that this brother stood in Oliver Goldsmith's mind not only for himself but for their father—and that he feared to approach the head of a family whose patience had been so cruelly tried by his vagaries. On the other hand, home was still Lissoy, and to Lissoy he chose to write—not to his sister but to her husband, Daniel Hodson ; the need to acknowledge his good offices made an easier opening. The letter must be given in full for no other gives so complete a picture of the writer.

DEAR SIR,—It may be four years since my last letters went to Ireland,—to you in particular. I received no answer, probably because you never wrote to me. My brother Charles, however, informs me of the fatigue you were at in soliciting a subscription to assist me, not only among my friends and relatives, but acquaintance in general. Though my pride might feel some repugnance at being thus relieved, yet my gratitude can feel no diminution. How much obliged am I to you, to them, for such generosity, or (why should not your virtues have the proper name ?) for such charity to me at that juncture. Sure I am born to ill-fortune, to be so much a debtor and unable to repay. But to say no more of this : too many professions of gratitude are often considered as indirect petitions for future favours. Let me only add, that my not receiving that supply was the cause of my present establishment in London.—You may easily imagine what difficulties I had to encounter, left as I was without friends, recommendations, money, or impudence ; and that in a country where being born an Irishman was sufficient to keep me unemployed. Many in such circumstances would have had recourse to the friar's cord or the suicide's halter. But with all my follies, I had principle to resist the one, and resolution to combat the other.

I suppose you desire to know my present situation. As there is nothing in it at which I should blush, or which mankind could censure, I see no reason for making it a secret. In short, by a very little practice as a physician, and a very little reputation as a poet, I make a shift to live. Nothing is more apt to introduce us to the gates of the Muses than poverty ; but it were well if they only left us at the door. The mischief is, they sometimes choose to give us their company at the entertainment ; and want, instead of being gentleman-usher, often turns master of ceremonies.

Thus, upon learning I write, no doubt you imagine I starve ; and the name of an author naturally reminds you of a garret. In this particular I do not think proper to undeceive my friends. But whether I eat or starve, live in a first-floor, or four pair of stairs high, I still remember them with ardour ; nay, my very country comes in for a share of my affection. Unaccountable fondness for country, this *maladie du pais*, as the French call it ! Unaccountable that he should still have an affection for a place who never, when in it, received above common civility ; who never brought anything out of it except his brogue and his blunders. Surely my affection for is equally ridiculous with the Scotchman's, who refused to be cured of the itch, because it made him unco' thoughtful of his wife and bonny Inverary.

But now to be serious,—let me ask myself what gives me a wish to see Ireland again ? The country is a fine one, perhaps ? No. There are good company in Ireland ? No. The conversation there is generally made up of a smutty toast or a bawdy song; the vivacity supported by some humble cousin, who has just folly enough to earn his dinner. Then perhaps there's more wit and learning among the Irish? Oh, lord, no! There has been more money spent in the encouragement of the Padareen mare there one season, than given in rewards to learned men since the times of Usher. All their productions in learning amount to perhaps, a translation, or a few tracts in divinity, and all their productions in wit, just to nothing at all. Why the plague then so fond of Ireland? Then, all at once,—because you, my dear friend, and a few more who are exceptions to the general picture, have a residence there. This it is that gives me all the pangs I feel in separation. I confess I carry this spirit sometimes to the souring the pleasures I at present possess. If I go to the opera where Signora Columba pours out all the mazes of melody, I sit and sigh for Lishoy's fireside and " Johnny Armstrong's Last Good night," from Peggy Golden. If I climb Hampstead Hill, than where Nature never exhibited a more magnificent prospect, I confess it fine; but then I had rather be placed on the little mount before Lishoy gate, and there take in—to me —the most pleasing horizon in nature.

Before Charles came hither, my thoughts sometimes found refuge from severer studies among my friends in Ireland. I fancied strange revolutions at home; but I find it was the rapidity of my own motion that gave an imaginary one to objects really at rest. No alterations there. Some friends, he tells me, are still lean, but very rich; others very fat, but still very poor. Nay, all the news I hear of you is, that you sally out in visits among the neighbours, and sometimes make a migration from the blue bed to the brown. I could from my heart wish that you and she (Mrs. Hodson) and Lishoy, and Ballymahon, and all of you, would fairly make a migration into Middlesex: though, upon second thoughts, this might be attended with a few inconveniences. Therefore as the mountain will not come to Mahomet, why, Mahomet shall go to the mountain; or, to speak plain English, as you cannot conveniently pay me a visit, if next summer I can contrive to be absent six weeks from London, I shall spend three of them among my friends in Ireland. But first, believe me, my design is purely to visit, and neither to cut a figure nor levy contributions,—neither to excite envy, nor solicit favour; in fact my circumstances are adapted to neither. I am too poor to be gazed at, and too rich to need assistance.

You see, dear Dan, how long I have been talking about myself, but attribute my vanity to affection ; as every man is fond of himself, and I consider you as a second self, I imagine you will consequently be pleased with these instances of egotism. . . .

My dear sir, these things give me real uneasiness, and I could wish to redress them.   But at present there is hardly a kingdom in Europe in which I am not a debtor.   I have already discharged my most threatening and pressing demands, for we must be just before we can be grateful.   For the rest, I need not say (you know I am), your affectionate kinsman,

OLIVER GOLDSMITH.

December 27th, 1757.

That is, in the circumstances, a very valiant letter.   Goldsmith was at this moment in very grim poverty.   The man to whom he wrote was the man for whom Goldsmith's father had stripped his family so that Dan Hodson's wife should come suitably portioned.   The gratitude he had to express was for a service he had never received ; yet all through one feels an eagerness to convey real affection, while avoiding the hint that assistance would be welcome. There is no false pride, but there is real pride.   No one can blame a man for making himself appear slightly less needy than he is, when he writes to a well-to-do kinsman, who has already shown a desire to help.

An unlucky damage to the letter obliges us to guess what the things were which gave him " real uneasiness."   He may have referred to his mother's condition, or to his own sense that he had been unduly a burden on his family.   But what we have suffices to judge the young man—for it is a young man's letter, though he was now thirty.   It is the letter of a very courageous and affectionate young man— who is also a first-rate writer.   After his usage, when he has to face home with a bad account of his doings, *il paie d'esprit,* and tries at least to make it amusing.   There are hints here that he was to work up later ; the Padareen mare figures in the " Citizen of the World " ; and so does the notion about a traveller's expectation of changes at home :

I open every packet with tremulous expectation, and am agreeably disappointed when I find my friends and my country continuing in felicity. I wander, but they are at rest; they suffer few changes but what pass in my own restless imagination; it is only the rapidity of my own motion, that gives an imaginary swiftness to objects which are in some measure immoveable.

Peggy Golden, the old dairymaid, was soon to have the honour of print in " The Bee " : but, above all, here is an early hint for one of the loveliest passages in English prose, the opening to " The Vicar of Wakefield " : " All our adventures were by the fireside and all our migrations from the blue bed to the brown." Many an artist, prodigal enough of money, has been a good husband of the stock he really values, his ideas; and Oliver Goldsmith is a capital instance.

The ice was broken now between him and Lissoy and he may have felt himself less alone in the world and outcast. But things were going badly. In November of this year, 1597, Smollett had published a critical article by him on a translation of Ovid's " Fasti," yet no more work followed there. He was still working for Griffiths on a translation, the " Memoirs of a Protestant condemned to the Galleys of France for his Religion," and it appeared in February, 1758; but the translator is called " James Willingdon," and it is possible that Griffiths had paid for it before they parted company. At all events, about the New Year of 1758, Goldsmith was driven to forsake Grub Street and go back to Peckham to seek a living by the trade he detested. It was disagreeable, but with great respect to an invaluable predecessor, Forster is rather absurd in giving this phase a tragic significance. " At this point," he says, " there is evidence of despair. A stronger man, with a higher constancy and fortitude might . . . have pushed resolutely on, conquering the fate of those who look back when their objects are forward." I do not see the least indication that Goldsmith gave up his object; and his object was to distinguish himself by writing. The trouble about making the attempt, for a man unprovided of capital, is to live meanwhile. At Dr. Milner's table he had met the editor of a magazine for which Milner wrote, and had received an offer which he accepted, apparently with Milner's full approval ; indeed, the facts prove that Milner took a helpful interest in the fortunes of his assistant and probably watched his career with Griffiths sympathetically. Then there had been a quarrel ; Goldsmith had quarrelled with his bread and butter (though perhaps bread and dripping would be nearer the mark), and had tried to live as a free lance. He may have thought that the " Critical Review," Griffiths' rival, would be glad to snap him up ; but, in fact, after six months, he was obliged to look elsewhere for subsistence. At Peckham he had burnt no boats : no apology was needed for his former departure—though up to a point, failure had to be admitted. Nevertheless, he came back to live with a man who himself dabbled in literature, and he had acquired at least some trace of the professional stamp. He had found his feet in print ; to look for bread elsewhere than by journalism was not to forswear literature. Garth and Arbuthnot had earned reputation by their pens while they were earning money in their profession, which was one that Goldsmith always hoped to practise. And although nearly everybody who was first a schoolmaster and then a writer has been very glad to escape the class-room, Goldsmith was only the first of a long line who probably had compositions of their own in their heads while they watched boys doing a Latin prose.

Milner as it chanced was ill and gladly took back an usher who knew the ways of the school—and was, it seems, promoted to use the cane in the headmaster's absence : some persons recalled with pride later on that they had been chastised by the author of " She Stoops to Conquer." But this return to teaching was only a temporary expedient, and Milner evidently knew Goldsmith's desire to get into another way of living and backed it. One of his acquaintance, a Mr. Jones, was a director of the East India Company, and from him he begged a medical appointment for his usher. The promise was given and by August, 1758, Goldsmith was back again in Fleet Street. His " knack of hoping " was now in full play : and though India did not tempt him, and had then a reputation for unhealthiness far worse than West Africa to-day, there were golden visions. Passage money and outfit had to be found and he proposed to raise these by the publication of a book over his own name. It must have been written while he was at Peckham, for it was with the printer by August : and in the second week of that month he let fly a whole sheaf of letters to his friends at Lissoy. He had now something to ask of them which he felt that he could ask honourably.

The first of the flight went on August 7 to his cousin Edward Mills, who had been designed for the Bar in their college days, but had (as the letter puts it) been contented " to be merely a happy man—to be esteemed only by your acquaintance—to cultivate your paternal acres—to take unmolested a nap under one of your own hawthorns, or in Mrs. Mills's bed-chamber, which even a poet must confess, is rather the most comfortable place of the two."

Then after some appeal to memories of old friendship, Goldsmith comes to business :

I have a request, it is true to make ; but, as I know to whom I am a petitioner, I make it without diffidence or confusion. It is in short this ; I am going to publish a book in London, entitled " An Essay on the Present State of Taste and Literature in Europe." Every work published here, the printers in Ireland republish there, without giving the author the least consideration for his copy. I would in this respect disappoint their avarice, and have all the additional advantages as may result from the sale of my performance there to myself. The book is now printing in London, and I have requested Dr. Radcliff,[1] Mr. Lawder, Mr. Bryanton, my brother, Mr. Henry Goldsmith, and brother-in-law, Mr. Hodson, to circulate my proposals among their acquaintance. The same request I now make to you ; and have accordingly given directions to Mr. Bradley, bookseller in Dame-street, Dublin, to send you a hundred proposals. Whatever subscriptions pursuant to those proposals, you may receive, when collected, may be transmitted to Mr. Bradley, who will give

---

[1] A Fellow of Trinity with whom he had still some friendly relations after going down.

a receipt for the money, and be accountable for the books. I shall not, by a paltry apology, excuse myself for putting you to this trouble. Were I not convinced that you found more pleasure in doing good-natured things, than uneasiness at being employed in them, I should not have singled you out on this occasion. It is probable you would comply with such a request, if it tended to the encouragement of any man of learning whatsoever; what then may not he expect who has claims of family and friendship to enforce his?

A week later, another went off to Bob Bryanton, a much closer companion: Goldsmith reproaches him gently for not having written:

However, since you have not let me hear from you, I have in some measure disappointed your neglect by frequently thinking of you. Every day I do, I remember the calm anecdotes of your life, from the fireside to the easy-chair; recall the various adventures that first cemented our friendship,—the school, the college, or the tavern; preside in fancy over your cards; and am displeased at your bad play when the rubber goes against you, though not with all that agony of soul when I once was your partner.

Is it not strange that two of such like affections should be so much separated and so differently employed as we are? You seem placed at the centre of fortune's wheel, and let it revolve never so fast, seem insensible of the motion. I seem to have been tied to the circumference, and . . . [run]¹ disagreeably round like an whore in a whirligig. . . . [I sat]¹ down with an intention to chide. The truth is, my heart is respondent only to softer affections. And yet, now I think on't again, I will be angry. God's curse, sir! who am I? Eh! what am I? Do you know whom you have offended? A man whose character may one of these days be mentioned with profound respect in a German comment or Dutch dictionary; whose name you will probably hear ushered in by a Doctissimus Doctissimorum, or heel-pieces with a long Latin termination. Think how Goldsmithius, or Gubblegurchius, or some such sound, as rough as a nutmeg-grater, will become me? Think of that! God's curse, sir! who am I? I must own my ill-natured contemporaries have not hitherto paid me those honours I have had such just reason to expect. I have not yet seen my face reflected in all the lively

¹ Letter damaged.

display of red and white paint on any sign-posts in the suburbs. Your handkerchief weavers seem as yet unacquainted with my merits or my phisiognomy, and the very snuff-box makers appear to have forgot their respect. Tell them all from me, they are a set of Gothic, barbarous, ignorant scoundrels. There will come a day, no doubt it will—I beg you may live a couple of hundred years longer to see the day—when the Scaligers and Daciers will vindicate my character, give learned editions of my labours, and bless the times with copious comments on the text. You shall see how they will dish up the heavy scoundrels who disregard me now, or will then offer to cavil at my productions. How they will bewail the times that suffered so much genius to lie neglected. If ever my works find their way to Tartary or China, I know the consequence. Suppose one of your Chinese Owanowitzers instructing one of your Tartarian Chianobacchhi—you see I use Chinese names to show my own erudition, as I shall soon make our Chinese talk like an Englishman to show his. This may be the subject of the lecture :

' Oliver Goldsmith flourished in the eighteenth and nineteenth centuries. He lived to be an hundred and three years old . . . age may justly be styled the sun of . . . and the Confucius of Europe . . . learned world, were anonymous, and have probably been lost, because united with those of others. The first avowed piece the world has of his, is entitled an " Essay on the Present State of Taste and Literature in Europe "—a work still worth its weight in diamonds. In this he profoundly explains what learning is, and what learning is not. In this he proves that blockheads are not men of wit, and yet that men of wit are actually blockheads.'

But as I choose neither to tire my Chinese Philosopher, nor you, nor myself, I must discontinue the oration, in order to give you a good pause for admiration ; and I find myself most violently disposed to admire too. Let me, then, stop my fancy to take a view of my future self ; and, as the boys say, light down to see myself on horseback. Well, now I am down, where the devil is I ? Oh Gods, Gods, here in a garret, writing for bread, and expecting to be dunned for a milk-score. However, dear Bob, whether in penury or affluence, serious or gay, I am ever wholly thine,   OLIVER GOLDSMITH.

Give my—no, not compliments neither, but something . . . most warm and sincere wish that you can conceive, to your mother, Mrs. Bryanton, to Miss Bryanton, to yourself; and if there be a favourite dog in the family, let me be remembered to it.

That is the Master Noll of George's public-house in Ballymahon—where, we may be very sure, he delighted not only to talk over hare-hunting and the ball alley, but to display his "book-learned skill." As to the future—note already the emergence of a Chinese Philosopher. Ideas lay long germinating in that very odd mind.

Next day there was another letter, written with evident difficulty, to his cousin, who had played with him when he was a child and she a young girl—Contarine's daughter, Mrs. Lawder. Plainly he thinks that, so far back as those days in Leyden when he spent the money borrowed for his journey on a gift of bulbs, the kind old man had already closed his heart against him. After that, to come asking simply for a renewal of friendship would have been easy, but he must appear with a request; and his tone is much more constrained than in the other letters. But here also there must be almost full quotation:

If you should ask why, in an interval of so many years, you never heard from me, permit me, madam, to ask the same question. I have the best excuse in recrimination. I wrote to Kilmore from Leyden in Holland, from Louvain in Flanders, and Rouen in France, but received no answer. To what could I attribute this silence but displeasure or forgetfulness? Whether I was right in my conjecture I do not pretend to determine; but this I must ingenuously own, that I have a thousand times in my turn endeavoured to forget them, whom I could not but look upon as forgetting me. . . .

I was, madam, when I discontinued writing to Kilmore, in such circumstances, that all my endeavours to continue your regards might be attributed to wrong motives. My letters might be looked upon as the petitions of a beggar, and not the offerings of a friend; while all my professions, instead of being considered as the result of disinterested esteem, might be ascribed to venal insincerity. I believe, indeed, you had too much generosity to place them in such a light, but I could not bear even the shadow of such a suspicion. . . . I could not—I own I could not—continue a correspondence; for every acknowledgment for past favours might be considered as an indirect request for future ones. . . .

It is true, this conduct might have been simple enough, but yourself must confess it was in character. Those who know me at all, know that I have always been actuated by different principles from the rest of mankind, and while none regarded the interest of his friend more, no man on earth regarded his own less. I have often affected bluntness to avoid the imputation of flattery, have frequently seemed to overlook those merits too obvious to escape notice, and pretended disregard to those instances of good-nature and good sense, which I could not fail tacitly to applaud : and all this lest I should be ranked amongst the grinning tribe, who say " very true " to all that is said, who fill a vacant chair at a tea-table, whose narrow souls never moved in a wider circle than the circumference of a guinea, and who had rather be reckoning the money in your pocket than the virtue of your breast. All this, I say, I have done, and a thousand other very silly though very disinterested things in my time, and for all which no soul cares a farthing about me. God's curse, madam ! is it to be wondered, that he should once in his life forget you, who has been all his life forgetting himself ?

Faith ! Madam, I heartily wish to be rich, if it were only for this reason, to say without a blush how much I esteem you ; but, alas ! I have many a fatigue to encounter before that happy time comes, when your poor old simple friend may again give a loose to the luxuriance of his nature, sitting by Kilmore fireside, recount the various adventures of a hard-fought life, laugh over the follies of the day, join his flute to your harpsichord, and forget that ever he stayed starved in those streets where Butler and Otway starved before him.

But now I mention those great names—My uncle ! he is no more that soul of fire as when once I knew him. Newton and Swift grew dim with age as well as he. But what shall I say ? —his mind was too active an inhabitant not to disorder the feeble mansion of his abode ; for the richest jewels soonest wear their settings.

Then follows a statement of the proposal, as before, winding up with a little touch of the jesting swaggerer :

If I know Mr. Lawder (and sure I ought to know him), he will accept the employment with pleasure. All I can say—if he writes a book, I will get him two hundred subscribers, and those of the best wits in Europe.

The postscript keeps the same suggestion of discomfort :

Now see how I blot and blunder when I am asking a favour.

One has a sense that after he had issued his request for the third time, it seemed less easy than at first : that he anticipated refusal—or what he actually received, a silent answer.

In none of these letters it should be noticed, does he mention the object for which he wants the money ; but it would seem that he told his brother ; for, writing also to his brother-in-law Hodson, he says :

I suppose you have heard of my intention of going to the East Indies. The place of my destination is one of the factories on the coast of Coromandel, and I go in quality of physician and surgeon ; for which the Company has signed my warrant, which has already cost me 10*l*. I must also pay 50*l*. for my passage, and 10*l*. for my sea stores ; and the other incidental expenses of my equipment will amount to 60*l*. or 70*l*. more. The salary is but trifling, namely, 100*l*. per annum ; but the other advantages, if a person be prudent, are considerable. The practice of the place, if I am rightly informed, generally amounts to not less than 1000*l*. per annum, for which the appointed physician has an exclusive privilege, This, with the advantages resulting from trade, and the high interest which money bears, viz. : 20*l*. per cent., are the inducements which persuade me to undergo the fatigues of sea, the dangers of war, and the still greater dangers of the climate ; which induce me to leave a place where I am every day gaining friends and esteem ; and where I might enjoy all the conveniences of life. . . . I have no certainty it is true ; but why cannot I do as some men of more merit, who have lived on more precarious terms ?

I know you have in Ireland a very different idea of a man who writes for bread ; though Swift and Steele did so in the earliest part of their lives. You imagine, I suppose, that every author, by profession, lives in a garret, wears shabby clothes, and converses with the meanest company. Yet I do not believe there is one single writer, who has abilities to translate a French novel, that does not keep better company, wear finer clothes, and live more genteelly, than many who pride themselves for nothing else in Ireland. I confess it again, my dear Dan, that nothing but the wildest ambition could prevail on me to leave the enjoyment of the refined conversation which I am sometimes permitted to partake in, for uncertain fortune and paltry show.

Then follows the detailed request; but at its close the tone sags down into melancholy:

I know not how my desire of seeing Ireland, which had so long slept, has again revived with so much ardour. So weak is my temper, and so unsteady, that I am frequently tempted, particularly when low-spirited, to return home and leave my fortune, though just beginning to look kinder. But it shall not be. In five or six years I hope to indulge these transports. I find I want constitution, and a strong steady disposition, which alone makes men great. I will, however, correct my faults, since I am conscious of them.

This group of letters, and one more which is related to them, give us the most intimate picture of the man that we possess. Hereafter we must infer him from his public writings, except for the light thrown by occasional notes; and to this is added a mass of sketches by other and not too friendly hands. But here, at the turning-point in his life, we can look straight into his mind.

The letter to Hodson is assigned by Cunningham to November: at all events it was before December, which proved the critical month. We have now the facts of an episode which earlier biographers had left dim and vague. Goldsmith certainly had the promise of an appointment on the Coromandel Coast before he left Milner's school in August. Why was it not fulfilled? I quote now from Dr. Kirkpatrick's paper in which his knowledge of medical history supplements Miss Balderstone's acute deduction from a study of what was happening in India at that period:

In April, 1758, Count Lally landed at Pondicherry on the Coromandel coast, captured Fort St. David, and laid siege to Madras, wellnigh establishing a French supremacy in Southern India. The East India Company was most anxious to conceal the true state of affairs from the people at home, and allowed very

little information of the French success to leak out. Although
the public knew practically nothing of the matter, yet it is obvious
that the Company could not send out a medical officer to a civil
post in a district which was not then under its control. The
offer to Goldsmith was postponed, but not cancelled. In December, 1758, eight warships were fitted out, one of which was osten-
sibly intended for Madras, but all of which eventually arrived
there, and raised the siege in February, 1759. Goldsmith at
once recognized that if he could get any sort of post as surgeon
on this warship he would get a free passage and so save £50.
In view of this he applied to the Surgeons' Hall for a qualification for the post of Surgeon's Mate, but he was found " not
qualified " by the Court of Examiners on December 21, 1758.
The cause of his rejection is not recorded, and it has generally
been assumed that it was for want of knowledge, but it is very
much more likely that the rejection was due to his want of proper
indentures as an apprentice. About any deficiency in indentures
the Surgeons were very strict. Want of knowledge was too
common to attract much attention. . . . Goldsmith had never
served as an apprentice to a surgeon, and consequently he would
not be passed by any surgical board for any surgical post.

But he presented himself; and before he presented
himself, he must be at least decently dressed.

All these appeals to Ireland for subscriptions had produced nothing and by November Goldsmith turned again
to the magazines. One may fairly assume that he had failed
everywhere before he went back to Griffiths; but to
Griffiths he went back. Griffiths agreed to go security with
the tailor for a new suit of clothes on condition that Goldsmith provided four lengthy reviews for that month. It
was part of the bargain that by a given time the clothes were
to be paid for or returned.

Had Goldsmith been appointed, he might have raised the
money; but on December 21 he was turned down. Then
came Christmas, and Goldsmith owed money for his lodging; his landlord's wife came in crying, to say that the
bailiffs were going to seize her husband, and money must be
found. So, to meet this demand, the new clothes went to
the pawnshop. But there was still food to be bought and a

few days later Goldsmith, left with the four volumes which he had reviewed for Griffiths, pledged them also. Books did not then become the reviewer's perquisite.

Then down came Griffiths with a demand that the books should be returned and the suit paid for or sent back. Goldsmith wrote what excuses he could. The tone in which Griffiths replied may be inferred from the following letter :

Sir,—I know of no misery but a gaol to which my own imprudencies and your letter seem to point. I have seen it inevitable these three or four weeks, and, by heavens ! request it as a favour that may prevent somewhat more fatal. I have been some years struggling with a wretched being, with all that contempt which indigence brings with it, with all those strong passions which make contempt insupportable. What then has a gaol that is formidable ? I shall at least have the society of wretches, and such is to me true society. I tell you again and again I am now neither able nor willing to pay you a farthing, but I will be punctual to any appointment you or the taylor shall make ; thus far at least I do not act the sharper, since, unable to pay my debts one way, I would willingly give some security another. No, Sir, had I been a sharper, had I been possessed of less good nature and native generosity I might surely now have been in better circumstances. I am guilty, I own, of meannesses which poverty unavoidably brings with it, my reflections are filled with repentance for my imprudence but not with any remorse for being a villain, that may be a character you unjustly charge me with. Your books I can assure you are neither pawn'd nor sold, but in the custody of a friend from whom my necessities oblig'd me to borrow some money ; whatever becomes of my person, you shall have them in a month. It is very possible both the reports you have heard and your own suggestions may have brought you false information with respect to my character, it is very possible that the man whom you now regard with detestation may inwardly burn with grateful resentment, it is very possible that upon a second perusal of the letter I sent you, you may see the workings of a mind strongly agitated with gratitude and jealousy, if such circumstances should appear at least spare invective 'till my book with Mr. Dodsley shall be publish'd, and then perhaps you may see the bright side of a mind when my professions shall not appear the dictates of necessity but of choice. You seem to think Dr. Milner knew me not. Perhaps so ; but he was a man I shall ever honour ; but I have friendship only with the dead ! I ask pardon for taking up so much time. Nor shall I add to it by any other professions (but) that that I am Sir your Humble Servt.

OLIVER GOLDSMITH.

P.S. I shall expect impatiently the result of your resolutions.

This unhappy document the bookseller studiously preserved, endorsing it, " Received in January, 1759." He felt that it gave him the whip-hand of this recalcitrant apprentice. The end could only be one way, and Goldsmith got out of his obligations by an undertaking to write a Life of Voltaire which should be prefixed to a translation of the " Henriade "—by another hand.

Meanwhile, however, Smollett had commissioned two articles for the " Critical Review " of January and another for February : this source of employment lasted steadily till autumn. Dodsley still delayed publication of the " Enquiry."

Such was the position of Oliver Goldsmith after nearly two years' experience of professional authorship.

CHAPTER VI

THE AUTHOR'S FIRST BOOK

THINGS were bad for the adventurer at the beginning of 1759; there is no doubt of that. In London where he must carry on, make shift to get a living, there was no friend at his back. Milner was dead; Griffiths, from whom alone he had been able a few weeks back to get a minimum of assistance, was most unfriendly; his relations with the " Critical Review " were still precarious. It was not even yet definitely fixed in his mind that he must, could and would support existence by writing. The book on which he had counted, as young authors count, was delayed from month to month. Still it was something coming out, on a larger scale than he had yet seen in print.

On the other hand, in that home country which he still instinctively regarded as the base of his life, there was no active reply answering his discreet signals of distress. Oliver Goldsmith's mother was indeed in no position to help him, but it is clear that not even kind messages from her came across the sea. She was done with a son who had been nothing but a disappointment. It is plain enough too that the family at large had decided to let the shiftless one shift for himself. Quite probably they remembered the Fiddleback saga and were doubtful as to whether this forthcoming book might not be a new legend. In any case, Mr. Edward Mills and Mr. Bob Bryanton were likely to have a lively interest in the Padareen Mare; not so likely to be concerned with the " State of Polite Learning in Europe." They took the easy way of leaving " Master Noll's " letters unanswered. Henry Goldsmith tried to stir them, but nothing came of that either. In short,

Oliver Goldsmith had only one person left in Ireland from whom he could expect so much as the answer to a letter, and that was the clergyman with a wife and family to keep on forty pounds a year. To him Oliver wrote the last and longest of these epistles to his home circle.

There is a trace of constraint in the beginning, but, as the pen runs, how completely it passes off!

DEAR SIR,—Your punctuality in answering a man, whose trade is writing, is more than I had reason to expect; and yet you see me generally fill a whole sheet, which is all the recompense I can make for being so frequently troublesome. The behaviour of Mr. Mills and Mr. Lawder is a little extraordinary. However, their answering neither you nor me is a sufficient indication of their disliking the employment which I assigned them. As their conduct is different from what I expected, so I have made an alteration in mine. I shall, the beginning of next month, send over two hundred and fifty books, which are all that I fancy can be well sold among you, and I would have you make some distinction in the persons who have subscribed. The money, which will amount to sixty pounds, may be left with Mr. Bradley, as soon as possible. I am not certain but I shall quickly have occasion for it. I have met with no disappointment with respect to my East India voyage; nor are my resolutions altered; though, at the same time, I must confess it gives me some pain to think I am almost beginning the world at the age of thirty-one. Though I never had a day's sickness since I saw you, yet I am not that strong and active man you once knew me. You scarcely can conceive how much eight years of disappointment, anguish, and study, have worn me down. If I remember rightly, you are seven or eight years older than me, yet I dare venture to say, that if a stranger saw us both, he would pay me the honours of seniority. Imagine to yourself a pale melancholy visage, with two great wrinkles between the eyebrows, with an eye disgustingly severe, and a big wig; and you may have a perfect picture of my present appearance. On the other hand, I conceive you as perfectly sleek and healthy, passing many a happy day among your own children, or those you knew as a child. Since I knew what it was to be a man, this is a pleasure I have not known. I have passed my days among a parcel of cool designing beings, and have contracted all their suspicious manner in my own behaviour. I should actually be as unfit for the society of my friends at home, as I detest that which I am obliged to partake of here. I can now neither laugh nor drink, have contracted a hesitating disagreeable manner of speaking, and a visage that looks ill-nature itself; in short, I have thought myself into a settled melancholy, and an utter disgust of all that life brings with it—Whence this romantic turn, that all our family are possessed with? Whence this love for every place and every country but that in which we reside? for every occupation but our own? this desire of fortune, and yet this eagerness to dissipate?

He has his brother Charles in mind here, as well as himself: inevitably, in the letters that passed between them there must have been question of this other wanderer.

Then follows the passage which I have already quoted in part,[1] concerning the education of Henry's son. The rest must now be given: and even if there is a hint of Mr. Micawber in this philosophy, it is none the less likeable for that:

It is impossible to conceive how much may be done by a proper education at home. A boy, for instance, who understands perfectly Latin, French, Arithmetic, and the principles of the civil law, and can write a fine hand, has an education that may qualify him for any undertaking. And these parts of learning should be carefully inculcated, let him be designed for whatever calling he will. Above all things let him never touch a romance or novel; those paint beauty in colours more charming than nature; and describe happiness than man never tastes. How delusive, how destructive are those pictures of consummate bliss! They teach the youthful mind to sigh after beauty and happiness which never existed; to despise the little good which fortune has mixed in our cup, by expecting more than ever she gave; and in general, take the word of a man who has seen the world, and who has studied human nature more by experience than precept; take my word for it, that books teach us very little of the world. The greatest merit in a state of poverty would only serve to make the possessor ridiculous; may distress, but cannot relieve him. Frugality, and even avarice, in the lower orders of mankind, are

[1] See Chapter II, p. 42.

true ambition. These afford the only ladder for the poor to rise to preferment. Teach then, my dear sir, to your son thrift and economy. Let his poor wandering uncle's example be placed before his eyes. I had learned from books to be disinterested and generous, before I was taught from experience the necessity of being prudent. I had contracted the habits and notions of a philosopher, while I was exposing myself in the very situation of the wretch who thanked me for my bounty. While I am in the remotest part of the world, tell him this, and perhaps he may improve from my example.

Now he turns to the thought of those from whom he must have felt himself deliberately cut off : and surely there is a sweetness in the nature that shows no trace of resentment—reasonable or unreasonable—against his sentence of exile :

My mother, I am informed, is almost blind ; even though I had the utmost inclination to return home, under such circumstances I could not : for to behold her in distress without a capacity of relieving her from it, would add too much to my splenetic habit. Your last letter was much too short, it should have answered some queries I had made in my former. Just sit down as I do, and write forward until you have filled all your paper ; it requires no thought, at least from the ease with which my own sentiments rise when they are addressed to you. For, believe me, my head has no share in all I write ; my heart dictates the whole. Pray, give my love to Bob Bryanton, and intreat him, from me, not to drink. My dear sir, give me some account about poor Jenny. Yet her husband loves her ; if so, she cannot be unhappy.

Last come his own affairs, and the budding author pours out his communications freely :

I know not whether I should tell you—yet why should I conceal those trifles, or indeed anything from you ?—there is a book of mine will be published in a few days, the life of a very extraordinary man—no less than the great Voltaire. You know already by the title, than it is no more than a catch-penny. However I spent but four weeks on the whole performance, for which I received twenty pounds. When published, I shall take some method of conveying it to you, unless you may think it dear of the postage, which may amount to four or five shillings. However, I fear you will not find an equivalent of amusement. Your last letter, I repeat it, was too short : you should have given me your opinion of the design of the heroic-comical poem which I sent you : you remember I intended to introduce the hero of the poem, as lying in a paltry alehouse. You may take the following specimen of the manner, which I flatter myself is quite original. The room in which he lies, may be described somewhat this way :

> The window, patched with paper, lent a ray,
> That feebly show'd the state in which he lay.
> The sandy floor, that grits beneath the tread :
> The humid wall with paltry pictures spread :
> The game of goose was there exposed to view,
> And the twelve rules the royal martyr drew ;
> The seasons, fram'd with listing, found a place,
> And Prussia's monarch show'd his lamp-black face.
> The morn was cold ; he views with keen desire
> A rusty grate unconscious of a fire.
> An unpaid reck'ning on the frieze was scor'd,
> And five crack'd teacups dress'd the chimney board.

And now imagine after his soliloquy, the landlord to make his appearance, in order to dun him for the reckoning :

> Not with that face, so servile and so gay,
> That welcomes every stranger than can pay,
> With sulky eye he smoak'd the patient man,
> Then pull'd his breeches tight, and thus began, &c.

All this is taken, you see, from nature. It is a good remark of Montaigne that the wisest men often have friends, with whom they do not care how much they play the fool. Take my present follies as instances of regard. Poetry is a much easier, and more agreeable species of composition than prose, and could a man live by it, it were not unpleasant employment to be a poet. I am resolved to leave no space, though I should fill it up only by telling you, what you very well know already, I mean that I am your most affectionate friend and brother,

OLIVER GOLDSMITH.

After this, the umbilical cord was cut : Oliver Goldsmith no longer thought of succour or support from Ireland. But he never ceased to think how he could make return to the man who stood by him with affection and in whom was preserved the tradition and example of their father. Henry Goldsmith was no gainer in money; but the dedication of " The Traveller " remains to preserve his memory. The money, when Oliver Goldsmith had any to spend or to lend, went elsewhere; scores of needy Irishmen dipped into that ill-fastened purse, and his own kindred were among them. But that was still a long way off. Yet the first real step on the road that led to well-paid literary work and recognized position was taken only a couple of months after this letter went out. " An Enquiry into the Present State of Learning in Europe " appeared in April, 1759, printed for R. and J. Dodsley in Pall Mall. No author's name appeared, but the appropriate circles always could inform themselves as to authorship : London's literary world was not then so big a place. Two sentences adorned the title-page, one in Greek, saying " I have friendship for philosophers ; but none for sophists and pedants, and may I never have " : and one in Latin : " It were endurable if those who pull down our buildings knew how to build." In these, I take it that Goldsmith offered proof of his ability to be sententious in both the classical tongues, for no scholar that I know can trace them to another author.

The " Enquiry " cannot be classed among the small handful of works by which Goldsmith acquired and retains his rank as a writer; yet it is of great importance for the study of the man and of his work. The writing itself is not yet entirely characteristic because he is not yet at ease with his public; he is self-consciously writing for print; he is not the Goldsmith whom we have already in the letter that has just been quoted. There is too much of the antithetic style which Johnson had already carried to excess, and to which this new writer added some over-fondness for alliteration : for instance in this paragraph of the Introduction where he hunts the letter—especially the damnatory *d*s :

Complaints of our degeneracy in literature as well as in morals, I own, have been frequently exhibited of late ; but seem to be enforced more with the ardour of devious declamation, than the calmness of deliberate inquiry. The dullest critic, who strives at a reputation for delicacy by showing he cannot be pleased, may pathetically assure us, that our taste is upon the decline ; may consign every modern performance to oblivion, and bequeath nothing to posterity except the labours of our ancestors, or his own. Such general invective, however, conveys no instruction ; all it teaches is, that the writer dislikes an age by which he is probably disregarded.

But it differs essentially from Johnson's style in this, that it is the prose of a poet—though a poet of an age which renounced all in poetry that was lyrical. Nevertheless it is a poet, a philosophic poet, who sets out the function of poetry in general culture :

Those who behold the phenomena of nature, and content themselves with the view without inquiring into their causes, are perhaps wiser than is generally imagined. In this manner our rude ancestors were acquainted with facts ; and poetry, which helped the imagination and the memory, was thought the most proper vehicle for conveying their knowledge to posterity. It was the poet who harmonized the ungrateful accents of his native dialect ; who lifted it above common conversation, and shaped its rude combinations into order. From him the orator formed a style ; and though poetry first rose out of prose, in turn it gave birth to every prosaic excellence. Musical period, concise expression, and delicacy of sentiment, were all excellencies derived from the poet ; in short, he not only preceded, but formed the orator, philosopher, and historian.

From this the author proceeds to what may be called a common-form account of the genesis of criticism :

Critics, sophists, grammarians, rhetoricians, and commentators, now begin to figure in the literary commonwealth. . . . Libraries were loaded, but not enriched with their labours. . . . They now took upon them to teach poetry to those who wanted genius ; and the power of disputing to those who knew nothing of the subject in debate.

Then comes, what was to be characteristic of this author, the appeal to " nature " :

Common sense would be apt to suggest, that those rules were collected, not from nature, but a copy of nature, and would consequently give us still fainter resemblances of original beauty. It might still suggest, that explained wit makes but a feeble impression ; that the observations of others are soon forgotten, those made by ourselves are permanent and useful. But, it seems, understandings of every size were to be mechanically instructed in poetry. . . . Metrodorus, Valerius Probus, Aulus Gellius, Pedianus, Boethius, and a hundred others, to be acquainted with whom might show much reading and but little judgment ; these, I say, made choice each of an author, and delivered all their load of learning on his back.

First and last, Oliver Goldsmith stood for direct contact with life, and a hatred of jargon. " We may be assured that the generality of mankind never lose a passion for letters while they continue to be either amusing or useful," he asserts. But it would be tedious to attempt a summary of the little book's philosophy of literature. Two sentences will give the pith of what Goldsmith preached :

It were to be wished that we no longer found pleasure with the inflated style that has for some years been looked upon as fine writing and which every young writer is now obliged to adopt, if he chooses to be read. . . . Let us instead of writing finely try to write naturally.

Goldsmith was to do much more later by example than here by precept, and a great deal even in this tract sounds inflated if set beside a page of the " Vicar " or " The Citizen of the World."

Yet even in this early and still amateurish work there is already a delightful writer. The matter of it is indeed no great matter. But if we had a similar work by one of the *vagantes* who swarmed out of Ireland in the ninth and tenth centuries, we should be less obliged to reconstruct the beginnings of modern Europe by conjecture. Goldsmith had read a great deal in Latin, Greek, English and French, and not a little in Italian : his only contact with polite society must have been such as could be gained by a penniless student, attending academic disputations. But he carried a noticing eye wherever he went and is not content to tell us that in France ladies " contributed not a little to prevent the decline of literature and philosophy " ; he testifies that he had " seen as bright a circle of beauty at the chemical lectures of Rouelle as gracing the court of Versailles." Even if we admit that he knew Versailles only by report (though he may have stood at the doors when courtiers assembled), at all events he had attended the lectures. Again, he gives an amusing though perhaps somewhat sketchy picture of the Virtuosi and Filosofi in Italy—lit up with one flash of style, when he denounces those who, like the Filosofi, had been schooled " to *think in track*—only adopt such opinions as their universities, or the inquisition, were pleased to allow."

When we come to Germany, a lively dislike gives spirit to the writing. With sound good sense, he condemns the Germans for continuing to write in Latin instead of studying their own tongue, and points to the result in a swarm of pedants :

Guilty of a fault too common to great readers, they write through volumes, while they do not think through a page. Never fatigued themselves, they think the reader can never be weary ; so they drone on, saying all that can be said on the subject, not selecting what may be advanced to the purpose. Were angels to write books, they never would write folios.

The merit of his own writing lies, and he knows it, in what cannot be got by mere reading. " Though the sketch I have drawn be general," he says, " yet it was for the most part taken on the spot." There is admirable observation in his chapter on the difficulty of establishing a comparison between the literatures of England and of France. One country is " an island little visited by travellers of discernment," developing its own local peculiarities unrestrained by criticism or by imitation. On the other hand, " an universal sameness of character appears to spread itself over the whole continent; particularly the fools and cox-combs of every country abroad seem almost cast in the same mould " :

The French pictures, therefore, of life and manners are imme-diately allowed to be just, because foreigners are acquainted with the models from whence they are copied. The Marquis of Molière strikes all Europe. Sir John Falstaff, with all the merry men of Eastcheap, are entirely of England, and please the English alone.

But for biographical interest, we must turn to the chap-ters " On rewarding Genius in England " : and " Of the Marks of Literary Decay in England and France." The complaints of an author are no new topic in literature ; yet with Goldsmith they assume a special character. He disapproves too lavish a provision ; such rewards act " like employments at court, rather as bribes to silence, than incentives to competition. . . . Authors, like running horses, should be fed not fattened." Genius should have its " proper encouragements—subsistence and respect " ; but of the two he is more concerned about the respect, and more angry at the lack of it.

Those who are unacquainted with the world are apt to fancy the man of wit as leading a very agreeable life. They conclude, perhaps, that he is attended to with silent admiration, and dic-tates to the rest of mankind with all the eloquence of conscious superiority. Very different is his present situation. He is called an author, and all know that an author is a thing only to be laughed at. His person, not his jest, becomes the mirth of the company. At his approach, the most fat unthinking face brightens into malicious meaning. Even aldermen laugh, and revenge on him the ridicule which was lavished on their forefathers.

And again in a passage which is pathetically self-revealing, he pleads that the author should be treated " as a child of the public " :

And indeed a child of the public he is in all respects, for while so well able to direct others, how incapable is he frequently found of guiding himself ! His simplicity exposes him to all the insidious approaches of cunning; his sensibility, to the slightest invasions of contempt. Though possessed of fortitude to stand unmoved the expected bursts of an earthquake, yet of feelings so exquisitely poignant as to agonize under the slightest disappointment. Broken rest, tasteless meals, and causeless anxiety shorten his life, or render it unfit for active employment; prolonged vigils and intense application still farther contract his span, and make his time glide insensibly away.

These generalities could at least make him no enemies; but in the next chapter Goldsmith localizes his attack. He complains of the flood of criticism in Reviews, newspapers and magazines:

If there be any, however, among these writers, who, being bred gentlemen and scholars, are obliged to have recourse to such an employment for subsistence, I wish them one more suited to their inclinations; but for such who, wholly destitute of education and genius, indent to the press, and turn mere bookmakers, they deserve the severest censure. These add to the sin of criticism the sin of ignorance also. Their trade is a bad one, and they are bad workmen in the trade.

Further on comes a complaint against the fashion of "a disgusting solemnity of manner," which must, both in prose and poetry, "banish all that agreeable trifling which, if I may so express it, often deceives us into instruction":

Were these Monthly Reviews and Magazines frothy, pert, or absurd, they might find some pardon; but to be dull and dronish is an encroachment on the prerogative of a folio.

Then comes the first shot of a battle that was to last through Goldsmith's literary career, and end in his triumph:

However, by the power of one single monosyllable our critics have almost got the victory over humour amongst us. Does the poet paint the absurdities of the vulgar, then he is low; does he exaggerate the features of folly to render it more thoroughly ridiculous, he is then very low. In short, they have proscribed the comic or satirical muse from every walk but high life; which, though abounding in fools as well as in the humblest station, is by no means so fruitful in absurdity.

When Goldsmith made it a cause of breaking with Griffiths that his manuscripts were mutilated, we may safely assume that this " one single monosyllable " figured in the argument. Goldsmith's idea of what a magazine article should be is familiar to us, and it is very unlike his contributions to the " Monthly Review " as we have them. But whether it was wise for a young author to attack by name the periodical for which he had been working is another matter : especially after that episode about the pawnshop. Indeed, I can hardly believe that this passage, which appeared in April, 1759, would have been written after the dreadful letter of that January. Probably the thing was already in type, composed when Goldsmith, expecting to take ship for Coromandel, was all for a parting fling at dunces and disagreeable booksellers.

Naturally enough, according to his nature, Griffiths set one of his minions to belabour the rebel. Kenrick, a very unamiable specimen of the hack, wrote a notice which appeared in the " Monthly Review " for November :

Notwithstanding our author talks so familiarly of us, the great, and affects to be thought to stand in the rank of Patrons, we cannot help thinking that in more places than one he has betrayed, in himself, the man he so severely condemns for drawing his quill to take a purse. We are even so firmly convinced of this, that we dare put the question home to his conscience, whether he never experienced the unhappy situation he so feelingly describes in that of a Literary Understrapper ? His remarking him as coming down from his garret, to rummage the bookseller's shop for materials to work upon, and the knowledge he displays of his minutest labours, give great reason to suspect he may himself have had concerns in the bad trade of book-making. *Fronti nulla fides*. We have heard of many a Writer who " patronized only by his bookseller," has nevertheless, affected the Gentleman in print, and talked full as cavalierly as our Author himself. We have even known one hardy enough publicly to stigmatize men of the first rank in literature for their immoralities, while conscious himself of labouring under the infamy of having, by the vilest and meanest actions, forfeited all pretensions to honour and honesty. If such men as these, boasting a liberal education, and pretending to genius, practise at the same time those arts which bring the Sharper to the cart's tail or the pillory, need our Author wonder that " learning partakes the contempt of its professors " ?

Within three years the " Monthly " printed an apology for this " undesigned offence "—so quick was Goldsmith's rise to a position which no bookseller could neglect. But more serious damage to him followed from the chapter on the Stage, which complains bitterly of the present conduct of the theatre—where Garrick was omnipotent.—No new play has a chance; before it can reach the public " it must be tried in the Manager's fire, strained through a licenser, and purified in the Review or the Newspapers of the day."

Old pieces are revived and scarcely any new ones admitted. The actor is ever in our eye, and the poet seldom permitted to appear. . . . What must be done? only sit down contented, cry up all that comes before us, and admire even the absurdities of Shakespeare.

Goldsmith goes on to repel the charge of literary impiety; but in fact he was aware that there is much bad writing in Shakespeare. Now that Mr. A. E. Housman has said as much, why should we not all admit it ?—though we need not go so far as this angry young man who declared that " the revival of these pieces of forced humour, far-fetched conceit, and unnatural hyperbole, which have been ascribed to Shakespeare, is rather gibbeting than raising a statue to his memory." Certainly Goldsmith cannot be commended as a critic, but at least he declined to " think in track." It does not matter to our estimate of his character how he permitted himself to speak of Shakespeare: the point is, that we have here a young man who plainly from the very beginning wanted to write plays, and who squared up at the God Almighty of that day's theatre. Everybody knew who was meant when he said that devotion to Shakespeare was " rather a trick of the actor, who thinks it safest acting in exaggerated characters." Yet that, if injudicious, was fair hitting: the description of " partisans, who understand the force of combination, trained up to vociferation, clapping of hands and clattering of sticks," might pass : but it was not wise to suggest that managers deliberately produced old pieces because they regarded " third nights "—(the author's perquisite) as " disagreeable drawbacks upon the profits of the stage."

It was not long before Goldsmith was asking a favour that Garrick could withhold—and was answered that his " unprovoked attack " barred the way. In short, he had been very unwise. Yet the resentment of his attacks had this much consolation. He had been read. He began to be somebody. The *literati* took notice of him. One of them indeed had sought him out already, even before the " Enquiry " appeared. This was Percy of the *Reliques*, to whom Grainger (poet of the Sugar Cane) had introduced the poet at his habitual coffee house. Percy showed perhaps a want of tact, for he discovered Goldsmith's address and went to call in Green Arbour Court. Yet what he saw, he described later only to emphasize the depth of squalor from which Goldsmith lifted himself into " the best societies of London " ; and one may say now, what he himself refrains from suggesting, that not many clergymen so well placed as Percy would have continued to cultivate such an acquaintance :

The Doctor was writing his " Enquiry," &c., in a wretched dirty room, in which there was but one chair, and when he, from civility offered it to his visitant, himself was obliged to sit in the window. While they were conversing, someone gently rapped at the door, and being desired to come in, a poor ragged little girl of very decent behaviour, entered, who, dropping a curtsie, said, " My mamma sends her compliments, and begs the favour of you to lend her a chamber-pot full of coals."

There is no need to dwell here on the other writings by which in 1759 Goldsmith warded off famine. All are reviews, and criticism did not interest him. Yet it is interesting to find him writing of Spenser that " no poet more enlarges the imagination" and curious that he should deplore the reviving of many Spenserian words : " a language already too copious has been augmented by an unnecessary reinforcement." His conception of a literary style, unduly influenced by the ruling French ideas, discarded all desire for richness. Thought should take shape in simple graceful form, without emphasis or colour. But if his interest in Spenser is not inspired by literary allegiance, yet a fellow-feeling makes him kind to the Elizabethan :

The ordinary of Newgate, we are told, has but one story, which serves for the life of every hero that happens to come within the circle of his pastoral care ; however unworthy the resemblance appears, it may be asserted, that the history of one poet might serve with as little variation for that of any other. Born of creditable parents, who gave him a pious education ; however, in spite of all their endeavours, in spite of all the exhortations of the minister of the parish on Sundays, he turned his mind from following good things, and fell to—writing verses ! Spenser, in short, lived poor, was reviled by the critics of his time, and died at last in the utmost distress.

That review appeared in the month when Percy saw the young lady come in to borrow coal.—There is a notable passage also too in his review of Young " On Original Composition " :

Of genius there are two species, an earlier and a later ; or, call them infantine and adult. An adult genius comes out of nature's hand, as Pallas out of Jove's head, at full growth and mature. Shakespeare's genius was of this kind : on the contrary, Swift had an infantine genius, which, like other infants, must be nursed and educated, or it will come to nought. Men are often strangers to their own abilities : genius, in this view, is like a dear friend in our company under disguise, who, while we are lamenting his absence, drops his mask, striking us at once with equal surprise and joy. Few authors of distinction but have experienced something of this nature at the first beamings of their unexpected genius, on the hitherto dark composition.

Goldsmith had no liking for Swift, as a later passage in this review shows. But he was interested by the fact that at his own age, one-and-thirty, Swift had published nothing.

CHAPTER VII

THE MAGAZINE WRITER

GOLDSMITH was now fully launched in the trade into which he had been drawn by a natural compulsion. He had not chosen to be a literary hack; but there was no other job that he was fit for, and he had certainly wanted to be a writer. Everybody who has that impulse wants to write according to his own fancy, and this man's desire was for highly finished, delicate, deeply-meditated work. But that offered no living; if he was to subsist by his pen, it must travel fast, faster than real thought could feed it. Journalism, as Stevenson said, is a school of cheap finish; yet the habit of writing much is in itself a training, like a pianist's or a billiard player's. The test, is whether a man can retain a feeling for finish which is not cheap, and a habit of gradually accumulating thought. Swift, for instance, was perpetually scribbling trifles even in the years when he was slowly perfecting "Gulliver," just as a great artist may be unable to sit at table without beginning to sketch on the menu card. It is a different matter when the scribbling must be done to order; the difficulty then is to keep a margin of reserve which is not expended from day to day. Yet from that margin Goldsmith gradually drew within the next four years his "Vicar of Wakefield" and his "Traveller"—composed, nobody knows when or how, but written certainly in the intervals of a weekly task that demanded on the average a matter of five pages daily.

From the autumn of 1859, that is to say within three years after he first apprenticed himself to Griffiths, he had at last the free use of his own discretion. A new employer,

Wilkie of St. Paul's Churchyard, engaged him to produce a weekly magazine of two sheets, that is thirty-two pages. Johnson's " Rambler " was to be the model. Goldsmith probably found his own title, " The Bee," and at all events furnished the entire contents. If he was to write for magazines, he could now follow his notion of what a magazine should be. The first number contained an Introductory essay, a couple of epigrams (imitated from the Spanish), one of them in English, one in Latin elegiacs ; some " Remarks on our Theatres " ; the " Story of Alcander and Septimius " translated from a Byzantine historian ; a " Letter from a Traveller " ; and " A Short Account of the late Mr. Maupertuis."

All this for two guineas—say, six of our money—to the author ! But it was a living ; and it was not all just hackwork. The essayist now gets a chance to try his hand ; and a good deal of it seemed to Goldsmith worth reprinting six years later when he had a reputation to lose. One of these selected papers was the Introduction, which opens with a manifest touch of self-study, by sketching the " whimsically dismal figure " cut by " a man of real modesty who assumes an air of impudence." And then comes raillery, with a sharp edge to it, of the way in which Magazines are made. " One writer, for instance," an imaginary publisher assures him, " excels at a plan, or a title page. Another works away at the body of the book, and a third is a dab at an index." But " The Bee " refuses to pursue any fixed plan ; " wherever pleasure presented, I resolved to follow." The reader must take his chances : only one thing is promised : " neither war nor scandal shall make any part of it." There was a deal to be written about wars, when Mr. Pitt was launching thunderbolts ; and scandal never fails ; but neither of these topics was ever to Goldsmith's liking. " Happy could any effort of mine, but for a moment, repress that savage pleasure some men find in the daily accounts of human misery." He had to rely on wit ; but that " generally succeeds more from being happily addressed, than from its native poignancy " :

A *bon mot*, for instance, that might be relished at White's, may lose all its flavour when delivered at the Cat and Bag-pipes in St. Giles's. A jest calculated to spread at a gaming-table, may be received with a perfect neutrality of face, should it happen to drop in a mackerel-boat. We have all seen dunces triumph in some companies, when men of real humour were disregarded, by a general combination in favour of stupidity.

Goldsmith always knew that there were places where he could make people laugh; but he was never sure that London was one of them.

The " Remarks on our Theatres " show that close attention which this unsuspected dramatist was already giving to his art:

There is something in the deportment of all our players infinitely more stiff and formal than among the actors of other nations. Their action sits uneasy upon them; for as the English use very little gesture in ordinary conversation, our English-bred actors are obliged to supply stage gestures by their imagination alone. A French comedian finds proper models of action in every company and in every coffee-house he enters.

It would " be inexcusable in a comedian to add anything of his own to the poet's dialogue " (note the use of " poet "), " yet as to action he is entirely at liberty " : and he illustrates it by citing two clever pieces of business invented by French actors—the latter of which terminates in a broadly farcical effect, " dull enough in the recital : but the gravity of Cato could not stand it in the representation."

In short, there is hardly a character in comedy, to which a player of any real humour might not add strokes of vivacity that could not fail of applause. But instead of this, we too often see our fine gentlemen do nothing through a whole part, but strut, and open their snuff-box; our pretty fellows sit indecently with their legs across, and our clowns pull up their breeches. These, if once, or even twice repeated, might do well enough; but to see them served up in every scene, argues the actor almost as barren as the character he would expose.

National characteristics change little in the course of centuries, it would seem.

The story of Alcander and Septimius betrays already that tolerance of the extremely improbable in fiction which for many readers mars enjoyment of the " Vicar." On the other hand, the " Letter from a Traveller " shows us Goldsmith's mind turning over those emotions and reflections that were to be the stuff of his first poem. Finally, in a short article, Maupertuis is commended for having introduced the learning of the English to France and made Newton famous across the Channel.

In the second number an essay on dress introduces one of those dramatic sketches of which Addison and Steele had set the example. Goldsmith was to exploit this vein more successfully later : but in this number his characteristic excellence is to be found rather in those reflections which I have already quoted, on his early happiness when he " thought cross-purposes the highest stretch of human wit."

Another article on the theatre gives a detailed study of Mademoiselle Clairon, with advice addressed chiefly to English actresses, but containing one notable compliment : Garrick alone is excepted from the criticism that English players never open with sufficient reserve, and therefore lose the " power of rising in the passion of the scene." However, in a later number, criticizing the farce " High Life below Stairs," he makes amends to Mrs. Clive— " But what need I talk of her ? Since, without the least exaggeration she has more true humour than any actor or actress upon the English or any other stage I have seen."

With the third number we come to the reflections of a habitual borrower :

Every man who has seen the world, and has had his *ups and downs* in life, as the expression is, must have frequently experienced the truth of this doctrine and must know that to have much, or to seem to have it, is the only way to have more.

Detailed illustration from experience with tailors is given ; Mr. Griffiths would probably have censured it as " low." But then follows a line of thought leading back to bitterness—" Pity is incompatible with friendship," for " friendship is made up of esteem and pleasure : pity is composed of sorrow and contempt " :

It is at best but a short-lived passion, and seldom affords distress more than transitory assistance. With some it scarcely lasts from the first impulse till the hand can be put into the pocket ; with others it may continue for twice that space, and on some of extraordinary sensibility, I have seen it operate for half an hour. But last as it may, it generally produces but beggarly effects ; and where, from this motive, we give farthings, from others we give always pounds. In great distress, we sometimes, it is true, feel the influence of tenderness strongly ; when the same distress solicits a second time, we then feel with diminished sensibility, but, like the repetition of an echo, every new impulse becomes weaker, till at last our sensations lose every mixture of sorrow, and degenerate into downright contempt.

He illustrated this acid philosophy by the history of Mr. Dick Wildgoose who, starting with a prosperous fortune, refused many offers of assistance, but later, needing them, found they were not renewed, and finally reached the point of paying calls just as the cloth was laying for dinner—only to be obliged " to return and mend his appetite by a walk in the Park." The moral follows :

You then, O ye beggars of my acquaintance, whether in rags or lace ; whether in Kent-street or the Mall ; whether at the Smyrna or St. Giles's ; might I advise you as a friend, never seem in want of the favour which you solicit. Apply to every passion but pity, for redress. You may find relief from vanity, from self-interest, or from avarice, but seldom from compassion.

That is as deep in cynicism as any passage one can find in Goldsmith. Out of an empty stomach, as well as out of a full heart, the mouth speaketh. But it was only in his journalism that he let the emptiness dictate ; his true philosophy sets compassion almost above all other virtues. And even in this same number of " The Bee " we find him setting down the considerations which should check his own strongest propensity : justice should come before generosity—and again there is a note of self-study :

Among men long conversant with books, we too frequently find those misplaced virtues, of which I have been now complaining. We find the studious animated with a strong passion for the great virtues, as they are mistakenly called, and utterly forgetful of the ordinary ones. . . . A man therefore, who has taken his ideas of mankind from study alone, generally comes into the world with a heart melting at every fictitious distress. Thus he is induced, by misplaced liberality, to put himself into the indigent circumstances of the person he relieves.

Yet again, against the voice of reason, one finds compassion crying out. "A City Night Piece" enlarges on these walkers of the streets who " have once seen happier days and been flattered into beauty. . . . Why, why was I born a man and yet see the suffering of wretches I cannot relieve ! . . . Why was this heart of mine formed with so much sensibility ! or why was not my fortune adapted to its impulse ! "

Perhaps from a sense that this cry of the heart departed from " The Bee's " habitual lightness of tone, he followed it with some airily impudent verses, too well known to need quoting—his Elegy on Mrs. Mary Blaize, pawnbroker, of Kent Street in Southwark :

> She freely lent to all the poor,—
> *Who left a pledge behind.*

The fifth number opened with an essay in praise of frugality : Goldsmith seemed to be looking for the qualities to eulogize in which he was most to seek. Incidentally one may note that his examples of " political frugality " are drawn from Holland, where as usual he had kept his eyes and ears open. But the paper which followed is the one by which " The Bee " is remembered : it contained his allegory of the "Fame Machine—a small carriage, Berlin fashion " whose coachman was " but a few days returned from the Temple of Fame to which he had been carrying Addison, Swift, Pope, Steele, Congreve and Colley Cibber." He was now back for another coachful but was not prepared to let the author of " The Bee " command a seat.

He " expected better passengers " : and a couple of other applicants were also repelled, protesting. One of these was Goldsmith's fellow-countryman, Arthur Murphy, whose " Orphan of China " had been produced at Drury Lane a few months earlier and Goldsmith had praised it highly in the " Critical Review " for excellence of writing. The coachman, casting an eye on Murphy's literary luggage, hoped that in time he might find a place, " as he seemed to have read in the book of nature, without a careful perusal of which none ever found entrance to the Temple of Fame." But the Irishman had to make way for another applicant :

This was a very grave personage, whom at some distance I took for one of the most reserved, and even disagreeable figures I had seen ; but as he approached, his appearance improved, and when I could distinguish him thoroughly, I perceived that in spite of the severity of his brow, he had one of the most good-natured countenances that could be imagined. Upon coming to open the stage door, he lifted a parcel of folios into the seat before him, but our inquisitorial coachman at once shoved them out again. " What ! not take in my Dictionary ! " exclaimed the other in a rage. " Be patient, sir," replied the coachman, " I have drove a coach, man and boy, these two thousand years ; but I do not remember to have carried above one Dictionary during the whole time. That little book which I perceive peeping from one of your pockets, may I presume to ask what it contains ? " " A mere trifle," replies the author ; " it is called ' The Rambler.' " " ' The Rambler,' " says the coachman, " I beg, sir, you'll take your place ; I have heard our ladies in the court of Apollo frequently mention it with rapture ; and Clio, who happens to be a little grave, has been heard to prefer it to ' The Spectator ' ; though others have observed, that the reflections, by being refined, sometimes become minute."

This passage makes the first link that we know of between Goldsmith and the Great Cham who was a well-known figure in Fleet Street. The two men did not actually meet till some eighteen months later.—Hume who came next for a place in the Machine got in for his History

DR. SAMUEL JOHNSON
From a portrait by Sir Joshua Reynolds in the National Portrait Gallery

though he was rejected for his sceptical essays ; and
Smollett, rejected for his history, got in for his novels—
which, after the fashion of the day, he was inclined to
pooh-pooh. However, Goldsmith with a pen in his hand
was never frightened of anybody, and spoke his mind as
befitted a philosopher about even the most eminent citizens
of the Republic of Athens—even about those who could
commission his work, and Smollett had already done so.
Evidently the paragraph was not ill-taken, for in the next
year Goldsmith was a frequent contributor to Smollett's
" British Magazine." In truth the author of " Roderick
Random " could not well be displeased when the coachman, in reply to his own disparagement of such " trifling,"
replied that he remembered Cervantes and Segrais among
former passengers. But what an odd commentary it is
on the " Fame Machine " that Goldsmith in 1759 should
have bracketed the author of " Don Quixote " with a
Frenchman whose name only professional students recognize to-day !

" The Bee's " honey gathering did not last long : eight
numbers finished it. But in Goldsmith's own judgment
it included some of his best work, for when he collected
his essays in 1765 many from it were included. One which
deserves attention is his paper on Education. In it occurs
the often-quoted passage about an usher's hard lot ; but
there is much else that modern opinion agrees with. If
the schools, for instance, were " kept a little out of town,
it would certainly conduce to the health and vigour of
perhaps the mind as well as the body." And he disapproves the idea of " inuring children to cold, to fatigue
and to hardship." There is a plea too for some instruction
in the facts of " natural philosophy "—and in general for
a less strictly scholastic course of studies. On the other
hand, he has no tolerance for the attempt to coax children
into learning :

Whatever pains a master may take to make the learning of the
languages agreeable to his pupil, he may depend upon it, it will
be at first extremely unpleasant. . . . Attempting to deceive

children into instruction of this kind is deceiving ourselves ; and I know no passion capable of conquering a child's natural laziness but fear.

No " French without Tears " for this philosopher. And for all his softheartedness, he is for the good boarding-school, since it is from one another, not from their masters, that boys really learn. " It is true, a child is early made acquainted with some vices in a school, but it is better to know these when a boy, than be first taught them when a man ; for their novelty then may have irresistible charms."

Yet perhaps the most important for a biographer among these early papers, is " An Account of the Augustan Age in England." Incidentally, it has interest because Gold-smith seems to have fixed for the first time on the writers of Queen Anne's time this epithet—adopted already in Italy for the age of Leo X and in France for that of Louis XIV. " The Bee " can never have had critical authority : its flight was too short ; and this is not one of the essays which Goldsmith chose to reprint. But in the preface to that collection he remarks that, although the various publi-cations in which they first appeared were short-lived, and therefore his contributions " shared the common fate with-out assisting the bookseller's aims or extending the writer's reputation," still the essays did not lack circulation. " If there be a pride in multiplied editions, I have seen some of my labours sixteen times reprinted and claimed by different parents as their own." There may therefore have been wide diffusion of this particular paper, which indeed made special appeal to professional writers, for it dealt with the conditions of their trade. In Queen Anne's age there was, Goldsmith held, " a just balance between patron-age and the press." " Before it men were little esteemed whose only merit was genius ; and since, men who can prudently be content to catch the public, are certain of living without dependence." In other words, under Queen Anne, you had to write to please the really great ; now, you need only please the booksellers. It is not difficult to earn a living, he suggests, but the rewards are not according to merit. In particular, poetry, by which Goldsmith means all imaginative composition, finds no patrons. "At present, were a man to attempt to improve his fortune, or increase his friendship by poetry, he would soon feel the anxiety of disappointment. The press lies open, and is a benefactor to every sort of literature, but that alone."

Yet in fact a poem was to make the turning-point in Goldsmith's own career. Is it true to say that he was a poet who at first did not write poetry because prose paid better? I think not. He was a poet, but of a limited and specialized kind whose excellence does not develop early. Nothing could have stopped Wordsworth and Shelley from writing poetry in their young manhood; it was urgent with them as a bird's song; and this is true of all the lyrists. Goldsmith had been rhyming since he was a child; an epigram of his Edinburgh days was somehow preserved and printed after his death—the sort of thing any smart young fellow might have written. Now, at one-and-thirty he was still rhyming. Three or four things appeared in " The Bee " as has been noted, two of them excellent in their way—the satiric elegy on Madam Blaize who kept a pawnshop and the satiric " gift " addressed to some one of the young ladies who helped him to spend his few shillings :

> Say, cruel Iris, pretty rake,
>   Dear mercenary beauty,
> What annual offering shall I make
>   Expressive of my duty?

Prior or Gay could not have done better, and when " The Bee " had ended, Goldsmith immediately began contributing to another spawn of the day, " The Busybody," where his satire, " The Logicians Refuted," was actually announced as Swift's, and even came to be included in several editions of " Swift's Poetical Works " :

> Logicians have but ill defin'd
> As rational the human mind;

Reason, they say, belongs to man,
But let them prove it if they can.
Wise Aristotle and Smiglecius,
By ratiocinations specious,
Have strove to prove with great precision,
With definition and division,
Homo est ratione præditum;
But for my soul I cannot credit 'em;
And must in spite of them maintain,
That man and all his ways are vain;
And that this boasted lord of nature
Is both a weak and erring creature.
That instinct is a surer guide
Than reason,—boasting mortals' pride;
And that brute beasts are far before 'em,
Deus est anima brutorum.
Who ever knew an honest brute
At law his neighbour prosecute,
Bring action for assault and battery,
Or friend beguile with lies and flattery?

Not many better imitations are to be found of Swift's essays in *la bagatelle*; it is indeed a deal more like Swift than like Goldsmith. But in the prose essays, even when the writer's chief concern was to fill his sixteen pages, one finds the philosopher speaking. That was the essential urge with him, his need for expression. When he was to be a poet, it was by suffusing with emotion and adorning with exquisite illustration the simple doctrines which were to him philosophy. In one of these papers—" The Sentiments of a Frenchman on the Temper of the English "—he defines what the word meant to him : " Philosophy is no more than the art of making ourselves happy : that is, of seeking pleasure in regularity, and reconciling what we owe to society with what is due to ourselves." It was an instinctive creed, a wisdom of the heart. Nobody was likely to care much for it while it was stated as an abstraction; but it penetrated like sunlight when the Vicar of Wakefield described his own attitude to life : " As some men gaze with admiration on the colours of a tulip, or

he wing of a butterfly, so I was by nature an admirer of
happy human faces."

In these early stages of Goldsmith's adventures, there
are two things to trace : the material progress, steps up
the ladder which led to literary reputation with its rewards
in cash and credit ; and the gradual advance of a great
writer towards discovery of what was in him to say : or
in one phrase, the making of a poet.

Several magazines and their directors had the honour
of keeping Oliver Goldsmith alive during the year 1760 :
there was " The Ladies' Magazine " as well as " The Busybody " : there was, on a more important scale, " The
British Magazine or Monthly Repository for Gentlemen
and Ladies," conducted by " T. Smollett, M.D., and
others." To this, it seems, Goldsmith furnished more
than a score of papers, though we can only be certain as
to four of them, which he included in the Collected Essays.
But beyond doubt Goldsmith felt that he owed Smollett
a good turn, and repaid him in a fashion familiar to literary
gentlemen in all ages. When Newbery started the " Public
Ledger " and engaged Goldsmith to contribute, one of the
first papers that he got was the " Description of a Wow-
wow " which, as the reader learnt, " was a confused heap
of people of all denominations assembled at a public-house
to read the newspapers, and to hear the tittle-tattle of the
day." There was a deal of high military and political
discussion on foreign affairs ; but in the course of this an
Oxford scholar, led there by curiosity, pulled out of his
pocket a new magazine and read from it the " Adventures
of Sir Launcelot Greaves " to the entire satisfaction of the
audience. " ' That piece, gentlemen,' " said the scholar
when he had finished his reading, " ' is written in the very
spirit and manner of Cervantes ; there is great knowledge
of human nature and evident marks of the master in almost
every sentence.' "

Smollett had a right to be pleased. But Goldsmith
had now found for the first time means to write something

less fugitive than those descriptions of Wow-wows, of London " clubs," or of public rejoicings for victory, which interest us to-day only by the light they throw on manners in the time when Mr. Pitt, not yet Lord Chatham, was at the pinnacle of fame. " The Public Ledger " was a new venture published daily by Francis Newbery—a very honest and kindly man, of whom, we are told on good authority, Goldsmith never spoke without respect. He had given the essayist a column to fill twice a week, and when the paper had been running a fortnight there appeared, on January 24, 1760, a letter, unsigned, addressed from Amsterdam to " Mr. ****, Merchant in London." Its purport was to be an introduction :

The bearer of this is my friend, therefore let him be yours. He is a native of Honan in China, and one who did me signal services, when he was a mandarine, and I a factor at Canton. By frequently conversing with the English there, he has learned the language, though entirely a stranger to their manners and customs. I am told he is a philosopher; I am sure he is an honest man : that to you will be his best recommendation.

Five days later, Lien Chi Altangi reported in a much longer letter to his friend at Amsterdam the impressions of a first sea-journey and a first glimpse of London. But the third letter, like the rest of the series (except for three or four replies from China), is addressed to Fum Hoam, first President of the Ceremonial Academy of Moscow. Before all was done, a hundred and twenty-seven of these papers had appeared, spread over a year and a half; Goldsmith had achieved a journalist's success ; he had created a " feature " in his paper.

The idea was not original : Montesquieu's " Lettres Persanes " were universally known ; and so late as in 1757 Horace Walpole had published a " Letter from Xo Ho, a Chinese Philosopher at London, to his friend Lien Chi at Peking." Goldsmith was in fact never an inventor of forms ; he made his own of what was common property (a hard thing to do, as Horace observes). But the philo-

sophic vagabond (now dignified into " a poor philosophic
wanderer ") found a new and amusing angle from which
to look at the world of which he had seen so much with
eyes that were so unworldly. It is well to quote from the
first of Lien Chi's commentaries, for a venture of this kind
must make its mark at once; and here probably is what
caught the town in the beginning of 1760:

The streets of Nankin are sometimes strewed with gold leaf;
very different are those of London: in the midst of their pave-
ments a great lazy puddle moves muddily along; heavy-laden
machines, with wheels of unwieldy thickness, crowd up every
passage; so that a stranger, instead of finding time for observation, is often happy if he has time to escape from being crushed
to pieces.

The houses borrow very few ornaments from architecture;
their chief decoration seems to be a paltry piece of painting hung
out at their doors or windows, at once a proof of their indigence
and vanity: their vanity, in each having one of those pictures
exposed to public view; and their indigence, in being unable to
get them better painted. In this respect, the fancy of their
painters is also deplorable. Could you believe it? I have seen
five black lions and three blue boars in less than the circuit of
half a mile; and yet you know that animals of these colours are
nowhere to be found except in the wild imaginations of Europe.

From these circumstances in their buildings, and from the
dismal looks of the inhabitants, I am induced to conclude that
the nation is actually poor; and that, like the Persians, they
make a splendid figure everywhere but at home. The proverb
of Xixofou is, that a man's riches may be seen in his eyes; if
we judge of the English by this rule, there is not a poorer nation
under the sun. [Letter 2.]

So launched, the philosopher went on, describing the
manners of the English, their clothes (" I have seen a lady,
who seemed to shudder at a breeze in her own apartment,
appear half naked in the streets "); their notions of liberty:
of politeness; and their passion for newspapers: (" Thus
at night he returns home full of the important advices of
the day: when lo! awaking next morning, he finds the

instructions of yesterday, a collection of absurdity or palpable falsehood.")

Soon, however, feeling a need for variety in the series, Goldsmith brings incident into play ; and as always, he is no niggard with catastrophe. A dispatch from China informs Lien that his possessions, his wife and his daughter have been seized by the Emperor ; only his son has escaped by stealth and run off to seek his wandering father. In return Lien Chi evinces his familiarity with the writings of Confucius—whom for the purpose in hand Goldsmith did not fail to study. Indeed, his most miscellaneous reading enabled him always to cite authorities almost as exotic and impressive as those which the rogue in the " Vicar " had at his tongue's end. But from this high strain we pass to comedy—or farce : the philosopher reports to his distant friend upon the virtues of those " well-disposed daughters of hospitality " who accosted him in the streets. A sequel shows the disillusionment, and leads to observations on monogamy as it is practised in England.

And now, I think, the vein or ironic comment began to run out. Agreeable information was given instead by a sketch of the Chinaman's journey across Asia, and observations on it—not always strictly exact, as for instance, when " the brown savage of Thibet " is represented as " nesting in the branches of the pomegranate which supplies his food." But we come back to England, and by a discourse on funeral customs are led to Westminster Abbey. It is in the Abbey that Lien Chi first makes acquaintance with " The Man in Black." Henceforward Goldsmith has two personages on his stage ; dialogue relieves the monotony and The Man in Black makes large contribution to the commentary on manners. Moreover, as has been already seen, he tells his story, which is, in its main outlines, the history of his creator. It is he also who guides the Chinaman to a club of authors (" at the sign of the Broom near Islington ").

On their first visit they draw a blank : the door is beset with bailiffs. But at the second venture they are luckier and over pipe and mug assist when "a poet in shabby finery" pays sixpence for the privilege of reading a "heroical description of Nature, sketched in my own apartment." And so Goldsmith works into this convenient hold-all the lines which three years earlier he had sent to his brother, but with a new exordium:

> Where the Red Lion flaring o'er the way,
> Invites each passing stranger that can pay;
> Where Calvert's butt, and Parson's black champagne,
> Regale the drabs and bloods of Drury-lane;
> There in a lonely room, from bailiffs snug,
> The muse found Scroggen stretch'd beneath a rug. . . .

There is also a new and much-applauded couplet for the close.

> A night-cap deck'd his brows instead of bay,
> A cap by night—a stocking all the day!

"You must know, gentlemen, that I am myself the hero"; so the poet said. If he was not speaking for the Goldsmith of 1760, he certainly was for the Goldsmith of 1757.

As the series goes on, what between one device and another, the essayist contrives to express himself on whatever excites his feelings. Rumour of Voltaire's death produces valiant eulogy, though neither Voltaire nor his country was then in fashion among the English. Later, in circles far removed from those of Scroggins, Goldsmith did not hesitate to rebuke Reynolds because the painter, in a picture of Dr. Beattie, had shown all the vices in flight before this divine; and the leading Vice had Voltaire's features. "Dr. Beattie and his book," he said, "will not be known in ten years; but your allegorical picture on the fame of Voltaire will live for ever to your disgrace as a flatterer."—"Tristram Shandy" is, none too fairly, denounced for obscenity; Goldsmith was seldom a lenient judge of his contemporaries, and never a good critic. But Sterne offended him by the liberties which he took with his audience and which Goldsmith set down as clowning. Nobody ever had more scrupulously good manners in print than Goldsmith himself and he resented applause of what he thought unmannerly.

When the series had been running for about half a year, another character was introduced, Beau Tibbs: I prefer him in his later incarnation when he appears in those gay verses concerning the " Haunch of Venison." However, Beau Tibbs was evidently a popular favourite and he with Mrs. Tibbs and their friend the pawnbroker's widow, helped the Man in Black to show Lien Chi the humours of Vauxhall, and other aspects of London. At the end of the series, all had to be married and live happy ever after; the Chinese philosopher's son had miraculously arrived, bringing the beautiful damsel whom he had miraculously rescued and who miraculously proved to be in exactly the right degree of relationship to him. They were the bride and bridegroom. Mr. and Mrs. Tibbs assisted; and it looked very much as if the Man in Black and the widow might also make a match of it. However, some difference of opinion about the carving of a turkey dispelled that danger: I suppose Goldsmith thought that a gentleman so closely resembling himself, if he married at all, could only join up with a pawnshop—and felt that it would be carrying the jest a little too far to consummate the alliance even in fiction.

But the invented machinery of the series, so far as it has one, need concern us little : it is the man one looks for, and almost every essay is Oliver Goldsmith in little. None is more characteristic than that which illustrates " The Distresses of the Poor " by sketching the life of a common soldier, with its quietly ironic ending.

Had I the good fortune to have lost my leg or the use of my hand on board a King's ship and not a privateer, I should have been entitled to clothing and maintenance during the rest of my life ; but that was not my chance ; one man is born with a silver spoon in his mouth, and another with a wooden ladle. However, blessed be God ! I enjoy good health and have no enemy in the world that I know of but the French and the justice of the peace. [Letter 219.]

Many illustrate Goldsmith's personal peculiarities. For instance, he upholds the importance of good clothes. In one gaudy assemblage the Chinaman found the conversation more vulgar than he could have expected—till he learnt that they were lackeys. "Yet," he adds, "I still continued to venerate their dress; for dress has a kind of mechanical influence on the mind." The irony is manifest here, but I find no trace of it when the same philosopher observes: "Every extravagance in dress proceeds from a desire of becoming more beautiful than nature made us; and this is so harmless a vanity that I not only pardon but approve it. A desire to be more excellent than others is what actually makes us so."

This philosophy Goldsmith continued to practise and to preach till the end. In the last of his books, his "Animated Nature," after discussing the prepossessions produced in our judgment by a lack of eloquence in the eye, he goes on:

This extends even to the cut of people's clothes and we should for such reason, be careful even in such trifling particulars, since they go to make up a part of the total judgment which those we converse with may form to our disadvantage. The first impression we generally produce arises from our dress and this varies in conformity to the manner in which we desire to be considered. The modest man, or he who wishes to be thought so, desires to show the simplicity of his mind by the plainness of his dress.

We have always to remember that Goldsmith always wanted to shine and thought—with good reason—that he had shining parts. But he knew they were not on the outside : so he trusted to help from his tailor. A description (in Letter 77) of what happened when Lien Chi went to buy silk for a nightcap gives us a fair idea of how bargains were sold to Oliver Goldsmith.

Letter 97 gives us his taste in poetry. What he would like, but finds quite forgotten, are "those sallies which mend the heart while they amuse the fancy." What he cannot abide, is the ode : "All odes, epodes, and monodies whatsoever shall hereafter be deemed too polite, classical, obscure and refined to be read, and certainly above human comprehension."

There is an attack on actors for being monstrously overpaid and for having four mistresses when two should content them—but this is common form among angry authors ; and there is also anger against the preference given in the Press to the literature of kings, chams and mandarins. " A man here who should write and honestly confess that he wrote for bread might as well send his manuscript to fire the baker's oven." Yet these hungry folk, he insists, are the best writers.

Did I desire to be well served, I would apply only to them who made it their trade and lived by it. Be assured, my friend, that wit is in some measure mechanical, and that a man long habituated to catch at even its resemblance, will at last be happy enough to possess the substance. By a long habit of writing he acquires a justness of thinking, and a mastery of manner, which holiday-writers, even with ten times his genius, may vainly attempt to equal. [Letter 93.]

Yet in another letter he admits that the case of writers is not as when Otway and others starved :

The few poets of England no longer depend on the great for subsistence ; they have now no other patrons but the public, and the public collectively considered, is a good and a generous master. It is, indeed, too frequently mistaken as to the merits of every candidate for favour ; but to make amends, it is never mistaken long. [Letter 84.]

The critics—for whom he has no good word—are the persons to blame for puffing the amateur and high-placed author ; and the blame, to his mind, is grave ; here Goldsmith speaks with a touch of passion :

In a polished society, that man, though in rags, who has the power of enforcing virtue from the press, is of more real use than forty stupid brachmans, or bonzes, or guebres, though they preach never so often, never so loud, or never so long. [Letter 57.]

There is no doubt that Goldsmith, like his Vicar, had a desire to do good and a belief that it could be done by preaching ; but he had more faith in the lay preacher who was " capable of deceiving even indolence into wisdom." Children could not be cajoled into grammar, he saw that ; but grown men and women, he never ceased to believe, might be charmed into virtue. It was a sententious age, but he had even beyond his contemporaries the impulse to moral persuasion. Something, indeed, nudged his elbow at times as he wrote : but he disregarded, or rather, faced the hint of inconsistency. " As it has been observed that none are better qualified to give advice than those who have taken the brunt of it themselves, so in this respect I find myself perfectly authorized to offer mine."

Some of it is very good advice : for instance, Letter 66, on the difference between love and gratitude. It is easy, he says, to earn gratitude ; the problem is how to confer favours in such a way as to forgo gratitude and win love. " We never reflect on the man we *love*, without exulting in our choice, while he who has bound us to him by *benefits* alone, rises to our idea as a person to whom we have in some measure forfeited our freedom." This is an excellent example of Goldsmith's " philosophy," which rested not on any formal system, but on an essential knowledge of mankind.

Two apologues follow, illustrating the truth that " it is better to have friends in the passage through life than grateful dependents." That of the philosopher Mencius is admirably apposite : the other, concerning a fiddler and his wife, has no very strict relevance. But as a piece of prose narrative it is as good as anything in " The Vicar of Wakefield," and shall be quoted to prove that this writer was now fully made :

A fiddler and his wife, who had rubbed through life, as most couples usually do, sometimes good friends, at others not quite so well, one day happened to have a dispute, which was conducted with becoming spirit on both sides. The wife was sure she was right, and the husband was resolved to have his own

way. What was to be done in such a case ? the quarrel grew
worse by explanations, and at last the fury of both rose to such
a pitch, that they made a vow never to sleep together in the same
bed for the future. This was the most rash vow that could be
imagined, for they still were friends at bottom, and besides, they
had but one bed in the house ; however, resolved they were to
go through with it, and at night the fiddle-case was laid in bed
between them, in order to make a separation. In this manner
they continued for three weeks ; every night the fiddle-case being
placed as a barrier to divide them.

By this time, however, each heartily repented of their vow ;
their resentment was at an end, and their love began to return ;
they wished the fiddle-case away, but both had too much spirit
to begin. One night, however, as they were both lying awake
with the detested fiddle-case between them, the husband happened to sneeze ; to which the wife, as is usual in such cases,
bid God bless him : " Aye but," returns the husband, " woman,
do you say that from your heart ? " " Indeed, I do, my poor
Nicholas," cries his wife, " I say it with all my heart." " If so
then," says the husband, " we had as good remove the fiddle-
case." [Letter 66.]

There you have at the very end a perfect example of
Goldsmith's humour—the tenderest in all English humor-
ists. Gentle irony runs through the whole, flooding back
on each sentence as it is uttered with a lovely irradiation
of silent laughter.

As an example of his complete mastery in more ornate
prose, take this passage from the 73rd Letter :

Life sues the young like a new acquaintance : the companion,
as yet unexhausted, is at once instructive and amusing ; its company pleases ; yet, for all this, it is but little regarded. To us,
who are declined in years, life appears like an old friend ; its
jests have been anticipated in former conversation ; it has no
new story to make us smile, no new improvement with which
to surprise ; yet still we love it : destitute of every agreement
still we love it ; husband the wasting treasure with increased
frugality, and feel all the poignancy of anguish in the fatal
separation.

How short a step it is from such a prose meditation to

such poetry as Goldsmith was to write! Indeed in these papers we already find first hints of what was to be developed in " The Traveller"; for instance, in the very first of Lien Chi's letters:

The farther I travel I feel the pain of separation with stronger force; those ties that bind me to my native country and you, are still unbroken. *By every remove, I only drag a greater length of chain.*

And again in Letter 103:

There is something so seducing in that spot in which we first had existence, that nothing but it can please. Whatever vicissitudes we experience in life, however we toil, or wheresoever we wander, our fatigued wishes still recur to home for tranquillity: we long to die in that spot which gave us birth, and in that pleasing expectation opiate every calamity.

It is clear that the series had been successful; it was at once reprinted as a book, and three editions appeared in Goldsmith's life. Its popularity must have lasted close on a century, for when Dickens was projecting " Master Humphrey's Clock," with a dialogue on current events between Gog and Magog, he wrote of planning " something between ' Gulliver's Travels ' and ' The Citizen of the World.' "

But the collected papers appeared in 1761 without the author's name, and a preface which begins lightheartedly ends in bitterness:

I cannot help wishing that the pains taken in giving this correspondence an English dress, had been employed in contriving new political systems, or new plots for farces. I might then have taken my station in the world, either as a poet or a philosopher, and made one in those little societies where men club to raise each other's reputation. But at present I belong to no particular class. I resemble one of those animals, that has been forced from its forest to gratify human curiosity. My earliest wish was to escape unheeded through life; but I have been set up for halfpence, to fret and scamper at the end of my chain. Though none are injured by my rage, I am naturally too savage to court any friends by fawning, too obstinate to be taught new tricks, and too improvident to mind what may happen. I am appeased, though not contented. Too indolent for intrigue, and too timid to push for favour, I am—But what signifies what am I?

A couplet from the Greek anthology follows, which reads being translated:

Hope and good luck, good-bye; I reached my port, and have no more to do with you; make the next comers your fools.

Not a cheerful valedictory—coloured perhaps by remembrance that Newbery had thought five pounds quite enough payment for the right to make a book of the essays. But there is more than that in the words: there is the angry sense that such a genius had received so little recognition.

For, what a writer! "Fret and scamper at the end of my chain." Who else in that century could have found words that so bit in the image? Swift perhaps: yet Swift never had the poet's imagination that can see the tragic figure in a chained monkey. This prose-writer was a poet—as this passage of his prose would prove if it stood alone.

CHAPTER VIII

JOHNSON ENTERS

THE close of 1760 may be taken as the turning-point in Goldsmith's career. Between his "Citizen of the World" and his work for Smollett's Magazine he must have earned something like £150 in the year—not far short of £500 nowadays. Work at the current rates crowded in on him: he became editor of the "Ladies' Magazine" and published in it his fragmentary "Life of Voltaire"; and when "The Citizen of the World" stopped, Newbery found plenty of prefaces and compilations for him. In short, he was well away from the starvation line: and he changed his abode from the squalor of Green Arbour Court to a decent lodging off Fleet Street in Wine Office Court. At this abode formal recognition of his status in the Republic of Letters was accorded to him. On May 31, 1761, Percy brought Johnson to supper with the journalist.

Both in his "Bee" and in his Chinese Letters Goldsmith had paid cordial tribute to Johnson's eminence as a writer. But there is a passage also in one of the Letters (the 74th, published in 1760) in which Lien Chi describes how he was invited to meet one of those officially reckoned as "great men"; and to my mind it reads as if inspired by what Goldsmith had been hearing about Johnson:

I came according to appointment. The venison was fine, the turtle good, but the great man insupportable. The moment I ventured to speak, I was at once contradicted with a snap. I attempted by a second and a third assault, to retrieve my lost reputation, but was still beat back with confusion. I was resolved to attack him once more from entrenchment, and turned the conversation upon the government of China: but even here he asserted, snapped, and contradicted as before. Heavens, thought I, this man pretends to know China even better than myself! I looked round to see who was on my side, but every eye was fixed in admiration on the great man : I therefore at last thought proper to sit silent, and act the pretty gentleman during the ensuing conversation.

When a man has once secured a circle of admirers, he may be as ridiculous here as he thinks proper ; and it all passes for elevation of sentiment, or learned absence. If he transgresses the common forms of breeding, mistakes even a tea-pot for a tobacco-box, it is said that his thoughts are fixed on more important objects : to speak and to act like the rest of mankind, is to be no greater than they. There is something of oddity in the very idea of greatness ; for we are seldom astonished at a thing very much resembling ourselves.

Whether that was written with a thought of Johnson or no, it represents Goldsmith's permanent attitude towards Johnsonolatry. Nothing could ever shake his independence of mind, and he thought that a man should have elbow-room in conversation ; there was always a touch of resentment in his relation to the Great Cham. But admiration and affection always had the better of this ; and if one searches through Boswell, the finest and the most penetrating things ever said about Johnson, as well as the wittiest, are attributed to Goldsmith, by a chronicler who certainly had no love for him.

If only Boswell had been present at that first meeting! Percy tells us nothing. But Boswell was not yet on the scene. When he arrived, Goldsmith was already established as a member of that literary circle which—thanks to Boswell's unique talent—is incomparably more familiar to us than that other famous group which preceded it in the last years of Queen Anne. But we do not really see him in it until after May 16, 1763, the consecrated date on which Boswell at last attained to his long-desired familiarity with Samuel Johnson. Goldsmith was busy in these years with compilations and other drudgery that it would be tedious to enumerate. Yet there is one excellent piece of work among them. He had found means to make excursions to Tunbridge Wells and to Bath (it seems, for the sake of his health, for his hardy body began to give trouble). Bath gave him the notion of writing a life of Beau Nash, which was, as it could hardly fail to be in such hands, a very entertaining study. The interest for Goldsmith's biography lies in the comments on Nash's character—and particularly on his benevolence.

He had pity for every creature's distress, but wanted prudence in the application of his benefits. He had generosity for the wretched in the highest degree at a time when creditors complained of his justice. . . . He rather fancied that misery was an excuse for indolence and guilt. It was a usual saying of his, when he went to beg for any person in distress that they who could stoop to the meanness of solicitation must certainly want the favour for which they petitioned.

Surely another person besides Nash was in Oliver Goldsmith's mind when he wrote such criticism; and he does not fail to note that " of all the immense sums which Nash lavished upon real or apparent wretchedness, the effect, after a few years, seemed to disappear." Nevertheless, his conclusion upon the whole matter is, I think, to be looked for in these sentences : " This gentleman's simplicity in trusting persons whom he had no previous reasons to place confidence in, seems to be one of those lights in his character which, while they implicate his understanding, do honour to his benevolence. The low and timid are ever suspicious." —In short, Goldsmith was always disposed to think the better of a man for being in such ways a fool.

Another production of these years was the " History of England," announced as " told in a series of Letters from a Nobleman to his Son." Probably Goldsmith found an ironic satisfaction in exploiting the preferential consideration given to " noble authors," and the device took. Various noble authors were fixed upon by guesses, and for several years Lord Lyttelton was believed to be the writer. But before long booksellers were only too anxious to father on Goldsmith whatever should be attributed to him, and, perhaps for the sake of his masterpieces, the hack-work continued to sell and be read. So late as 1844, we find gentlemen and ladies in " Coningsby " discussing a new political doctrine whose outline Mr. Disraeli left rather vague. " ' But they say it requires a deuced deal of reading,' continued Mr. Cassilis. ' One must brush up one's Goldsmith.' "—Even the hack-work of this accomplished pen was warranted to wear.

By the middle of 1763, when we begin to see Goldsmith through Boswell's eyes, it was possible for Boswell to write : " At this time I think he had published nothing with his name, though it was pretty generally known that one Dr. Goldsmith was the author of ' An Enquiry ' . . . and of ' The Citizen of the World.' " But already, at his third meeting with the great man, Boswell had been told by Johnson : " Dr. Goldsmith is one of the first men we now have as an author, and he is a very worthy one too. He has been loose in his principles, but he is coming right."

It is important to study the first references to this couple ; for Boswell was a reporter of genius, incapable, I believe, of tampering with the record ; but he sets down phrases without always appreciating their context. Speaking of his first acquaintance with Goldsmith, he observes :

Goldsmith's respectful attachment to Johnson was then at its height ; for his own literary reputation had not yet distinguished him so much as to excite a vain desire of competition with his great Master. He had increased my admiration of the goodness of Johnson's heart, by incidental remarks in the course of conversation, such as, when I mentioned Mr. Levett, whom he entertained under his roof, " He is poor and honest, which is recommendation enough to Johnson " ; and when I wondered that he was very kind to a man of whom I had heard a very bad character, " He is now become miserable, and that insures the protection of Johnson."

Now the truth is that Johnson and Goldsmith, when speaking to Boswell as to a new acquaintance, expressed their opinion as if it were to be delivered *urbi et orbi*. It was in each case almost a challenging pronouncement. Later, when they spoke not so much to Boswell as before him, when he had become their constant associate, both men gave way to little bursts of spleen or of slighting comment, directed against each other. Boswell sets down these also without mitigation—perhaps rightly—leaving his readers to assess for themselves how much seriousness in each case was behind the speech.

What seems to stand out clear is that Johnson, fully established in reputation, took under his ægis this other writer whose name was as yet considered as of no value, or worse than none, by the booksellers. This fits in with the testimony of Garrick's biographer, another Johnsonolater, Davies, the ex-actor turned bookseller:

The first man of the age, one who for the extensiveness of his genius and benevolence of his mind is superior to envy and mean jealousy which adhere so closely to most authors, and especially to those of equivocal merit, took a special pleasure in introducing Dr. Goldsmith to his intimate friends, persons of eminent rank and distinguished abilities.

We may, I think, go farther, and say that Johnson's interest in his protégé had a missionary character. Percy relates that, going to fetch Johnson for that first visit in 1761, he was amazed to find his friend in " a new suit of clothes, a new wig nicely powdered," and altogether quite unlike his usual self. He ventured to ask the reason. " Why, sir," said Johnson, " I hear that Goldsmith, who is a very great sloven, justifies his disregard of cleanliness and decency by quoting my practice ; and I am desirous this night to show him a better example." Such an example indeed was not likely to be lost on one who thought that money spent on dress added to the sum of human cheerfulness. But I think that other phrase " he has been loose in his principles," implies that Johnson had been talking seriously to him about " idle women."

At all events, the big ugly man who had emerged famous from the purlieus of Alsatia took the ugly little man by the hand and introduced him to good company—even to the best. He introduced him to Joshua Reynolds, to whom, as I think, Oliver Goldsmith owed even more than to Johnson. This frayed and battered sensitive needed a gentler handling than it was in Johnson's nature to give. Reynolds never lost patience with any of Goldsmith's absurdities or imprudences, and they were many; he never hustled or harried him in talk. What is more, he saw under the uncouth mask. Northcote remarks: " There is a very fine portrait which is the only original one of Dr. Goldsmith, now at Knowle, painted by Sir Joshua. . . . I remember Miss Reynolds said of this portrait that it was a very great likeness of the Doctor; but the most flattered picture she ever knew her brother to have painted." In other words, Goldsmith's daily intimates never knew what Goldsmith was like till Reynolds showed them.

Moreover, it was Reynolds who in 1763, while Goldsmith had as yet no public recognition, suggested the foundation of "The Club." He and Johnson launched it and they appear to have included Goldsmith as a matter of course. Northcote, writing down the list of twelve who formed the original membership, puts Goldsmith's name after those of Reynolds and Johnson. It is true that, when Northcote wrote, Goldsmith's outstanding position had been long unquestioned and with one exception the other nine names were not celebrated. But there is the exception; and Burke comes half-way down the list, as if he had been among the afterthoughts.

Percy was a member and he had been the first man with a standing in literary society to seek out Goldsmith. But it seems that some of the others turned up their noses at the ugly duckling; so at least it is suggested by the egregious Sir John Hawkins: " As he wrote for the booksellers, we at the Club looked on him as a mere literary drudge, equal to the task of compiling and translating, but little capable of original and still less of poetical composition." Hawkins himself got in because he had been a member of a club which Johnson had founded some fourteen years earlier in Ivy Lane, and which was proposed as the model for this new assembly that was to meet at seven o'clock every Monday at the Turk's Head in Gerrard Street.

Such clubs were a feature of London life in those days and Goldsmith had always used this means of providing himself with society. "For," he writes in the fourth number of "The Bee" (turning his amusements into copy):

although such as have a knowledge of the town, may easily class themselves with tempers congenial to their own; a countryman who comes to live in London finds nothing more difficult. With regard to myself, none ever tried with more assiduity, or came off with such indifferent success. I spent a whole season in the search, during which time my name has been enrolled in societies, lodges, convocations, and meetings without number.

The essay goes to describe how he had tried the "Choice Spirits" where everybody had to oblige with a song or recitation and the evening went very merrily: "Every man had his say, and he saw no reason why he should not be heard as well as the rest," so that the whole became "one universal shout," when to the general dismay "the landlord came to acquaint the company that the reckoning was drank out." Apparently, all comers found two shillings a head and it went to supply a punch bowl, but punch bowls have their limits.—Then there was the Muzzy Club, "men of prudence and foresight every one of them, and some worth forty thousand." Here it was guaranteed that there should be "no confusion or bawling," and the pledge held. "The members kept a profound silence, each with a pipe in his mouth and a pewter pot in his hand, and with faces that might easily be construed into absolute wisdom. Happy society, thought I to myself, where the members deliver nothing rashly." Yet, "every time the pipe was laid down I expected it was to speak; but it was only to spit."—Quitting this "dumb society," he tried the "Harmonical":

The landlord was himself founder. The money spent is four-pence each; and they sometimes whip for a double reckoning. To this club few recommendations are requisite, except the intro-ductory fourpence and my landlord's good word, which, as he gains by it, he never refuses.

We all here talked and behaved as everybody else usually does on his club night; we discussed the topic of the day, drank each other's healths, snuffed the candles with our fingers, and filled our pipes from the same plate of tobacco. The company saluted each other in the common manner. Mr. Bellowsmender hoped Mr. Curry-comb-maker had not caught cold going home the last club-night; and he returned the compliment by hoping that young Master Bellowsmender had got well again of the chin-cough. Doctor Twist told us a story of a parliament-man with whom he was intimately acquainted; while the bug-man, at the same time, was telling a better story of a noble lord with whom he could do anything. A gentleman in a black wig and leather breeches, at t'other end of the table, was engaged in a long narrative of the Ghost in Cock-lane : he had read it in the papers of the day, and was telling it to some one that sat next him, who could not read. Near him Mr. Dibbins was disputing on the old subject of religion with a Jew pedlar, over the table, while the president vainly knocked down Mr. Leathersides for a song. Besides the combinations of these voices, which I could hear altogether, and which formed an upper part to the concert, there were several others playing under-parts by themselves, and endeavouring to fasten on some luckless neighbour's ear who was himself bent upon the same design against some other.

When every allowance is made for caricature, it has to be allowed that the Turk's Head was a great advance on any society in which Goldsmith had before found himself. It was indeed the high top-gallant of clubdom, and within a few years the most respectably distinguished persons were fighting to get in. Probably also, the first years before it became the fashion were those in which it was most agreeable.

Hawkins says that " a lady distinguished for beauty and taste in literature "—(Mrs. Montague the bluestocking)— " asked the members more than once to dinner at her house. . . . Curiosity was her motive and possibly a desire of intermingling with our conversation the charm of her own." He thinks also that it was she who brought into use the name of the " Literary Club "—" a distinction which it never assumed itself."

We do not know if Goldsmith was of the company at Mrs. Montague's, but at least his life now began to know an element which must have completely dropped out of it. For years he can scarcely have had speech with an educated woman. Reynolds's household, where he was soon familiar, gave him that amongst other good things, though it does not seem that either of the sisters shared their brother's affection for this odd friend—whom everybody looked down on, all the more because he was expected to be formidable, and was not. For it seems clear that in the Club Goldsmith was something of a misfit and never wholly at his ease there. He was vain, so at least all his associates tell us, and vanity made him jealous. These are not uncommon failings among authors, or for that matter, among fishermen, lawn-tennis players, politicians, or any seekers after eminence. Hans Andersen, one of the most lovable natures that ever bestowed beauty on the world, was vain to absurdity; like Goldsmith, he was not vain enough to conceal his hurt vanity. Now the Club must have been a kind of ordeal for a man with Goldsmith's temper and in his circumstances. If he had been elected a year or so later, after his first blazing success, things would have been different; men would have been forced to adjust their opinion of his personality to the admitted quality of his published work. They would have prided themselves too much on their own discernment to set down a man of proved literary genius for a commonplace companion. Unluckily this did not happen so. He came in on the recommendation of Reynolds and Johnson, and he had to make good his title to wit in such encounters as went on at that surprising assembly. We know how Johnson talked; we know also what Johnson thought of Burke as a talker. " His stream of mind is perpetual. I cannot say he is good at listening. So desirous is he to talk that if one is speaking at this end of the table, he'll speak to somebody at the other end." Between such combatants, what chance was there for Oliver Goldsmith to get a word in ? He had always a tendency to hesitate which nervousness increased. Besides, his idea of good company was something less athletic and gladiatorial : he wanted fun ; and he liked to have the chance of making fun.   Now, in the Club he was overpowered, and outside the Club he found himself saddled with the terror that the exploits of Johnson and Burke had created.   Northcote in his talks with Hazlitt said : " As Sir Joshua's companions were chiefly composed of men of genius, they were often disputatious and vehement in argument. . . .   Lord B—— (probably Bathurst), intimate with the painter, had conceived such a formidable idea of all those persons who had gained great fame as literary characters, that I have heard Sir Joshua say, he verily believed he could no more have prevailed upon this noble person to dine at the same table with Johnson and Goldsmith, than with two tygers."   And again Northcote tells us that he has frequently " seen the whole company struck with an awful silence at the entrance of Goldsmith, but that Goldsmith has quickly dispelled the charm, by his boyish and social manners, and he then has soon became the plaything and favourite of the company." Elsewhere we have it on the same authority that Goldsmith was painfully aware how " whenever he entered into a mixed company he struck a kind of awe on them that deprived him of the enjoyment and freedom of society," and how consequently he used deliberately to play the fool " in order to bring himself to the wished-for level."   Another passage in Northcote's " Life of Reynolds " illustrates exactly what this meant.   Garrick had one day been dining there and left the room—it was supposed, to depart : but presently he was found in the area, reducing a negro page-boy to convulsions by his imitation of a turkey-cock. Goldsmith, he says, played the same sort of antics ; but it was much more in character when Garrick did the turkey, as we may well believe : and no doubt the Club was strongly of the same opinion.

However, nothing gives us the impression of Goldsmith in a friendly house so well as Northcote's account of his own introduction.   Just come to London as apprentice to Reynolds, he had expressed a great desire to meet the

author : and very shortly Goldsmith came to dine. Thereupon Sir Joshua, " with a designed abruptness," said " This
is Dr. Goldsmith. Pray why did you wish to see him ? "
Northcote in a hurry blurted out, " Because he is a notable
man." There was a burst of laughter, because in those
days " notable " was a special word of praise for housewives,
and the epithet in this sense was " so very contrary to the
character and conduct of Goldsmith " that Reynolds vowed
he should " in future always be called ' the notable man.' "

About this time Newbery the publisher was so much
impressed by Goldsmith's lack of the ' notable ' qualities
that he took in hand to provide for his well-being. A lodging was hired in the convenient country village of Islington
where Mrs. Fleming agreed for fifty pounds a year to
provide the subsistence necessary for a journeyman of letters.
Newbery paid her and deducted the amount from what was
due to Goldsmith. He paid also on Goldsmith's account
fifteen pounds to Mr. William Filby, tailor ; and doled out
pocket money, a guinea or two at a time. It was the sort of
arrangement that Mrs. Milner had suggested to the usher,
and probably not a bad one.

Goldsmith was at Islington in 1763 from August to
November and again from April to June in 1764 ; and in
the quieter surroundings he was writing, over and above
his compilations, work of a very different nature. Reynolds came out one day to look him up and found him
seated at a table with papers before him, but not stirring ;
his eyes were on a little dog in another corner of the room
learning to sit up and beg : his hand was stretched out to
keep the dog's attention. Reynolds walked quietly forward, looked over the writer's shoulder at the page, and saw
it was verse : the ink was wet on the second line of a couplet :

> By sports like these are all their cares beguiled ;
> The sports of children satisfy the child.

But if a literary hack deserts hack-work to write imaginative literature, there is likely to be trouble with his creditors :
and so we come to the most famous story in the saga which

tells how Johnson came to the rescue. "I shall give it authentically," says Boswell, "from Johnson's own exact narration":

I received one morning a message from poor Goldsmith that he was in great distress, and as it was not in his power to come to me, begging that I would come to him as soon as possible. I sent him a guinea, and promised to come to him directly. I accordingly went as soon as I was drest, and found that his landlady had arrested him for his rent, at which he was in a violent passion. I perceived that he had already changed my guinea, and had got a bottle of Madeira and a glass before him. I put the cork into the bottle, desired he would be calm, and began to talk to him of the means by which he might be extricated. He then told me that he had a novel ready for the press, which he produced to me. I looked into it, and saw its merit; told the landlady I should soon return, and having gone to a bookseller, sold it for sixty pounds. I brought Goldsmith the money, and he discharged his rent, not without rating his landlady in a high tone for having used him so ill.[1]

Sixty pounds was not, as it would be now, an advance on possible royalties: it was a payment in full, and of course Newbery got a great bargain. But if we put the equivalent at £200 to-day, it must be allowed that it was, as Johnson afterwards said to Boswell, "a sufficient price." The immediate effect on Goldsmith's mind may be gathered from what he told Cooke in later years. "It was a sum I was so little accustomed to receive in a lump that I felt myself under the embarrassment of Captain Brazen in the play, whether I should build a privateer or a playhouse with the money."

Indeed, financially, it marks a turning-point in his fortunes. Not that this accession of wealth made any marked difference to Goldsmith's solvency; a sieve never becomes capable of holding water. But Johnson had recognized and he had imposed his view on Newbery, that here was work of a kind worth serious payment; and from this time

[1] Austin Dobson has shown that this episode did not take place at Islington and consequently Mrs. Fleming was not the severe landlady. He assigns the scene to Wine Office Court.

on, Goldsmith could get money in lumps. However, the publisher was not immediately decided to act practically on Johnson's advice. " He had such faint hope of profit by his bargain," Johnson told Boswell, " that he kept the manuscript by him for a long time." How long, we do not know ; we cannot date the transaction. What we do know is the date of the publication which once for all decided Goldsmith's position in literature. On the 19th of December, 1764, an announcement appeared : " This day is published, price one shilling and sixpence, ' The Traveller,' or, a Prospect of Society, a Poem. By Oliver Goldsmith, M.B."

It was the first time that work by this author, who had already written as much as would fill several volumes, was published with his name attached : and it should be observed that he added the letters indicating his professional qualification. In the previous year he had already used them in signing an agreement (for a work which was never written) with Dodsley ; and it seems that the literary world knew him first and last as " Dr. Goldsmith." No record exists of the grant of this degree from any university, but Dr. Kirkpatrick says that at this period medical degrees were granted on occasion by Dublin University without examination and even without residence or study in the college. Goldsmith was a graduate in Arts of the University, and the conclusion is that the degree was granted to him *in absentia*. Dr. Kirkpatrick suggests that on his visit to Bath in 1762 he may have met some member of the Board of Trinity who could be persuaded to secure him this favour.

Another fact of biographical interest must be set out before considering this poem itself and its effect on Goldsmith's fortunes. Dedications were still in vogue, and on occasion were still rewarded—though, as Goldsmith had written very plainly, the book-buying public was now superseding all these other patrons. Yet to pay such a compliment was a recognized and respected method for a man to advance his future, and Goldsmith must have either known men who might serve him, or been able to reach them through other members of the Club. What he did, however, was to inscribe the work to a man who had neither money nor influence, his brother.

It was indeed, as the opening sentences showed, the only natural dedication :

To The Rev. Henry Goldsmith

DEAR SIR,

I am sensible that the friendship between us can acquire no new force from the ceremonies of a Dedication ; and perhaps it demands an excuse thus to prefix your name to my attempts, which you decline giving with your own. But as a part of this Poem was formerly written to you from Switzerland, the whole can now, with propriety, be only inscribed to you. It will also throw a light upon many parts of it, when the reader understands that it is addressed to a man, who, despising fame and fortune, has retired early to happiness and obscurity, with an income of forty pounds a year.

No one doubts that Goldsmith had an affectionate heart ; but it is not always remembered with what dignity, even at his neediest, he maintained the independence of a man of letters. The best that he had to give was neither for sale nor for barter.

CHAPTER IX

"THE TRAVELLER" AND "THE VICAR OF WAKEFIELD"

ALL poetry, except the very greatest (and perhaps this exception should not be made), appeals more fully to the contemporaries of its author, means more to them, than to any subsequent age. They understand it better, living under the same influences of the time as those which helped to mould it. There is therefore always a tendency to over-praise contemporary work. But at the same time, literature divides itself into camps, and there are hostilities of the moment which influence judgment, and result in this, that those who do not overpraise often damn out of mere pre-judice. Goldsmith most singularly escaped this reaction. For instance, all Gray's prepossessions were against Gold-smith, and Goldsmith had helped to strengthen them. Nevertheless, Goldsmith's poetry found so strong an echo in the mood of the time that Gray responded to it instinc-tively, and his richly-equipped judgment confirmed the instinctive praise.

In London Johnson, of course, set the tone by pronounc-ing " The Traveller " to be the finest poem since Pope's death. This was to put it before Gray's " Odes " and even before his " Elegy " : but neither Johnson nor Goldsmith ever valued Gray at his worth. Collins and Smart were to them merely examples of mad unhappy genius. The writer then in vogue was Churchill, who had just died : but the real competitor against Goldsmith in that period was John-son himself. If he decided that " The Traveller " was a finer poem than either " London " or " The Vanity of

Human Wishes," it does not lessen the credit of his generosity to say that the world has agreed with him.

He has indeed a sort of paternal proprietary interest in the poem, which, if we may trust a good witness, might never have seen the light but for him. " The manuscript lay by the doctor for some years without any determined idea of publishing," Cooke says, " till persuaded to it by his friend Dr. Johnson, who gave him some general hints towards enlarging it."—One must inquire what this means.

Part of the poem, he tells his brother, was " written to you from Switzerland," and we know from Boswell that there was collaboration in the completing of it. Johnson furnished one line which has no great merit or importance ; but he actually wrote the concluding five couplets. Goldsmith substituted one couplet (that about " Luke's iron crown "), but with this exception the lines that sum up the poem's philosophy were contributed by Johnson. It is not believable that any writer would have allowed so marked an interference had there not been discussion at earlier stages while the work took shape.

Can we conjecture with any plausibility which parts of the poem were written before Johnson came in to advise ? I think so.

It is a moral essay. It is in the main very like a versification of one of Goldsmith's prose essays. We are told by Cooke that his method in writing verse was to set down in prose the substance of what he wanted to say and then transpose it into the other medium. Now, this is not the way in which poetry is normally written ; it differs from prose in quality as dancing does from walking ; it is normally a dance of thoughts and of words which convey emotion ; and thoughts and words present themselves dancing— gravely or gaily, in a simple or elaborate rhythm ; but they come in rhythm. It is not believable that Goldsmith when he sat down to write the verses about Madam Blaize or his " Elegy on the Death of a Mad Dog," began with a draft in prose. These things, trifles no doubt, but long-lived trifles, are in the tradition of natural English verse. "The Travel-ler" for the most part is in that other tradition which Pope and his circle imposed for a time on England, according to which the excellence of verse lies in a happy sententiousness: Swift describes it:

> In Pope I cannot read a line
> But with a sigh I wish it mine.
> When he can in one couplet fix
> More sense and wit than I in six.

I must try later on to examine the case for this kind of poetry; but here my concern is to see if a line of cleavage can be traced between earlier and later in "The Traveller." On the face of it, the preluding lines which look back on his whole course of travel, from Scheldt to Po, could not have been written while he was still in Switzerland; and one couplet in them may have its original sketch in the passage already quoted from one of the first "Letters from a Citizen of the World."[1] That was written early in 1760. By the end of 1764 it had become:

> Where'er I roam, whatever realms to see,
> My heart untravell'd fondly turns to thee;
> Still to my brother turns, with ceaseless pain,
> And drags at each remove a lengthening chain.

Then, with what appears a calculated abruptness, the poem passes from this note of yearning to a sudden passionate greeting:

> Eternal blessings crown my earliest friend,
> And round his dwelling guardian saints attend.

One has the sense here of a fresh beginning: and, in fact, here perhaps the poem first began. It was written first, I think, to express not a philosophic thesis but a mood: the Wanderer, "thinking long" for home, pictures home's happiness, and contrasts it with his own futile pursuit of "some fleeting good, that mocks me with the view."

Yet if he captures nothing, and can find "no spot of all the world his own," what the eye beholds, it possesses:

[1] P. 151.

"Creation's heir, the world, the world is mine!" But there is no lasting satisfaction in such philosophy.

> And oft I wish amidst the scene to find
> Some spot to real happiness consign'd,
> Where my worn soul, each wandering hope at rest,
> May gather bliss to see my fellows blest.

At that part, I believe, the fragment stopped; and Johnson, reading it, said, "Why not go on? Why not illustrate from your travels that happiness can be everywhere, and is nowhere by prescriptive right?" At all events, from this point forward the poem assumes definitely the appearance of a moral essay written "to show" (as the Dedication says) "that there may be equal happiness in states that are differently governed from our own; that each state has a particular principle of happiness, and that this principle in each may be carried to a mischievous excess."

Success was not dazzling, but the little book went into its fourth edition by August. We get some idea of what in it found special favour, when we read how, as Boswell was helping Johnson into his great-coat one evening, the big man fell to declaiming the passage about Britain and "the lords of human kind." He went on till the tears started to his eyes. Yet there is nothing pathetic in the passage. Johnson was merely experiencing one of those symptoms of the response to poetry which Professor Housman has analysed. This particular one is described by him as "a constriction of the throat and a precipitation of water to the eyes"; and he would doubtless agree that if these lines produced that physical effect on Johnson, they were poetry to Johnson.

Johnson's enthusiasm communicated itself, or imposed itself, for the general tendency in Goldsmith's circle was almost to incredulity. "I believe that he wrote it," said one of them, "and let me tell you that is believing a great deal." Johnson, when asked long after whether the partiality of Goldsmith's friends had not unfairly pushed on "The Traveller," answered baldly, "Why no, sir; the partiality of his friends was always against him; it was with difficulty we could give him a hearing." But perhaps the most eloquent utterance recorded came from Miss Reynolds. When she had heard Johnson read the poem from beginning to end a few days after it came out, her comment was, " Well, I never more shall think Dr. Goldsmith ugly." It is evident that other people than Miss Reynolds decided to change their attitude to Goldsmith. They would never more think him simply a scribbler. Cooke tells a story how one of the other Irishmen by whom Oliver Goldsmith was constantly surrounded congratulated him on his success and pressed him to come and celebrate it. This was Hugh Kelly, soon to be a successful rival. Goldsmith said that he was really so full up of engagements that it was difficult. " Let me see, to-night I dine with Burke; next day with Nugent, and the day after that with Topham Beauclerc. I'll tell you what I'll do for you, my boy, I'll dine with you on Saturday." Cooke tells it as an example of his blundering way of expressing himself—" what I'll do for you." But even if success had gone a little to his head, it was the fact that he had become the fashion, and his friends who were already his friends, like Burke, were proud to produce him. Nugent, afterwards Lord Clare, seems to have first met him at this period. But the big genial Irishman who paraded his brogue took enthusiastically to his fellow-countryman, and it was a lasting intimacy between the hard-driven writer for bread and this wealthy aristocrat.

From this new state of affairs, Goldsmith's inferiority complex felt relief; and he sought to mark the advance by those means to which he attached so much value. He appeared, Cooke says, " in a more professional scarlet great-coat, buttoned close under the chin, and a physical wig as was the fashion of the time." A doctor's wig was large and, later on, Goldsmith joked about it in his " Animated Nature " :

Another point of view which men have in dressing is to take up more room in the world than Nature seems to have allotted them. The largeness of the doctor's wig arises from the same pride with the beau's queue. Both want to have the size of their understanding measured by the size of their heads.

But in 1765 Goldsmith was anxious as anyone to increase the space he took up, and suffered privations from his desire to cut a fashionable figure. " He declined visiting many of those public places which were formerly so convenient to him in point of expense," Cooke says, " and which contributed so much to his amusement. ' In truth,' said the Doctor (a favourite phrase of his), ' one sacrifices something for the sake of good company, for here I'm shut out of several places where I used to play the fool very agreeably.' "

Another step upward was his move to better quarters, on the Library Staircase in the Temple. Meanwhile he received some practical recognition of his altered position when two booksellers came with a proposal to republish his essays—paying ten guineas apiece for the right to reprint with his name what had been, as he said in his preface, " regularly reprinted twice or thrice a year and conveyed to the public through the kennel of some engaging compilation. As these entertainers of the public, as they call themselves, have partly lived upon me for some years, let me now try if I cannot live a little upon myself " : and he quotes the story of a fat man in a shipwreck who " when the sailors were taking slices from his posterior insisted, with great justice, on having the first cut for himself."

Goldsmith, now that he was fairly done with anonymous journalism, always gave himself airs of great superiority towards the " engaging compilations " by which he had so long subsisted. But his finances were as yet far from solid. There was enough for him to live by, no doubt, but not enough to cut a dash or play Sir Bountiful. Money, when he had it, escaped at every pore : one of Cooke's stories illustrates the leakage.

Lloyd, an author who collaborated with Churchill, came up to Goldsmith one morning in the Chapter Coffee House and asked how he did. Goldsmith, not knowing the man, returned his inquiries with an air of distant civility till Lloyd said there should be no ceremony. " I am Lloyd, you are

Dr. Goldsmith, we should know each other as brother poets and literary men ; will you please sup with me here this evening and meet half a dozen honest fellows ? " Goldsmith accepted, the company of authors and booksellers was merry and " the glass circulated to a late hour in the morning," when Lloyd left the room and was heard loud and angry in debate with the tavern-keeper. Goldsmith ran to the rescue and asked what was the matter : " Only that this very cautious gentleman has refused to take my note for the reckoning." " You are forgetting," said the other, " that you owe me fourteen or fifteen pounds already ; and since you have made things public, I say here that I will take neither your word nor your note." " Pooh, pooh," said Goldsmith who had a keen fellow-feeling, " it's not the first time a gentleman was short of cash : will you take my word for the reckoning ? " " Most certainly, Doctor, and for as much more as you like." Lloyd stepped over to the inn-keeper. " Why then, send in another case of wine and add it to the bill." Naturally, Goldsmith had to foot the whole.

There was, however, a possibility that literary success might bring solid rewards in another way than through the bookseller. Percy was in those days preparing his " Reliques," and discussions with him upon the ballad-form set Goldsmith to writing his " Edwin and Angelina." This poem, since Percy was chaplain at Northumberland House, he wrote out and addressed to the Countess—profiting no doubt by Percy's introduction. She was pleased enough with it to have some copies " printed for the amusement of the Countess of Northumberland." This was before " The Traveller " had appeared. After that public success, Goldsmith received an invitation to call on the Earl. While he waited for audience, Sir John Hawkins arrived and was at once shown in. His account is well known but deserves to be printed in full.

I made my business as short as I could, and, as a reason, mentioned that Doctor Goldsmith was waiting without. The Earl asked me if I was acquainted with him : I told him I was, adding what I thought likely to recommend him. I retired, and staid in the outer room to take him home. Upon his coming out, I asked him the result of his conversation. " His lordship," says he, " told me he had read my poem," meaning the " Traveller," " and was much delighted with it ; that he was going lord-lieutenant of Ireland, and that, hearing that I was a native of that country, he should be glad to do me any kindness." And what did you answer, asked I, to this gracious offer ? " Why," said he, " I could say nothing but that I had a brother there, a clergyman, that stood in need of help : as for myself I have no dependence upon the promises of great men : I look to the booksellers for support ; they are my best friends, and I am not inclined to forsake them for others." Thus did this idiot in the affairs of the world trifle with his fortunes, and put back the hand that was held out to assist him ! Other offers of a like kind he either rejected or failed to improve, contenting himself with the patronage of one nobleman, whose mansion afforded him the delights of a splendid table, and a retreat for a few days from the metropolis.

The nobleman referred to was Nugent, Lord Clare, and he would probably have kicked anybody downstairs who called him Goldsmith's " patron."

Northumberland told Percy afterwards that if he had known how to serve Goldsmith he would have done so ; for instance, that if he had been aware of his desire to travel, he would have got him a salary on the Irish establishment. The request for help to his brother—then curate at Athlone —was probably regarded as an impertinence better not mentioned.

Nothing was to take away from Goldsmith the claim that he was the first great writer in England who lived entirely by the earnings of his pen. Johnson had done it, and even established himself as a kind of literary dictator, before he accepted a pension. In his case the provision was only needed because of the man's inveterate indolence. If he had to make shifts barely to live, it was because he would not work. Goldsmith, on the other hand, was a marvel of industry. Even on the basis of selling work for tens of pounds which ultimately brought the trade thousands, he contrived to make a very appreciable income. This improvidence was different from Johnson's who would not work. Goldsmith would work, but he would not save, even to keep him till the next ship came home.

But he demonstrated beyond yea or nay the truth which he repeatedly maintained, that the professional author can when writing vast quantities of mere hack-work also produce work as finished and as durable as even that of men whose genius does not need to cash itself in petty coin; and that it will, moreover, be more workmanlike. Gibbon and Burke may last as long as Goldsmith; they have, each in his way, a greater importance, and have rendered perhaps greater service to the intellect of their nation. Goldsmith's value in that respect is less specific; you can no more set it apart for estimate than the worth of a day's sunshine. But consider them as writers, and comparison turns the balance clearly. Gibbon had positively a bad influence as a writer of English prose; Burke is not an example to imitate. But Goldsmith's is a prose that every wise man would imitate if he could. It not only carried on the manner of Addison and Swift but adds to it a suppleness and charm not to be matched in their writings.

But the finest examples of it had not yet been given in the year of which I have been writing: "The Vicar of Wakefield" did not appear till the spring of 1766. To the world at large Goldsmith is, and is rightly, known by his one novel. It was not so with his contemporaries. His "notability," to adopt the word which Northcote blundered on to, came from "The Traveller" and its pendant, and, later, from the plays. Yet the novel, and it only, has the master quality of this delightful writer—his humour. The plays have his fun, which in spite of the critics sent London into fits of laughter. But in the "Vicar" we observe a charitable Christian gentleman, well educated, who is something of a philosopher, but not very wise in worldly wisdom; we see him lovable in prosperity, but displaying all his foibles; then we are shown how admirable he can be in adversity, yet even under the most improbable load of misfortunes he remains the same human being, watched with the same

Vicar

indulgent hint of laughter. I do not know of any other book that deals so tenderly with vanity in a really good man. It is, of course, not a portrait of the author, but it is a picture based on loving remembrance of the author's father, and the family likeness is unmistakable. The foibles which Goldsmith indicates with so light a touch were Goldsmith's own—though in the son they were much intensified; the folly, the lack of ordinary shrewdness in life's ordinary affairs, was Goldsmith's—but he had more of it. Yet so also was the wisdom—and here the son made rich addition to what he received from inheritance and from instruction. One of a family " all equally generous, credulous, simple and inoffensive," he was launched into a world for which (in his own judgment) home training had given him no sufficient preparation; his father's lack of worldly wisdom had made it too easy for him to fall into follies. A desire for experience, which was indeed the prompting of genius, led him to adventure, in which he was constrained to many courses which, to put it mildly, he could not have contemplated with satisfaction. Not only the desire for extended knowledge but most ordinary frailties led him into difficulties; he was a borrower who often did not repay, and such borrowers do not easily retain self-respect. Yet his worst irregularities can be matched from the history of many more famous in literature who not only indulged their passions, but bilked their creditors and plundered their friends to get means for the indulgence. From a soil so treated, Baudelaire, for instance, grew his " Fleurs du Mal " : Goldsmith grew the " Vicar of Wakefield." He had put his inherited philosophy to tests far more really mordant than those which the Vicar's underwent in the story, and they left it enriched but in its essence unaltered. Goethe testifies :

It is not to be described, the effect that Goldsmith's ' Vicar ' had upon me, just at the critical moment of intellectual development. That lofty and benevolent irony, that fair and indulgent view of all infirmities and faults, that equanimity under all changes and chances, and the whole train of kindred virtues, proved my best education.

No doubt such an effect can only be produced on a reader subject to the same influences under which the writer worked : we are all attuned to contemporary wave-lengths. Yet it would be a very wise man (or perhaps a very unwise one) who could read the " Vicar " without acquiring some philosophy from it. Goldsmith is far more our contemporary than Richardson, Fielding, Smollett or Sterne, partly because his enchanting style is more constantly in the best English tradition, less marked with the peculiarities of an age ; still more, because charm never goes out of fashion, and, more than these others, he has the quality of charm ; but, above all, because he goes deeper than any of them ; because he is a better philosopher.

All that he had to say is best said in the " Vicar," though he said much of it in other ways and in other places ; and much of what he preached elsewhere in theory is here given by example. Also, though he is everywhere among the most autobiographic of authors, it is from the " Vicar " that we learn most about his history, the people he came from, and about the man he was.

Oliver himself is all through the book. He is, of course, the wandering son who sketches his adventures—though, to be sure, Oliver Goldsmith had little about him of the handsome young soldier who won the heart of Miss Arabella Wilmot. But I have no doubt that Goldsmith wrote from vivid recollection when he says, describing a meeting between the wanderer and an Irish student returning from Louvain, in which the " conversation turned upon topics of literature : " I always forgot the meanness of my circumstances when I could converse upon such subjects."

He is also, though by dramatic impersonation, Mr. Burchell : there is no mistaking the sketch of a man " who carried benevolence to an excess when young." The novelist has asked himself, What should I be, had I been born to a great fortune ? Here is part of the answer :

He loved all mankind ; for fortune prevented him from knowing that there were rascals. Physicians tell us of a disorder, in which the whole body is so exquisitely sensible that the slightest touch gives pain : what some have thus suffered in their persons, this gentleman felt in his mind : the slightest distress, whether real or fictitious, touched him to the quick, and his soul laboured under a sickly sensibility of the miseries of others. Thus disposed to relieve, it will be easily conjectured he found numbers disposed to solicit ; his profusions began to impair his fortune, but not his good-nature—that, indeed, was seen to increase as the other seemed to decay : he grew improvident as he grew poor ; and, though he talked like a man of sense, his actions were those of a fool. Still, however, being surrounded with importunity, and no longer able to satisfy every request that was made him, instead of *money*, he gave *promises*. They were all he had to bestow, and he had not resolution enough to give any man pain by a denial.

The consequences are set out in the story : but as if to emphasize the identity, we are told that Sir William Thornhill (known to the Primrose family as Mr. Burchell) " in his own whimsical manner, travelled through Europe on foot." Yet there is a more significant similarity in another trait of this eccentric, " who was known in our neighbourhood by the character of the poor gentleman, that would do no good when he was young."

He would at intervals talk with great good sense ; but, in general, he was fondest of the company of children, whom he used to call harmless little men. He was famous, I found, for singing them ballads, and telling them stories, and seldom went out without something in his pockets for them—a piece of gingerbread, or an half-penny whistle.

At the Peckham Academy, and on the pavement outside Green Arbour Court (if there was a pavement), this is how (by recorded testimony) Oliver Goldsmith behaved. And in later days when he was famous, we hear what happened when he went to dine with the elder Colman, author and theatrical manager. Colman's son, a boy of eight, was there ; Goldsmith called him over after dinner and took him on his knee, whereupon the brat slapped his face with such energy that he left the mark of his fingers on it. Chastisement followed and the brat was sent upstairs to howl by himself, which he continued to do, till after a while the door opened, and in came Goldsmith carrying a candle, and proffering consolation—which was rejected. Thereupon the comforter, setting the candle on the floor, "fell to conjuring"; collected three hats, produced three coins, said, "Look, these are England, France and Germany"—and put one coin carefully under each hat. Then suddenly saying "Presto!" he lifted the hats, and there were England and France and Germany all under one crown. By this time, tears and sulks were done with; it was evident that a person of such gifts should be cultivated: and after that whenever Goldsmith came to Colman's house, the unmannerly boy was now the first to run to him. "Thenceforward," Colman says, telling the story in his "Random Recollections," "we were always cordial friends and merry playfellows"—for the three years that remained of that companionship.

Throughout the "Vicar" whatever incoherences and inconsistences may be detected in the conduct of Mr. Burchell-Thornhill—and there are plenty—in one respect he is always himself: he never forgets to bring gingerbread for the small boys, which he distributes "a letter at a time." This writer knew all about gingerbread and its distribution.

But chiefly and most intimately Oliver Goldsmith is Moses. It is through the person of Moses that he can laugh most freely at the family characteristics—and he loved to laugh loud. We cannot suppose that Oliver ever went to sell a horse and brought back a gross of green spectacles, for if he had, Mrs. Hodson would certainly have told us so. But I am sure that when Goldsmith described the sisters "mighty busy in fitting out Moses for the fair: trimming his hat, brushing his buckles, and cocking his hat with pins," he wrote from memory of his own preparations for some such outing. Whether he ever had "a coat made of that cloth they call thunder-and-lightning which though grown too short was much too good to throw away," I would not be certain, nor about the waistcoat of gosling green, nor the hair tied with a broad black ribband : but I am confident that when the Vicar says that the hour for dinner " was taken up in innocent mirth between my wife and daughters, and in philosophical argument between my son and me," Oliver was the philosophic Moses. Whenever Moses is made to dispute, he disputes in good set phrases, very reasonably ; yet his zeal for encounter is not always prudent. We have, for instance, the occasion when young Squire Thornhill, by a string of cheap logic-patter, turned the laugh most effectively against " poor Moses, who sat the only dismal figure in a group of merry faces : nor did he offer a single syllable more during the whole entertainment." Plenty of stories in Boswell and the other chroniclers show us the creator of Moses reduced to the condition which is here so feelingly described.

There is also a passage in which Mr. Primrose the younger describes his reactions to a position which must have often faced Oliver Goldsmith. " I had still half a guinea left and of that I thought Nature herself should not deprive me ; but in order to be sure of this, I was resolved to go instantly and spend it while I had it, and then trust to occurrences for the rest." Such we may be sure was Oliver Goldsmith's practical as opposed to his theoretical philosophy.

It is important to study the presentment of Mrs. Primrose. She is seen always with humour, as a rule with indulgent humour, but never with tenderness. Home to Goldsmith meant the family ; it meant walking out, drinking tea, country dances, and forfeits : in summer, sitting out under a hedge of hawthorn and honeysuckle : when the days drew in, it meant burning nuts on Hallowe'en, blindman's buff, hot cockles, questions and commands, and hunt the slipper—all the round of simple pleasures. But, for this son who called it up to mind from overseas, the centre of affection in the family was the father. The mother was simply, as Dr. Primrose himself puts it, " a good natured notable woman, and, as for breeding, there were few country ladies who could show more. She could read any English book without much spelling; but for pickling, preserving, and cookery, none could excel her." At dinner " she took the lead, for, as she always insisted upon carving everything herself, it being her mother's way, she gave us upon these occasions the history of every dish." The main interest in her life was matchmaking for her daughters; and when the young Squire Thornhill appeared on the scene " she had the most lucky dreams in the world which she took care to tell us in the morning with great solemnity and exactness." As the intimacy with their landlord grew she " laid a thousand schemes to entrap him: she would sometimes tell the squire that she thought him and Olivia extremely of a size and would bid both stand up to see which was tallest."

I cannot help suspecting that Oliver Goldsmith as a small boy saw some such arts as this employed to promote attachment between his eldest sister and the well-to-do young Mr. Hodson. Possibly also he remembered how he, who was once her special darling, found her turn completely against him when he had given cause. In the novel, on the news of Olivia's flight with her lover, it is the mother who heaps hard names on the girl; and she does not spare reproaches when the Vicar brings Olivia back, penitent and abandoned. In short, Mrs. Primrose, though she insists that a man must be well provided with birth and fortune to match in such a family as hers, is not represented as a lady: whereas the Vicar with all his simplicity is not only a scholar and a Christian but a gentleman in every word and thought. " The mother makes us most ": it is a true saying for most men; but it was not true for Oliver Goldsmith.

It seems clear, since no letters appear to have passed between her and him during his absence, although he wrote to his other kindred, that she had definitely washed her hands of him. This should be borne in mind when we read a story told by Northcote that on learning of her death (which happened in 1770) he immediately dressed himself in a suit of grey clothes trimmed with black such as is commonly worn for second mourning ; and when Miss Reynolds asked him whom he had lost replied " a distant relation." Northcote observes with justice that his conduct was a " kind of Irish bull " since those who did not know of his mother's death would not expect him to wear mourning at all, and those who did would think the dress not proper for so near an occasion. Miss Reynolds, when she came to hear the truth, " thought it very brutish in him to call her a distant relation." I see no reason to question Northcote's story, though Forster does ; and I should explain it by an unwillingness to make a parade of grief in excess of what was felt—as if the man had thought out for himself what should truly express his feeling, without regard for usage : and the answer, with its double meaning, was designed to avoid an explanation that he would have found it painful to make.

But whether some scruple about sincerity moved him or no, it was undoubtedly a blunder to offer a mark of respect which would be construed by all who knew the facts as the opposite. There is no denying that Goldsmith's intellectual processes often led him to absurd conclusions on matters of conduct. On the other hand, his thinking on subjects of large general import is often most distinguished, and nowhere better exemplified than in this novel —which indeed he made a vehicle for his whole philosophy.

There is one notable example in the harangue upon liberty, which the Vicar addresses to a company as to whose quality he is mistaken. This is indeed " a harangue extended beyond the rules of good breeding," as Dr. Primrose himself admits ; and æsthetically it cannot be defended, except as illustrating the good man's abundant readiness to testify without regard to fitness of place or hearers. But considered as a discourse upon the case for monarchy, it is interesting for its light upon Goldsmith's views. All men are " originally equal," but in practice some become masters ; it is entailed upon humanity to submit, and the wisest course is to have one tyrant instead of many, and to keep him as far off as possible.   The rich and wealthy desire to undermine the king's power that they may increase their own; the rabble are their subordinates; hope lies in the middle class which subsists between the very rich and the very rabble.   Among them "are generally to be found all the arts, wisdom and virtues of society."   It is they who must fend off such a state as may be seen " in Holland, Germany, or Venice, where the laws govern the poor, and the rich govern the law."—That is Goldsmith's protest against what nearly a hundred years later Disraeli denounced as the attempt to introduce a Venetian constitution.

Indeed he need hardly have gone abroad for his examples, to prove that, as he puts it elsewhere, " monarchy was the best government for the poor to live in and commonwealths for the rich."   England's monarchy was by then no very strong protector of the poor, and England was a grand country for the rich.   " I am glad to have lived in a Whig world," said the old Lord Houghton when modern Radicalism began to get the upper hand.   But the Vicar of Wakefield, when he has told how he established Christian decency and humane society within the confines of a jail, proceeds to preach to the legislators who maintain the jails and fill them; and he testifies valiantly against the abuse of capital punishment, which was then applied to almost every offence against property.

All our possessions are paled up with new edicts every day, and hung round with gibbets to scare every invader.

I cannot tell whether it is from the number of our penal laws, or the licentiousness of our people, that this country should show more convicts in a year than half the dominions of Europe united. Perhaps it is owing to both; for they mutually produce each other.   When, by indiscriminate penal laws, a nation beholds the same punishment affixed to dissimilar degrees of guilt, from perceiving no distinction in the penalty, the people are led to lose all sense of distinction in the crime, and this distinction is the bulwark of all morality.

. . . It were to be wished then, that . . . we made law the

protector, but not the tyrant of the people. . . . We should then find . . . that very little blood will serve to cement our security.

This philosopher was in advance of his age by several generations. But the " Vicar of Wakefield " shows us also that Goldsmith put limits to the efficacy of philosophy :

The consolations of philosophy are very amusing, but often fallacious : it tells us, that life is filled with comforts, if we will but enjoy them, and, on the other hand, that though we unavoidably have miseries here, life is short and they will soon be over. Thus do these consolations destroy each other ; for, if life is a place of comfort, its shortness must be misery, and if it be long, our griefs are protracted.

Generations of country clergy had contributed to the strange product that was called Oliver Goldsmith ; he had in him very strongly the instinct to preach, and held strong views about the true methods of preaching. Almost as soon as he got the chance to choose his own subjects he wrote in " The Bee " of 'Eloquence,' and the fifth of his essays has to do with preaching. He is severe alike upon the ignorance of " the vulgar of England who are the most barbarous and the most unknowing of any in Europe," and upon their teachers, " who with the most pretty gentlemanlike serenity deliver their cool discourses."

When I think of the Methodist preachers among us, how seldom they are endued with common sense, and yet how often and how justly they affect their hearers, I cannot avoid saying within myself—had these been bred gentlemen, and been endued with even the meanest share of understanding, what might they not affect ! Did our bishops, who can add dignity to their expostulations, testify the same fervour, and intreat their hearers, as well as argue, what might not be the consequence !

This essay was not one of those he reprinted : perhaps because when he collected them, he remembered that in the " Vicar," then due to appear, he would be coming up for judgment as a preacher. The Vicar's sermon delivered in jail is a sermon addressed to the wretched, by one who felt the pinch. "They who would know the miseries of the poor," the Vicar says, "must see life and endure it."

To the miserable, philosophy can bring no comfort; nothing is left but the promises of happiness in heaven.

Only let us try for them, and they will certainly be ours; and, what is still a comfort, shortly too: for if we look back on past life, it appears but a very short span, and whatever we may think of the rest of life, it will yet be found of less duration; as we grow older, the days seem to grow shorter, and our intimacy with Time ever lessens the perception of his stay. Then let us take comfort now, for we shall soon be at our journey's end.

That was how Goldsmith thought that a good clergyman should preach the gospel. He did not content himself with showing the Vicar at work as a practical Christian to establish decent order among jailbirds, and encouraging them even to earn a few pence by industry. The Vicar has to testify of the faith that is in him; but Goldsmith refrains from making him do this until he is faced with a worse affliction than the unhappiest of his companions. His son has been brought in fettered and wounded, with a capital charge against him to which there is no defence; he has attempted to obtain redress of wrong by manslaying; and it is to this son that he first addresses himself " to fit us both for eternity." Then as an afterthought he adds: " But let us not be niggardly in our exhortations and let all our fellow-prisoners have a share."

Dramatically, then, the sermon has full justification: it is indeed the climax of the book; it is the Vicar's final response to calamity when it has done its worst. " I am now raised above this world and all the pleasures it can produce. From this moment I break from my heart all the ties that held it down to earth."

But a biographer has to face the question whether Goldsmith really believed what he preached through the mouth of his vicar. Could he square his belief with his conduct? Only a very imperfect answer can be given.

Whether Goldsmith was a practising member of the

Church of England, whether for instance he was a communicant, we do not know. We do know that in his writings he laid little stress on this. But I think there was a candour in the man's mind, a frank attitude to truth, which would have prevented him from presenting even dramatically such a discourse as the Vicar's, had he not believed in future rewards and punishment meted out by a guiding providence. That he himself did not act so as to ensure reward and avoid punishment was another matter. We know that in his final sickness his doctor asked him if his mind was at ease; and we know his answer: "No, it is not." We are told also that when he went to France in company with the Horneck ladies (may their memory be blessed!) they asked him on a Sunday, since there was no Protestant church for them to go to, if he would read the service. He refused, and again refused: "I do not think myself good enough." In short he was a philosopher who did not live according to the dictates of his reason, and a Christian who did not obey the teaching of his religion. But his mind was never at ease and I am sure it was not philosophy that troubled him. He might at any time have defended his conduct in argument; I do not think he would ever have justified it to any one remotely resembling his father, his brother or the Vicar of Wakefield. He was the prodigal son, forgiven because he would never have dared to count on a welcome home.

That is what seems to me centrally important in this philosophic idyll. It would be absurd to criticize its construction from the standpoint of probability. Just as in "Candide" Voltaire heaps one misfortune after another on his hero, showing in burlesque the confident reactions of his philosophy to even extravagant affliction, in order to reduce optimism to an absurdity, Goldsmith puts his Vicar's Christianity through a series of imaginary tests, in order to bring it out shining and triumphant. We laugh as Voltaire wants us to laugh. It is not so easy to believe with Goldsmith, and yet we do believe. We believe that

courage and goodness can win through anything—although
we must postulate a next world to put things right. But
the story is credible because the hero is so human: because
we never entirely cease to laugh at him a little. In this
respect—in this only—Goldsmith outdoes Fielding as a
novelist. Squire Western is brought before us with a
force of creation that Goldsmith never approached:
Sophia on occasion can speak nervous good sense: neither
Olivia nor the other Sophia is ever such real solid flesh
and blood. But Mr. Allworthy, in whom Fielding set
out to present a good man, is throughout seen without
humour; whereas, whenever we can look at Dr. Primrose
with dry eyes, we smile as we watch him.

As to the writing, much has been quoted already;
Goldsmith himself (in relating the Odyssey of young Mr.
Primrose) speaks of "the easy simplicity of my style and
the harmony of my periods," as unavailing excellencies.
We can see them displayed in a single paragraph of the
Vicar's narration after he had talked to his womenfolk
against trying to be fine ladies when they had come down
in the world:

This remonstrance had the proper effect: they went with great
composure, that very instant, to change their dress; and the next
day I had the satisfaction of finding my daughters, at their own
request, employed in cutting up their trains into Sunday waist-
coats for Dick and Bill, the two little ones; and, what was still
more satisfactory, the gowns seemed improved by this curtailing.

CHAPTER X

TO THE THEATRE

IT is little short of marvellous to our notions that Goldsmith having written the "Vicar of Wakefield" should not have attempted to repeat his success. I had thought for some time that this argued a great advance in the commercial understanding of literature since Goldsmith's day: but Goldsmith himself corrects me. The 97th Letter in "The Citizen of the World" opens thus:

It is usual for the booksellers here, when a book has given universal pleasure upon one subject, to bring out several more upon the same plan; which are sure to have purchasers and readers, from that desire which all men have to view a pleasing object on every side. The first performance serves rather to awake than satisfy attention; and, when that is once moved, the slightest effort serves to continue its progression: the merit of the first diffuses a light sufficient to illuminate the succeeding efforts: and no other subject can be relished, till that is exhausted.

It is not surprising, then, that after some time Newbery pressed him to write, say, a "Curate of Donington"; and one would like to say that Goldsmith himself rejected what he calls this "method of writing to the dregs." In fact, it seems that he made the attempt, but he must have made it half-heartedly, for the story was never completed, and fortunately has escaped preservation. He was a hack writer, yet also a very fine artist guided by a sure instinct: so good a writer that whatever came from his pen was stamped with his graceful impress and had the quality of his mind. But what he wrote from the depths of his nature was never written to order, to meet a demand. It had the spontaneity of a great artist, and a sure instinct guided him to a sense of his own limitations. The usual need for money prompted him to disregard the instinct, but nature was stronger than the need. In poetry, as I hope to show, he had only one deep central emotion to express, and the need for expression was not yet exhausted. In the creation whose medium was prose, he had proved to himself and to the world that he possessed the gift of creating characters who were natural and living, in the most fantastic situations. That is one necessary endowment of the novelist. But the other is a bent of mind which must be for ever making up stories. Walter Scott is the classic instance, he was at it from early boyhood; but a gifted writer of to-day, as versatile as Goldsmith, who would not choose to be ranked chiefly on his novels, tells me that his mind also has this bent, so that at all times a story of some kind is evolving itself in his inner consciousness; the natural play of his mind is invention and he is never without a story to write. It was not so with Goldsmith. Now and then incidents presented themselves to him, possibly invented, possibly reported : we can trace much of the " Vicar " in his earlier work. In the Life of Nash he relates an instance of Nash's generosity. A certain colonel who had run through his fortune gained the affections of an heiress and was aiming at an elopement when Nash discovered the intrigue, disclosed it to the father and the girl was taken from Bath out of harm's way. The colonel, pressed by his creditors, fled, enlisted as a private soldier with the Dutch, but returning to England entered a company of strolling players under an assumed name. Nash heard of this and thought he would give the colonel another chance with the lady who had now succeeded to her fortune and was being courted by an eligible peer. Accordingly he took the lady and her sister in his own carriage to Peterborough where the company was performing. When the colonel, "now degraded into the character of Tom in the ' Conscious Lovers,' appeared in that despicable situation on the stage," there was a recog-

nition; and things happened very much as they did in the
"Vicar" between young Mr. Primrose and Miss Arabella
Wilmot.—This is a single incident; but in the "British
Magazine" for July, 1760, Goldsmith recounted the
History of Miss Stanton. She was the daughter of a
country parson whose virtues Goldsmith describes much
as, later, he was to describe those of Mr. Primrose; a
professional seducer saw the beautiful girl, got into the
rector's house by a trick, persuaded them to be his guests
in a large mansion and succeeded in his designs. The
rest of the story is of no consequence, except that it is
evidently invented and a most improbable invention.—
Goldsmith's mind worked on this germ for a matter of
four years and the result shows how much his invention was
able to add—at times admirably. It is, for instance, perfectly credible that when the Vicar goes to jail he should
meet the rogue who had tricked first Moses and then
himself at a fair, and also that Squire Thornhill should
have used this rogue in the abduction of Olivia. But it is
by a brilliant piece of invention that this same rascally
Ephraim Jenkinson is made able to defeat Thornhill's
attempt to retain Miss Wilmot's fortune, pledged under the
marriage contract. Jenkinson, employed to find a sham
priest for a sham marriage with Olivia, had brought a
real one—not with any improbable desire to help beauty
in distress, but with the very natural design of blackmailing
his scoundrelly employer. When Goldsmith has to assign
a motive to a character he has created, his instinct teaches
him to find a real one—to "follow nature." Once he had
a situation, he could make people act naturally in it. But
his invention was by no means lavish in providing possible
situations for the dramatic display of character.

So from that time out, after one abortive attempt to
repeat success had warned him, he left the novel alone,
and went on bread-winning till the instinct which had before
urged him to creation should again bring about birth.
Bread-winning in this period, when Goldsmith was fully
established, meant compiling—*invita Minerva*. In "Retali-

ation " he dashes off a sketch of persons who, now that the critic Douglas is dead, go on doing what they are least fit for :

> Our Dodds shall be pious, our Kenricks shall lecture,
> Macpherson write bombast and call it a style,
> Our Townshends make speeches, and—I shall compile.

What he was compiling in these days was anthologies : " Poems for Young Ladies " and " Beauties of English Poetry Selected." Before considering these, it is well to consider Goldsmith as a critic ; and again for the most characteristic expression we must look in the " Vicar of Wakefield." Whatever he put there came from the bottom of his heart, and he found occasion there more than once to speak his mind on poetry.

First, when the family are happily at dinner in the midst of haymaking, Moses starts a discussion as to whether Mr. Gay or Ovid is the better poet :

" It is remarkable," cried Mr. Burchell, " that both the poets you mention have equally contributed to introduce a false taste into their respective countries, by loading all their lines with epithet. Men of little genius found them most easily imitated in their defects ; and English poetry, like that in the latter empire of Rome, is nothing at present but a combination of luxuriant images, without plot or connexion—a string of epithets that improve the sound without carrying on the sense."

This little debate is devised to introduce the ballad of " Edwin and Angelina " so that one need not dwell on it, except to point out Goldsmith's constant emphasis on simplicity. The next piece of criticism is also introductory ; but it is the Vicar who speaks. The little boy Bill has been asked for a song and says :

" Which song do you choose, ' The Dying Swan,' or the ' Elegy on the Death of a Mad Dog ' ? " " The elegy, child, by all means," said I ; " I never heard that yet : and Deborah, my life, grief, you know, is dry ; let us have a bottle of the best gooseberry wine, to keep up our spirits. I have wept so much at all sorts of elegies of late, that without an enlivening glass I am sure this will overcome me ; and Sophy, love, take your guitar, and thrum in with the boy a little."

There is no mistake that Goldsmith's taste was all for gaiety ; and I cannot but think that he had a very limited appreciation of Shakespeare and believed that most of the admiration professed for him was (in Mr. Burchell's word) Fudge. Here at all events is the conversation which passed when the Vicar, in his quest after Olivia, fell in with a strolling player walking beside the property cart :

"Good company upon the road," says the proverb, "is the shortest cut." I therefore entered into conversation with the poor player ; and as I once had some theatrical powers myself, I disserted on such topics with my usual freedom ; but as I was pretty much unacquainted with the present state of the stage, I demanded who were the present theatrical writers in vogue—who the Drydens and Otways of the day ?—"I fancy, sir," said the player, "few of our modern dramatists would think themselves much honoured, by being compared to the writers you mention. Dryden's and Rowe's manner, sir, are quite out of fashion : our taste has gone back a whole century ; Fletcher, Ben Jonson, and all the plays of Shakespeare are the only things that go down." —"How," cried I, "is it possible the present age can be pleased with that antiquated dialect, that obsolete humour, those over-charged characters, which abound in the works you mention ?" —"Sir," returned my companion, "the public think nothing about dialect, or humour, or character, for that is none of their business ; they only go to be amused, and find themselves happy when they can enjoy a pantomime, under the sanction of Jonson's or Shakespeare's name."—"So then, I suppose," cried I, "that our modern dramatists are rather imitators of Shakespeare than of nature."—"To say the truth," returned my companion, "I don't know that they imitate anything at all ; nor, indeed, does the public require it of them ; it is not the composition of the piece, but the number of starts and attitudes that may be introduced into it, that elicits applause. I have known a piece, with not one jest in the whole, shrugged into popularity, and another saved, by the poets throwing a fit of the gripes. No, sir, the works of Congreve and Farquhar have too much wit in them for the present taste."

When we turn to the two anthologies, we find, as was to be expected from the taste here suggested, that nothing is included which seemed to Goldsmith archaic. In the shorter collection, " Poems for Young Ladies," which is divided under the three heads of ' Devotional,' ' Moral ' and ' Entertaining,' Milton is represented under the first head by " Adam's Hymn to his Creator " from " Paradise Lost." But the section opens with a very long poem on " Destiny " by Mr. Boyse, and includes Mr. Ogilvie's " Day of Judgment." Under the ' Moral ' heading, " Edwin and Angelina " appears along with works by Mr. Glover (one of Goldsmith's Irish friends) and also " Marriage, a Vision " by Dr. Cotton. The ' Entertaining ' part is largely made up of passages from Dryden's Virgil and Pope's Homer : Gay also figures handsomely : Collins's " Oriental Odes " are given. Except for Dryden and Milton, and a couple of short things from Waller, there is nothing that dates earlier than Queen Anne's reign in this collection which, according to the preface, " offers in a very small compass the very flower of our poetry." I do not think Goldsmith wrote this ; but there is no doubt about his authorship of the introduction to the two volumes of " Beauties." In this he disclaims all desire for the recondite : " Every poem here is well known "—and popular. But also " Every poem has, as Aristotle expresses it, a beginning, a middle and an end, in which, however trifling the rule may seem, most of the poetry of our language is deficient."—And, indeed, how should one distinguish this progression in " Full fathom five her father lies " or in " Diaphenia like the daffadown-dilly " ? That was not what Goldsmith meant by poetry, and there is not a verse from Shakespeare here, or from anyone before Milton. We have, however, " Il Penseroso " and " L'Allegro," in which he says " a very notable critic " considers that Milton's powers are more fully displayed than elsewhere. Yet " the introduction in irregular measure is borrowed from the Italian and hurts our English ear."

Goldsmith was confidently of his own age, and, opening his selection with " The Rape of the Lock," comments : " It is probable that if our country were called upon to show a specimen of their genius to foreigners, this would be the work here fixed upon." So he begins with it—followed by Parnell's " Hermit." Then comes the Milton, next Gray's " Elegy," " a very fine poem but overloaded with epithet." Next, in Johnson's " London," " imitation gives us a much truer idea of the ancients than even translation could do." Shenstone's " Schoolmistress " is included because " though I dislike the imitation of our old English poets in general, it is justifiable for mock heroic ; the antiquity of the style produces a very ludicrous solemnity." Denham's " Cooper's Hill," and Dryden's " Ode on Alexander's Feast " (" more applauded perhaps than felt ") are among the very few choices from before 1700. He quotes, indeed, Waller's lines " On the Death of the Lord Protector " with a remark which gives the reason for this exclusiveness. " Our poetry was not quite harmonized in Waller's time, so that this, which would now be looked upon as a very slovenly sort of versification, was almost a prodigy of harmony."

We have to accept the fact that poetry did not mean to Goldsmith what it does to us. Two of his comments give us a clear idea of what he himself aimed at. One is on Ambrose Philips's " Epistle to Dorset from Copenhagen " with a description of the frozen sea which Goldsmith thinks " incomparably fine." A couplet gives an idea of it :

> The ships unmov'd the boist'rous winds defy
> While rattling chariots o'er the ocean ply.

This is a condensed and easily memorable expression of a scene ; one may find, Goldsmith probably thought he could find, as good examples in " The Traveller." Again he writes of Addison's " Letter from Italy "—" Few poems have done more honour to the English genius than this. There is in it a strain of political thinking that was at that time new in our poetry. Had the harmony of this been equal to that of Pope's versification it would be incontestably the finest poem in the language." Now, since " The Traveller " appeared, a 'strain of political thinking' had been linked to versification which in harmony yielded little to that of Pope: *ergo*—. Goldsmith may have hoped that the conclusion would be drawn.

However this anthology was not destined to great popularity : for it included two pieces by Prior, " Hans Carvel's Ring " and " The Ladle," which were considered to be indecorous—as indeed they are : and this checked the sale. It is some indication that Goldsmith was not as yet much used to drawing-rooms or he would have been aware how these would be received. Very justly critics have said that he never wrote an indelicate line (at least in the works by which he survives) and they are surprised by his tolerance for these versifications from the " Contes Nouvelles " and the like. But Miss Balderstone has printed the letter of reminiscences written for Percy by Goldsmith's elder sister, Mrs. Hodson, and it gives one instance of his precocious wit. Company was present at tea, and he, a small and rather ragged boy, made some awkward movement which disclosed, through a rent in his breeches, parts that are usually concealed. The ladies laughed and the small boy made verses about their exceeding interest in what they had seen. Miss Balderstone observes that Goldsmith's father cannot have been at all so refined as Dr. Primrose is represented. My reading of the case is that in Ireland, an old-fashioned country, the taste of Prior's day survived when it had been discarded in London —and that even after Goldsmith's death a country-bred lady would have been quite ready to laugh at the story of " Hans Carvel's Ring."

However it fared with his publishers, Goldsmith took a special satisfaction in this anthologizing for a reason with which others can sympathize. " Here," he told Cooke, " he did nothing but mark particular passages with a red pencil and for this he got two hundred pounds." That was " the art of profession." But he added, " a man shows his judgment in these selections and he may be often twenty years of his life cultivating that judgment." Forster, who checked over records of Goldsmith's finances, as we may be sure Goldsmith never did, lets us know that Goldsmith was putting a good skin on the story ; the actual figure paid by Griffin was £50. This may, however, only have been for one of the two. Anyhow this was certainly unusually good pay ; for at the end of 1767 Newbery paid him five guineas for compiling an English grammar. This also was no doubt a work of judicious selection, with red pencil, paste and scissors—but still !

Davies the bookseller did better by him when at the beginning of 1768 he organized a combination of publishers who should commission a History of Rome for which £250 was to be paid. It was expected that two years would be needed to complete it. Call this £750, it was still not a lavish provision ; but it would keep the wolf from the door ; and in such cases Goldsmith never failed to extract most of the price in advances. At this time— though not later—publishers could count that they would get work done when he undertook it.

Cooke has described for us " his manner of compiling " in one of the country lodgings where most of this work was done. He first read in a morning as much in the leading books from which he worked as would cover his next instalment, and marked on a sheet of paper the passages to his purpose :

He then rode or walked out with a friend or two who he constantly had with him, returned to dinner, spent the day generally convivially, without much drinking (which he was never in the habit of), and when he went up to bed, took up his books and paper with him, where he generally wrote the chapter or the best part of it, before he went to rest. This exercise cost him very little trouble, he said ; for having all his materials ready for him, he wrote it with as much facility as a common letter.

It was worth the booksellers' while to keep such a workman going. But nothing could keep him out of

difficulties : his expenditure was always nicely propor-
tioned to his income, or his credit ; when he earned more,
he was in debt for larger sums. Yet he never mortgaged
his time or his energy so completely that there was not the
margin available on which he could draw for work that
was not hack work ; and now he turned in a new direction.

Here I incline to make a distinction. His poem " The
Traveller " certainly was in its beginnings the outcome of
a need for self-expression ; it was the sad song of his
lonely emotions. " The Vicar " too was, I am sure, under-
taken from an impulse to put his philosophy in the form
which he—rightly—thought would be most persuasive.
Now, he thought of the theatre. Certainly no professional
literary man, and probably no one at all, can think of the
theatre without thinking of the money it may bring. At
the same time, in whatever Goldsmith did to express himself, there was always a philosophy to be expressed. He
had, as several of his essays prove, an ardent interest in
acting : he had also a vehement detestation of the current
fashion and standards in criticism of the drama. This
amiable and inoffensive citizen had the stuff of a champion
in him and he was determined to run full tilt against the
established idols. He loved fun, and fun was banished
from the boards : he would bring it back to them. But
the critics, he knew perfectly well, would say that he was
" low."

" Low " appears to have been used over a considerable
period by those whom we should call highbrow critics much
as their modern equivalents use " Victorian,"—for general
purposes of condemnation. Whatever is Victorian, to-day
" has no guts." Whatever in Goldsmith's day was of the
Restoration type was " low." Fielding had written in
" Tom Jones " of " That word ' Low ' by which the
modern judges of our theatre have happily succeeded in
banishing all humour from the stage and have made the
theatre as dull as a drawing-room." Another passage in
the same book is even more pertinent; it concerns the
puppet show that " was indeed a very grave and solemn

entertainment without any low wit or humour or jests."
The master of the show boasted of the improvements attained "by throwing out Punch and his wife Joan and
such idle trumpery." Mr. Jones could not agree in this
opinion, but was told that the best judges differed from
him, and that the showman would never consent to spoiling
the decency and regularity of his stage by introducing any
such low stuff on it. Thereupon a clerk in the company
told how he and his friends were "resolved to drive out
everything which is low from the stage. 'Nothing can
be more just,' cried the exciseman pulling his pipe from
his mouth. 'I remember I was in the footman's gallery
the night when this play of the Provoked Husband was
acted first. There was a great deal of low stuff about a
country gentleman come up to town to stand for a parliament-man ; and then they brought a parcel of his servants
on the stage, his coachman I remember particularly ; but
the gentlemen in our gallery could not bear anything so
low, and they damned it.'"

That was in 1749, and for the next twenty years the
clerk and the exciseman had their own way. Goldsmith
was facing a formidable array of prejudice when he determined in 1767 to act up to what he had preached so far
back as ten years earlier, in his first published book, the
"Enquiry" : "Does the poet paint the absurdities of
the vulgar, then he is *low* ; does he exaggerate the features
of folly to render it more thoroughly ridiculous, he is
then very *low*." That was written in 1758. Ten years
later Goldsmith set out on these two enterprises which
were condemned in advance by critical opinion. He
would "paint the absurdities of the vulgar" and he would
"exaggerate the features of folly" ; he would make people
laugh in spite of the critics ; and he hoped to make money
by doing so.

Money was badly needed, though at this period his way
of life was simple enough : Cooke describes it. After he
had moved to the Library Staircase, he provided himself
with country quarters by clubbing with a barrister in the

Temple, one Mr. Bott, to take "a country house on the Edgware Road at the back of 'Cannons.'" This place he called "Shoemaker's Paradise," because it had been built by a prosperous tradesman in that craft "who laid out half an acre with a small house, two rooms on a floor, with flying Mercuries, *jets d'eau*, and all the false taste which Mr. Murphy so happily ridicules in his farce of 'Three Weeks after Marriage.'" Here he worked at his compilations, as Cooke has described; but here also he certainly wrote more lasting work, and, when he was pleased with himself, would take a 'Shoemaker's Holiday' which, according to Cooke, was spent in the following innocent manner:

Three or four of his intimate friends rendezvoused at his chambers to breakfast about ten o'clock in the morning; at eleven they proceeded to the City-Road and through the fields to Highbury Barn to dinner; about six o'clock in the evening they adjourned to White Conduit House to drink tea; and concluded the evening by supping at the Grecian or Temple Exchange Coffee-houses, or at the Globe in Fleet-street. There was a very good ordinary of two dishes and pastry kept at Highbury Barn about this time (five-and-twenty years ago) at 10*d*. per head, including a penny to the waiter, and the company generally consisted of literary characters, a few Templars, and some citizens who had left off trade. The whole expenses of this day's fête never exceeded a crown, and oftener from three-and-sixpence to four shillings, for which the party obtained good air and exercise, good living, the example of simple manners, and good conversation.

Cooke goes on to deplore that "in the latter part of his life, when he exchanged these simple habits for those of the great, when he ate and drank with them, he contracted habits of expense which he could not individually afford." None the less, it is clear that even in this idyllic period he contrived to run into debt. Glover says: "Our Doctor had a constant levee of his distrest countrymen whose wants as far as he was able he always relieved; and he has often been known to leave himself even without a guinea in order to supply the necessities of others." Not a

doubt but these Bohemians were welcome at the Shoemaker's Paradise, and perhaps were there even when they
had no welcome.   At all events Cooke speaks of " a friend
or two whom he constantly had with him," and who
shared his walks.   It would be strange if Purdon, his contemporary at Trinity, who had done the translation from
Voltaire for which Goldsmith wrote an introduction, were
not often a guest.   But he passed off the scene at this
period ;   and Goldsmith made his epitaph :

> Here lies poor Ned Purdon from misery freed,
>   Who was once a bookseller's hack.
> He had such a damnable life in this world,
>   I don't think he'll wish to come back.

There were others left to draw on the industrious compiler
when he was in funds : still, Goldsmith felt himself able to
face the world, and he showed it notably.

The Grafton administration had just been formed in
1767, bringing in Lord North as Chancellor of the Ex-
chequer.   Lord Sandwich (" Jemmy Twitcher ") was in
charge of propaganda, and felt the need of assistance : for
Wilkes began to be troublesome.   One of his agents was
his chaplain, the Rev. Dr. Scott, and this scout approached
Goldsmith, as a handy pen.   " I found him," he said when
he told the story long after, " in a miserable set of chambers
in the Temple.   I told him my authority ; I told him that
I was authorized to pay most liberally for his exertions ;
and would you believe it ? he was so absurd as to say,
' I can earn as much as will supply my wants without
writing for any party ; the assistance you offer is therefore
unnecessary to me.'   And so I left him in his garret."

But although Goldsmith might take a high line when he
was asked to be one of Scott's under-spur-leathers on the
press, Goldsmith was hard up and he had been at work
on his comedy " The Good-natured Man " throughout
this year, 1767.   When he had finished it, he was advised,
very naturally, to offer it to Garrick—who was intimate
with Johnson, Reynolds and their circle.   Forster suggests
that he and Goldsmith had only met on the occasion when

(about 1760) Goldsmith was an applicant for the secretary-ship to the Society of Arts, and called to ask for Garrick's vote, and was refused because of his attack on theatrical management in his " Enquiry." Davies in his " Life of Garrick " says that on this earlier occasion, Goldsmith, instead of saying that he had written from misleading information, bluntly replied, " In truth he had spoken his mind and believed what he said was very right." It is impossible for us to believe that, in a London no bigger than Dublin is to-day, Garrick and Goldsmith never met during seven years in which both were friends of the same people. But I can easily believe that there lingered some touch of resentment in the actor's mind, first felt against an unrecognized author who so obstinately refused to retract ; and when the author, still unrecognized, became an original member of the Club into which the worshipped actor could not get admittance, the soreness rankled. Davies's account is worth reproducing because it seems to be true and sensible, so far as it goes :

The manager was fully conscious of his merit, and perhaps more ostentatious of his abilities to serve a dramatic author than became a man of his prudence : Goldsmith was, on his side, as fully persuaded of his own importance and independent great-ness. Mr. Garrick, who had been so long treated with the com-plimentary language paid to a successful patentee and admired actor, expected that the writer would esteem the patronage of his play as a favour : Goldsmith rejected all ideas of kindness in a bargain that was intended to be of mutual advantage to both ; and in this he was certainly justifiable ; Mr. Garrick could reason-ably expect no thanks for the acting a new play, which he would have rejected, if he had not been convinced it would have amply rewarded his pains and expense. I believe the manager was will-ing to accept the play, but he wished to be courted to it ; and the doctor was not disposed to purchase his friendship by the resignation of his sincerity. He then applied to Mr. Colman, who accepted his comedy without any hesitation."

But this is not the whole story. In the nature of things theatrical managers will always keep dramatic authors on

tenterhooks, because they have many considerations to
think of that do not present themselves to the author;
and if the manager is an actor-manager, the divergence is
greater than ever. Garrick played fast and loose with the
offer, first because he was not certain of the play's success.
It broke away from established tradition and any manager
would have hesitated. But the actor's point of view came
in to complicate matters. There were two contrasted
parts, Honeywood, the good-natured man, and Croaker
the pessimist. Garrick had at this time Powell with him,
the handsome *jeune premier*, cut out for Honeywood; and
he saw great possibilities for himself in Croaker. But
the trouble was that Goldsmith had invented a third
character which had great possibilities for somebody else;
and Garrick considered that Lofty by dividing the attention
would take off from the effect of contrast between Croaker
and Honeywood. He wanted the play altered so as to
reduce Lofty to insignificance: and Goldsmith very rightly
objected, though the financial pinch grew every day
sharper. Then by a sudden chance Colman at the rival
theatre, Covent Garden, fell in for money and was able to
bribe Powell away from Drury Lane. In the circumstances, Goldsmith offered the piece to Colman and it was
accepted. A letter from him to Colman shows that he had
been brought to a state of mind most suitably humble:
it is eloquent of what he had gone through:

TEMPLE GARDEN COURT, *July* 19*th*, 1767.

DEAR SIR,—I am very much obliged to you, both for your
kind partiality in my favour, and your tenderness in shortening
the interval of my expectation. That the play is liable to many
objections I well know, but I am happy that it is in hands the
most capable in the world of removing them. If then, dear sir,
you will complete your favours by putting the piece into such a
state as it may be acted, or of directing me how to do it, I shall
ever retain a sense of your goodness to me. And indeed though
most probably this be the last I shall ever write yet I can't help
feeling a secret satisfaction that poets for the future are likely to
have a protector who declines taking advantage of their dependent situation, and scorns that importance which may be acquired

by trifling with their anxieties. I am, dear sir, with the greatest esteem, your most obedient humble servant,

OLIVER GOLDSMITH.

Giving one of the few instances in which he showed reasonable prudence, Goldsmith wrote next day to Garrick explaining what he had done and apologizing for warmth at their last interview. He received a courteous reply. "It has been the business and ambition of my life to live upon the best terms with men of genius; and as I know that Dr. Goldsmith will have no reason to change his present friendly disposition towards me, I shall be glad of any future opportunity to convince him how much I am his obedient servant and well wisher."

The men had too many friends in common and were too well aware of each other's talent to quarrel if they could help it; and the end was friendship. Perhaps that came the easier because Goldsmith did not bring a fortune to the rival house. At this first encounter, the highbrows of the footman's gallery and elsewhere were too strong for him. When Honeywood, finding bailiffs in his house, has the brilliant idea of persuading them to pass for his acquaintances, and finds himself obliged to introduce them in that character to the admired Miss Richland, we nowadays think it very excellent fooling; and so have our forerunners this hundred and fifty years past. But in 1768 it was too 'low' and even had to be "retrenched in the representation." In short, the scene was cut out. The final outrage had been the bailiff's retort: "That's all my eye." Yet when the play was published, Goldsmith restored the scene—and even this offending line—"in deference to the judgment of a few friends who think in a particular way," and expressed his hope that "too much refinement will not banish humour and character from our, as it has already done from the French theatre. Indeed," he adds, "the French comedy is now become so very elevated and sentimental that it has not only banished humour and Molière from the stage, but it has banished all spectators also."

The unkindest cut of all was that at the same moment the rival house was reaping rich harvest with a play adapted to those persons who thought, not "in a particular way," but "in track." I shall quote Cooke's account of the whole as in it we have the facts set out by an intimate of Goldsmith's, and they disclose Goldsmith's worst weakness :

> The success of the comedy of "The Good-natured Man" fell infinitely short of what either the Author or his friends had calculated. During the run of it, in deference to the vitious taste of the public, he was obliged to omit the Bailiff Scene, and even with this sacrifice, it rather *dragged* through the remainder of the season. This irritated poor Goldsmith's feelings much, and what added to the irritation was, the very great success of "False Delicacy," a comedy written by the late Hugh Kelly, which appeared at the other house just at the same time.
>
> Of the superior merit of "The Good-natured Man," there could be but one opinion amongst judges of dramatic merit, but such was the taste of the town for sentimental writing, in which this comedy abounds, that "False Delicacy" was played every night to crowded audiences—ten thousand copies of the play were sold that season, and the Booksellers concerned in the profits of it not only presented the Author with a piece of plate, value 20*l.* but gave a public breakfast at the Chapter Coffee-house.

All this was wormwood to Goldsmith, who, though the type of his "Good-natured Man" in every other respect, yet, in point of Authorship, and particularly in poetry,

> "Could bear no rival near his throne."

He vented his spleen in conversations amongst his friends and coffee-houses, abused "False Delicacy" in very unguarded terms and said he would write no more for the stage, whilst the dramatic chair was usurped by such blockheads. What further widened the breach between the two rival authors was, their accidentally meeting in the Green-room at Covent Garden, where Goldsmith, thinking 'twas necessary to say something civil to Kelly, faintly wished him joy on the success of his piece, to which the other (who had heard all the strong things Goldsmith had said of his play) smartly enough replied, "I cannot thank you, because I cannot believe you." From that hour they never spoke to one another.

Cooke adds that if Kelly had been in distress and a failure, Goldsmith would have shared his last guinea with him. Nobody doubts that. This other failing was an ugly one. But it is fair to say that, as some of Goldsmith's friends observed, he said out what other people keep to themselves. It is not easy for an author to watch his rival's success with pleasure. But in this case, one must admit in fairness that Goldsmith, a sincere and scrupulous artist, resented the preference shown for what he knew to be bad work; and I at least believe that this was the true cause of bitterness.

His own rewards for the venture were certainly not negligible: I quote Cooke again:

Though the fame of his "Good-natured Man" did not bear him triumphantly through, yet, what with the profits of his three nights, and the sale of his copy-right, he netted *five hundred pounds*. With this and the savings made by some compilations, which he used to call "building of a book," he descended from his Attic storey in the Stair-case, Inner Temple, and purchased chambers in Brick-court, Middle Temple, for which he gave four hundred pounds. These he furnished rather in an elegant manner, fitted up and enlarged his library, and commenced quite a man of "lettered ease" and consequence.

Even a moderate appearance on the stage brought in then, as it does now, more cash than a successful book. But if from five hundred pounds you take four hundred, and furnish elegantly with the balance, you have not put the bailiffs out of sight. In order to live, Goldsmith must still be busily put to it to "write a volume every month." (So he once stated his output.) Still, his reputation, already very high, had now been enhanced by a new work of whose originality there could be no question. Boswell, indeed, has noted that Goldsmith took the character of Croaker from Suspirius in "The Rambler" and that he acknowledged as much to Johnson. Since Boswell also thought that Goldsmith modelled his style on Johnson's, it may be worth while to quote this :

I have now known Suspirius fifty-eight years and four months, and have never yet passed an hour with him in which he has not made some attack on my quiet.   When we were first acquainted, his great topic was the misery of youth without riches ; and whenever we walked out together, he solaced me with a long enumeration of pleasures, which, as they were beyond the reach of my fortune, were without the verge of my desires, and which I should never have considered as the objects of a wish, had not his unseasonable representations placed them in my sight. . . .

Suspirius has, in his time, intercepted fifteen authors in their way to the stage ; persuaded nine and thirty merchants to retire from a prosperous trade for fear of bankruptcy, broke off a hundred and thirteen matches by prognostications of unhappiness, and enabled the small-pox to kill nineteen ladies, by perpetual alarms of the loss of beauty.

Whenever my evil stars bring us together, he never fails to represent to me the folly of my pursuits, and informs me that we are much older than when we began our acquaintance, that the infirmities of decrepitude are coming fast upon me, that whatever I now get I shall enjoy but a little time, that fame is to a man tottering on the edge of the grave of very little importance, and that the time is at hand when I ought to look for no other pleasures than a good dinner and an easy chair. . . .

Yet, what always raises my resentment and indignation, I do not perceive that his mournful meditations have much effect upon himself.   He talks, and has long talked of calamities, without discovering, otherwise than by the tone of his voice, that he feels any of the evils which he bewails or threatens, but has the same habit of uttering lamentations, as others of telling stories, and falls into expressions of condolence for past, or apprehension of future mischiefs, as all men studious of their ease have recourse to those subjects upon which they can most fluently or copiously discourse.

Now, enter Croaker ; we can judge the extent of the indebtedness.

Croaker.   A pleasant morning to Mr. Honeywood, and many of them.   How is this ! you look most shockingly to-day, my dear friend. I hope this weather does not affect your spirits. To be sure, if this weather continues—I say nothing—But God send we be all better this day three months !

Honeywood. I heartily concur in the wish, though, I own, not in your apprehensions.

Croaker. May be not. Indeed, what signifies what weather we have in a country going to ruin like ours ? Taxes rising and trade falling. Money flying out of the kingdom, and Jesuits swarming into it. I know at this time no less than a hundred and twenty-seven Jesuits between Charing Cross and Temple Bar.

That is a live person, even if a " character part " ; but Goldsmith can put wit into his mouth. " When I'm determined, I always listen to reason because it can then do no harm," he tells his son ; and when Leontine expostulates—" An only son, sir, might expect more indulgence," he is pat with the answer : " An only father, sir, might expect more obedience." Is there not a great ring of Mr. Shaw as well as of Sheridan in these ?

However, there is this to be said. Goldsmith thought of writing comedy about what is called good nature. The obvious trick was to set off the good-natured man against an ill-natured one : but that would have thrown the sympathy on the other side and spoilt the satire ; so, looking for a foil, he may have found the suggestion in Johnson's paper and used it as neither Johnson nor Boswell could ever have done.

But the play for all its farcical humour is essentially a satire on weaknesses that Goldsmith knew well in himself. There is a hard saying attributed to Johnson in Northcote's " Life of Reynolds." Soon after Goldsmith's death, Miss Reynolds said, " Poor Dr. Goldsmith, I am exceedingly sorry for him ; he was every man's friend." " No, Madam," answered Johnson, " he was no man's friend." Northcote thinks that this meant that Goldsmith was no friend even to himself, " and when that is the case a man is rendered incapable of being of any essential service to the world." For my part, I am sure, first, that Johnson would never have used this phrase if he had known it would have come down to posterity; and secondly, that he meant no more than what is said at large in the " Good-natured Man "—" All the world loves him," says Jarvis the old servant. " Say rather," says Sir William, " that he loves all the world; that is his fault."

For, undistinguishing good will, " friendship as common as a prostitute's favour," and " ever complying with every opinion, never refusing any request," are only vanity in disguise, " attempting to please all by fearing to offend any "; and the stroke of these lashes certainly fell upon Oliver Goldsmith himself. He was philosopher enough to be aware of his own shortcomings: he was even aware of the shortcomings of philosophy. " That same philosophy is a good horse in a stable, but an arrant jade on a journey," says the shrewd old Jarvis. " Whenever I hear him mention the name on't, I'm always sure he's going to play the fool."

That is a " good line "; the play is full of " good lines "; but what was left of it when they took out the bailiffs, it is hard to guess. It is still played, I think, though chiefly by amateurs, and survives by virtue of its stable companion: as compared with which, it is intellectual comedy (especially if you drop the bailiffs). Goldsmith had not yet sufficiently made up his mind to set people laughing by giving them the sort of thing that he himself liked to laugh at—" nature and humour," sheer uproarious fun.

CHAPTER XI

SOCIAL LIFE AND "THE DESERTED VILLAGE"

GOLDSMITH'S position was now, after eleven years of professional authorship, fully established. He had the publishers ready to feed him with work and he had the best literary opinion emphatic as to his merits. Johnson, who had pronounced " The Traveller " to be the best poem since Pope's time, declared " The Good-natured Man " the best comedy since the " Provok'd Husband." Nothing like Croaker, he said, had been seen on the stage.

He had identified himself with the piece by contributing a ponderous prologue, of which this was the opening:

> Press'd by the load of life, the weary mind
> Surveys the general toil of human kind;
> With cool submission joins the lab'ring train,
> And social sorrow loses half its pain.

Then followed:

> Amidst the toils of this returning year,
> When senators and nobles learn to fear,
> Our little bard without complaint may share
> This bustling season's epidemic care.

It was so printed in " The Public Advertiser " as a puff preliminary; but Goldsmith got Johnson to drop the lines about senators and nobles—probably, Malone says, because he thought they might give offence. He also got " our little bard " changed to " anxious," because, according to Malone, he thought " little " might " diminish his dignity."

But in truth Johnson had conveyed, unconsciously, that attitude towards Goldsmith which made a difficulty in their relationship. The big dominant man could not help looking down on one who, to put it moderately, was neither big nor dominant. Eccentricity, even ungainliness of appearance, combined with striking talent may be rather a help than a hindrance to success : Johnson is the classic instance, but not the only one ; Wilkes, Charles Fox and Curran are others. But all these men had the power to display their talent in discourse ; Goldsmith was ugly in an insignificant way and had no gift for wordy battle. The anonymous " Life " which appeared in the year of his death describes him thus :

Dr. Goldsmith was in stature rather under the middle size and built rather more like the porter than the gentleman ; his complexion was pale, his forehead low, his face almost round and fretted with the smallpox ; but marked with the strong lines of thinking. If on the whole there was nothing in his appearance that would not rather prepossess the mind against him, yet to those who knew him there appeared a melting softness in his eye that was the genuine effect of his humanity.

Such a physical outfit is a bad handicap to any adventurer ; and even Johnson was liable like anyone else to be prejudiced through the eye. Besides, first impressions are indelible and Johnson met Goldsmith while he was still unknown and still in a garret : and Johnson helped him to recognition. Goldsmith, he told Boswell, was not one of his imitators ; and he " had great merit." " ' But, Sir, he is much indebted to you for his getting so high in the public estimation.' ' Why, Sir, he has perhaps got *sooner* to it by his intimacy with me.' " That was no doubt true, and Goldsmith was not unwilling to feel it ; but manifestly he did not therefore like to be permanently in a position of inferiority. Boswell, who accepted that position with enthusiasm, preferred very much to regard Goldsmith as standing naturally and properly on a level with himself ; and as a result we find in his pages Goldsmith represented as continuously and ungraciously in revolt against Johnson's ascendency. The only occasions when Boswell is fair to his rival is when he records some tribute paid by Goldsmith to Johnson. But it is necessary to review the whole relation.

Boswell arrived on the scene in 1763, when Goldsmith was already intimate with Johnson—so intimate that Johnson was suggesting lines for " The Traveller " ; and one of Boswell's own inimitable touches frankly reveals his own jealousy. The three had supped together at the Mitre, and Johnson before returning to the Temple must pay his nightly visit to drink tea with old Miss Williams. " Dr. Goldsmith being a privileged man went with him this night, strutting away and calling to me with an air of superiority, like that of an esoterick over an exoterick disciple of a sage of antiquity, ' I go to see Miss Williams.' I confess I then envied him this mighty privilege of which he seemed so proud ; but it was not long before I obtained the same mark of distinction."

Now my reading of the facts is that but for Boswell Goldsmith would have gone to drink tea without any sense of " mighty privilege " ; but that he perceived the neophyte's adoring envy and made a mock of it. Yet in the long run the Scot had the last word. He has presented himself in the picture with Johnson, a lovable but laughable figure : Goldsmith also is constantly seen as laughable, but not lovable.

However, here is one picture of the three, too pleasant not to be borrowed :

Another evening Dr. Goldsmith and I called on him, with the hope of prevailing on him to sup with us at the Mitre. We found him indisposed, and resolved not to go abroad. " Come then (said Goldsmith), we will not go to the Mitre to-night, since we cannot have the big man with us." Johnson then called for a bottle of port, of which Goldsmith and I partook, while our friend, now a water-drinker, sat by us. *Goldsmith.* " I think, Mr. Johnson, you don't go near the theatres now. You give yourself no more concern about a new play, than if you had never had anything to do with the stage." *Johnson.* " Why,

Sir, our tastes alter greatly. The lad does not care for the child's rattle, and the old man does not care for the young man's whore." *Goldsmith*. "Nay, Sir; but your Muse was not a whore." *Johnson*. "Sir, I do not think she was. But as we advance in the journey of life we drop some of the things which have pleased us; whether it be that we are fatigued and don't choose to carry so many things any farther, or that we find other things which we like better." *Boswell*. "But, Sir, why don't you give us something in some other way?" *Goldsmith*. "Ay, Sir, we have a claim upon you." *Johnson*. "No, Sir, I am not obliged to do any more. No man is obliged to do as much as he can do. A man is to have part of his life to himself. If a soldier has fought a good many campaigns, he is not to be blamed, if he retires to ease and tranquillity. A physician, who has practised long in a great city, may be excused, if he retires to a small town, and takes less practice. Now, Sir, the good I can do by my conversation bears the same proportion to the good I can do by my writings, that the practice of a physician, retired to a small town, does to his practice in a great city." *Boswell*. "But I wonder, Sir, you have not more pleasure in writing than in not writing." *Johnson*. "Sir, you *may* wonder."

"Such specimens of the easy and playful conversation of the great Dr. Samuel Johnson are, I think, to be prized," Boswell adds, and we may be sure that Goldsmith liked it best when it was easy and playful. On occasion he could even play the fool with this "tremendous companion" (as a frightened divine once described the great man): Cooke has a good passage on this. Goldsmith according to him conciliated Johnson's good opinion by "almost never contradicting him" and excused himself for this by saying—"'There's no chance in arguing with such a man; for, like the Tartar horse, if he does not conquer you in front, his kick from behind is sure to be fatal.'"

In his pleasantries before Johnson, however, he had less restraint, and used to say and do many things *cum privilegio*. As an instance of this, whilst they were at supper one night, *tête à tête* at the King's Head, Holborn, on rumps and kidneys, Johnson observed, "Sir, these rumps are pretty little things, but then

a man must eat a great many of them before he fills his belly."
"Aye, but," says Goldsmith, "how many of these would reach
to the moon?" "To the moon! aye, Goldy, I fear that ex-
ceeds your calculation." "Not at all, Sir," says Goldsmith, "I
think I could tell." "Pray then, Sir, let us hear." "Why, one
if it was long enough." Johnson growled at this reply for some
time, but at last recollecting himself, "Well, Sir, I have deserved
it; I should not have provoked so foolish an answer by so foolish
a question."

Goldsmith certainly much preferred this Tony Lumpkin
style of wit to the kind of argument in which "If Johnson's
pistol misses fire, he knocks you down with the butt-end
of it"—to quote the happiest of all his phrases. But if
there was to be set discussion, he liked to have his say,
and in the circles where Johnson moved it was apt to be
like one of the cricket matches when the hero goes in,
makes a century, declares the innings, and goes on to
bowl, while the wretched underling has to spend some
hours chasing balls in the deep field. The truth is that
talk to Goldsmith meant relaxation after a hard day's
work; Johnson, who in these years very seldom did any
work at all, considered conversation (as we have seen)
his main activity, by which he could do as much good as
by his writings, though not to so many people. And if
Goldsmith thought, as he did think, that he should get
an innings, and showed it as he did show it, Johnson
thought, and they all thought, that this was envy. It
was not cricket, it was not croquet, where the superior
performer has a right to go on as long as he can keep up
the masterly exhibition. To do Johnson justice, he had
no objection to another man who really could monopolize
the bowling. Burke might go on as long as he would,
for Burke also was a tiger. But Goldsmith was a rabbit
wanting to be a tiger, and we have ample record in Boswell
of the real tiger's contemptuous resentment.

Of our friend Goldsmith he said, "Sir, he is so much afraid
of being unnoticed, that he often talks merely lest you should
forget that he is in the company." *Boswell.* "Yes, he stands

forward." *Johnson.* "True, Sir; but if a man is to stand forward, he should wish to do it not in an awkward posture, not in rags, not so as that he shall only be exposed to ridicule." *Boswell.* "For my part, I like very well to hear honest Goldsmith talk carelessly." *Johnson.* "Why, yes, Sir; but he should not like to hear himself."

And again :

He said, "Goldsmith should not be for ever attempting to shine in conversation : he has not temper for it, he is so much mortified when he fails. Sir, a game of jokes is composed partly of skill, partly of chance, a man may be beat at times by one who has not the tenth part of his wit. Now Goldsmith's putting himself against another, is like a man laying a hundred to one who cannot spare the hundred. It is not worth a man's while. A man should not lay a hundred to one, unless he can easily spare it, though he has a hundred chances for him : he can get but a guinea, and he may lose a hundred. Goldsmith is in this state. When he contends, if he gets the better, it is a very little addition to a man of his literary reputation : if he does not get the better, he is miserably vexed."

One must go into this record fully, because, for all time and so much of eternity as concerns itself with English literature, Goldsmith will be seen in relation to Johnson ; Boswell has settled that. And it is a relation where he does not show to advantage, either because talk was the characteristic expression of that period, or because in that period one man specially gifted preserved the talk of a great talker ; and we know what Johnson's idea of a good talker was. "Burke's talk is the ebullition of his mind ; he does not talk from a desire of distinction, but because his mind is full." Of Goldsmith he said, "He was not an agreeable companion, for he talked always for fame. A man who does so, never can be pleasing." And elsewhere : "He was not a social man ; he never exchanged mind with you." Mind meant knowledge, reasoning based on erudition ; and Johnson rated Goldsmith low for knowledge. All that had been got by tramping through Europe with eyes open, by contact with all manner of

men, did not figure in his account. He had indeed a
very just opinion of Goldsmith's dexterity in handling
what is to be got out of books, and perhaps a not less
just one of his mind's furniture. " Goldsmith," he said,
" was a man who whatever he wrote did it better than
any other man could do. He deserved a place in Westminster Abbey ; and every year he lived would have
deserved it better. He had, indeed, been at no pains to
fill his mind with knowledge. He transplanted it from
one place to another ; and it did not settle in his mind ;
so he could not tell what was in his own books." But
he had a complete contempt for Goldsmith as a talker.
" No man was more foolish when he had not a pen in
his hand, or more wise when he had." Yet another
passage is more fully revealing :

Goldsmith being mentioned ; *Johnson*. " It is amazing how
little Goldsmith knows. He seldom comes where he is not
more ignorant than any one else." *Sir Joshua Reynolds*. " Yet
there is no man whose company is more liked." *Johnson*. " To
be sure, Sir. When people find a man of the most distinguished
abilities as a writer, their inferior while he is with them, it must
be highly gratifying to them. What Goldsmith comically says
of himself is very true,—he always gets the better when he argues
alone ; meaning, that he is master of a subject in his study, and
can write well upon it ; but when he comes into company, grows
confused, and unable to talk."

Now, that gives us two things. First, that, as Johnson
admitted, the partiality of his friends was against Goldsmith ; and secondly, that Reynolds said, No man's company was more liked. There were two attitudes towards
Goldsmith : that of Johnson and his worshippers ; the
other, that for which Reynolds had good right to speak.
And I do not suppose that Johnson really believed that
Reynolds enjoyed a sense of superiority when he saw
Goldsmith blundering.

In short, Goldsmith was something of a misfit in Johnson's company. Fundamentally, they were in sympathy ;
and Goldsmith saw far deeper into Johnson than ever

Johnson saw into Goldsmith. "Johnson to be sure has a roughness in his manner," he said to Boswell in the early days of their intercourse (when he still felt it necessary to explain Johnson to this new-comer), "but no man alive has a more tender heart. He has nothing of the bear but his skin." Yet superficially there was disagreement, and when it came to the Johnsonolaters, there was total misunderstanding. Boswell was bad, Mrs. Thrale and Tom Davies worse. Both make a fantastic contrast in their sketches of Goldsmith's character: "Such a compound of absurdity, envy and malice," Davies says, "contrasted with the opposite virtues of kindness, generosity and benevolence, that he might be said to consist of two distinct souls": and Mrs. Thrale, who heartily disliked him, complains that he was vulgar and had bad manners: with a great desire to please, he offended by attempts at drollery. Or, as she put it in a couplet, he was

> A poet, so polished, so paltry a fellow,
> A critic, historian, and vile punchinello.

This means at least that he had not tact; that he did not easily adapt himself to his company. Partly the trouble arose from his talking Irish, so to say, before English people; Davies affords a good illustration:

He went with some friends to see the entertainment of the Fantoccini, whose uncommon agility and quick evolutions were much celebrated. The doctor was asked how he liked these automatons. He replied, he was surprised at the applause bestowed on the little insignificant creatures, for he could have performed their exercises much better himself.

As the story is told elsewhere (for these instances of Goldsmith's "envy" went from one authority to another), we get the *ipsissima verba*: "Pooh, I could do it better myself." Now, any Irish person would have understood at once that this was meant for a joke, not perhaps a very grand joke, but a joke conveying a compliment. "The ludicrous here is to be found in the incongruity of the standard of measures:

for if a man says he could perform an action better than a mechanical toy performs it, he implies that the toy does it as well as some men." So a Johnsonian might have put it.[1]

The capital instance of this misunderstanding is found, however, in the story (first given, I think, by Boswell), that when Goldsmith went with Mrs. Horneck and her two beautiful daughters into France and Flanders, people crowded round the door and testified a desire to see these beautiful young women. "The ladies, willing to gratify them, came into a balcony and Goldsmith with them; but he presently withdrew himself with signs of mortification, saying 'There are places where I am the object of admiration also.'" In Northcote's manuscript memoir, this goes on—"He said this in a joke with laughter." But in his "Life of Reynolds" the tale appears as above, without this explanation, and has been endlessly quoted: though Ashe King, an Irishman, put, as he naturally would, the proper construction on it.

Why Northcote allowed it to appear as it did is a puzzle: but one Mr. Laird revised his manuscript, and probably told him that he was spoiling a good and well-established story. If so, it did not occur to Laird that he was contaminating one of the best sources of information about Goldsmith. Whatever comes to us from Reynolds's studio is free from the conventional attitude of contempt towards the poet who knew in Reynolds his best friend. It was in Reynolds's studio that he met the Hornecks who, I think, brought him the only real satisfaction he ever got from his contacts with the fashionable world. The Hornecks were of good family, coming, like many of Reynolds's friends, from the West of England. Catherine, the elder daughter, got the name of

[1] In studying the instances told of Goldsmith's absurdity or envy, I have often been reminded of a precaution taken in the "Spectator" when it was conducted by R. H. Hutton and Meredith Townsend. A sentence in some article of mine was editorially censured: I protested that the irony was obvious. "We make it a rule in the 'Spectator' never to admit irony: it leads to misunderstandings." Both these men knew the use of irony as well as any that ever read or wrote. But they also knew their English public.

"Little Comedy" from their poet friend. She married H. W. Bunbury, an amateur artist so accomplished that his work in caricature is remembered along with that of Rowlandson and Gillray; but he was a wealthy landowner, and the Bunburys' home, Barton Hall in Suffolk, became one of Goldsmith's favourite resorts for a country holiday. Mary Horneck, the younger, is still known to us by the name that Goldsmith found for her—the Jessamy Bride; and it keeps its fragrance. She did not marry till after Goldsmith's death, when she became the wife of Colonel Gwyn, a soldier of some distinction. She was, of course, painted by Reynolds, who has left us also a portrait of Mrs. Horneck—the perfectly well-dressed, well-bred English lady of that time. If only he had done the daughter also in her normal habit! But, unluckily, the young lady must have been inordinately pleased by her own appearance at some masquerade, for she insisted on being painted in Turkish costume, cross-legged in voluminous trousers, and crowned by an enormous turban. Very amusing to see, but not a bit the Jessamy Bride!

But these people, though they were part of the best society in England, were not typical of the fashionable world. With them Goldsmith was on a footing of real intimacy. Bunbury's study of him emphasizes, indeed, the inordinately long upper lip, the coarsely modelled mouth, and the disappearing chin, yet has no touch of unkindness: he gives as well as Reynolds does the unusual development of the forehead, and leaves an impression of rustic strength as well as rustic simplicity, which Reynolds refined away.

Still the man whom Bunbury shows us was ill-fitted to cut a figure in fashionable society and Horace Walpole helps us to see him in it:

I dined and passed Saturday at Beauclerk's, with the Edgecumbes, the Garricks, and Dr. Goldsmith, and was most thoroughly tired, as I knew I should be, I who hate the playing off a butt. Goldsmith is a fool, the more wearing for having some sense. It was the night of a new comedy, called "The School for Wives," which was exceedingly applauded, and which

MISS MARY HORNECK
afterwards Mrs. Gwyn (" The Jessamy Bride ")
From a portrait by Sir Joshua Reynolds owned by Lord Astor

Charles Fox says is execrable. Garrick has at least the chief hand in it. I never saw anybody in a greater fidget, nor more vain when he returned, for he went to the play-house at half-an-hour after five, and we sat waiting for him till ten, when he was to act a speech in " Cato " with Goldsmith ! that is, the latter sat in t'other's lap, covered with a cloak, and while Goldsmith spoke, Garrick's arms that embraced him made foolish actions. How could one laugh when one had expected this for four hours ?

To Walpole Goldsmith was " an idiot with flashes of parts "—and he was much more conscious of the idiot than of the parts. He, like Mrs. Thrale, could not stand the " vile punchinello." It was perhaps a foible in Goldsmith that he always wanted to make people laugh, even if they laughed at him. Garrick shared the foible, but then Garrick could be sure that laughter was a tribute.

This note of Walpole's belongs to 1773, but long before that the playwright and the actor who would never play for him had come on the friendliest terms. In 1769, a year after the troubles about the " Good-natured Man," we see the two of them in company at Boswell's along with the Great Cham :

He [Johnson, of course] honoured me with his company at dinner on the 16th of October, at my lodgings in Old Bond-street, with Sir Joshua Reynolds, Mr. Garrick, Dr. Goldsmith, Mr. Murphy, Mr. Bickerstaff, and Mr. Thomas Davies. Garrick played round him with a fond vivacity, taking hold of the breasts of his coat, and, looking up in his face with a lively archness, complimented him on the good health which he seemed then to enjoy ; while the sage, shaking his head, beheld him with a gentle complacency. One of the company not being come at the appointed hour, I proposed, as usual upon such occasions, to order dinner to be served ; adding, " Ought six people to be kept waiting for one ? " " Why, yes (answered Johnson, with a delicate humanity), if the one will suffer more by your sitting down, than the six will do by waiting." Goldsmith, to divert the tedious minutes, strutted about, bragging of his dress, and I believe was seriously vain of it, for his mind was wonderfully prone to such impressions. " Come, come " (said Garrick), " talk no more of that. You are perhaps the worst—

eh, eh." Goldsmith was eagerly attempting to interrupt him, when Garrick went on, laughing ironically, " Nay, you will always look like a gentleman ; but I am talking of being well or ill drest." " Well, let me tell you (said Goldsmith), when my taylor brought home my bloom-coloured coat, he said, ' Sir, I have a favour to beg of you. When any body asks you who made your clothes, be pleased to mention John Filby, at the Harrow, in Water-lane.' " *Johnson.* " Why, Sir, that was because he knew the strange colour would attract crowds to gaze at it, and that they might hear of him, and see how well he could make a coat even of so absurd a colour."

The story ends with a snub, as so often, a rub of the bear's rough coat.—It may be an Irish way of looking at it, but I should have thought that Goldsmith again was speaking in joke and had been amused by Mr. Filby's eagerness. However, on this occasion there is no sign that he resented Johnson's heavy hand.

The capital case of such a revolt is well known to readers of Boswell, but it is too characteristic to omit. It took place at a dinner given by the Dillys, booksellers, to a mixed company ; and after a while they got on to the subject of literature and liberty of conscience—as to which Johnson agreed with Swift and with Cromwell that man is free to think, but the state must control his utterance. Martyrs have only the right to suffer. Goldsmith raised the question whether a man, convinced of truth to which he should testify, may not be " as it were committing voluntary suicide," if he speaks. Johnson answered that " you could get men for fourpence a day to go without scruple to be shot at." " But," said Goldsmith, " have they a moral right to do this ? " Thereupon Johnson tossed and gored the pacifist. " Nay, Sir, if you will not take the universal opinion of mankind, I have nothing to say." And he went on to lay down that " before a man may be a martyr he must be persuaded that he has a particular delegation from heaven." *Goldsmith*—" How is this to be known ? Our first reformers were burnt for not believing bread and wine to be Christ——" *Johnson* (interrupting him)—" Sir, they were not burnt for not believing bread and wine to be Christ, but for insulting those who did believe it. And, Sir, when the first reformers began they did not intend to be martyred; and as many of them ran away as could."

That was the butt-end of the pistol and it stunned the interrupter efficiently, while the controversy passed into the more suitable hands of the Rev. Dr. Mayo, who, says Boswell, " never flinched, but after reiterated blows remained seemingly unmoved as at the first. Hence he obtained the epithet of the Literary Anvil." Blows resounded for a long time, " the scintillations of Dr. Johnson's genius flashed every time his opponent was struck."

During this argument, Goldsmith sat in restless agitation, from a wish to get in and *shine*. Finding himself excluded, he had taken his hat to go away, but remained for some time with it in his hand, like a gamester, who, at the close of a long night, lingers for a little while, to see if he can have a favourable opening to finish with success. Once when he was beginning to speak, he found himself overpowered by the loud voice of Johnson, who was at the opposite end of the table, and did not perceive Goldsmith's attempt. Thus disappointed of his wish to obtain the attention of the company, Goldsmith in a passion threw down his hat, looking angrily at Johnson, and exclaimed in a bitter tone, " *Take it*." When Toplady was going to speak, Johnson uttered some sound, which led Goldsmith to think that he was beginning again, and taking the words from Toplady. Upon which, he seized this opportunity of venting his own envy and spleen, under the pretext of supporting another person : " Sir " (said he to Johnson), " the gentleman has heard you patiently for an hour ; pray allow us now to hear him." *Johnson* (sternly). " Sir, I was not interrupting the gentleman. I was only giving him a signal of my attention. Sir, you are impertinent." Goldsmith made no reply, but continued in the company for some time.

After Johnson's own display was over, says Boswell :

He and Mr. Langton and I went together to THE CLUB, where we found Mr. Burke, Mr. Garrick, and some other members, and amongst them our friend Goldsmith, who sat silently brooding over Johnson's reprimand to him after dinner. Johnson perceived this, and said aside to some of us, "I'll make Goldsmith forgive me"; and then called to him in a loud voice, "Dr. Goldsmith,—something passed to-day where you and I dined; I ask your pardon." Goldsmith answered placidly, "It must be much from you, Sir, that I take ill." And so at once the difference was over, and they were on as easy terms as ever, and Goldsmith rattled away as usual.

Boswell certainly is a marvellous chronicler. He reproduces faithfully what he adored as Johnson's superb ascendency, moral and intellectual, without considering that it may strike his readers as brutality: and with the same fidelity he gives Goldsmith's words, leaving it to us whether the reconciliation shows childish inconstancy or admirable forbearance. But one thing he insists upon, and that is Goldsmith's resentment of Johnson's monopoly as a personal wrong. It surely might be construed as a protest on behalf of the company. Toplady, it should be observed, had not got one word in so far, except to express admiration for Johnson's "untwisting" of the difficulty; and Toplady after all was a man of considerable parts.

However, there is agreement of his contemporaries that Goldsmith was vain and did not like to remain in the shade when there was company. It is a kind of relief to regain contact with the indefatigable worker and the scrupulous artist in his study.—We need not linger over the worker. In 1769 he had finished his "History of Rome" and proceeded to contract for a "Natural History" (his "Animated Nature"), to make eight volumes at a hundred guineas each, payable volume by volume on delivery of the manuscript. But very soon precedence over this was given to a "History of England" in four volumes, which went rapidly on. But advances were asked and given, on both works; Goldsmith worked fast, but he spent faster. Miss Hawkins, worthy daughter of Sir John, has a story to the effect that he got an advance from Cadell for the English history, on the ground that he was pressed by his creditors; that Cadell advanced the money but doubted the pretext, and followed as far as Hyde Park Corner where he saw

Goldsmith get into a post-chaise " where a woman of the town was waiting for him ; with whom he went to Bath to dissipate what had been thus fraudulently obtained." So Miss Hawkins tells us—" kind father to her," the Irish would say. Forster has established that Cadell had no concern with the affair, and we are not bound to take the evidence of Miss Hawkins as holy writ. But it is clear that Goldsmith's friends believed that " women of the town " gave great assistance to tailors and needy Irish acquaintance in disposing of what this worker earned.

He was also at this time concerned, Cooke tells us, " in a fortnightly publication called ' The Gentleman's Journal,' in which he was assisted by Drs. Kenrick, Bickerstaff and another Gentleman who undertook the compilation part." Kenrick was an old and persistent enemy, but necessity and magazines make strange bed-fellows. Bickerstaff was one of the Irish tribe, familiar at the Wednesday Club in the Globe tavern where Goldsmith had gone back to playing the fool as he could not in Gerrard Street. The other gentleman was probably Mr. Paul Hiffernan, *ne plus ultra* of this type, like Bickerstaff, a medical, qualified or unqualified, and deplorably drunken. " This journal," Cooke adds, " was to do wonders both for original writing, criticism, &c., but, each depending on the industry of the other, after one or two numbers, it fell off exceedingly, and, I believe, hardly lived to its sixth month. When it ceased to be published, a friend was observing what an extraordinary death it had. ' Not at all, Sir,' says Goldsmith ; ' a very common case ; it died of too many doctors.' "

But behind all this hack-work the poet's brain was now actually shaping a work on which he had long pondered : and Cooke's account is too valuable not to be given in full :

Goldsmith, though quick enough at prose, was rather slow in his poetry—not from the tardiness of fancy, but the time he took in pointing the sentiment, and polishing the verification. He was, by his own confession, four or five years collecting materials in all his country excursions for this poem, and was actually engaged in the construction of it above two years. His manner of writing poetry was this : he first sketched a part of his design in prose, in which he threw out his ideas as they occurred to him ; he then sat carefully down to versify them, correct them, and add such further ideas as he thought better fitted to the subject. He sometimes would exceed his prose design, by writing several verses impromptu, but these he would take uncommon pains afterwards to revise, lest they should be found unconnected with his main design.

The Writer of these Memoirs called upon the Doctor the second morning after he had begun " The Deserted Village," and to him he communicated the plan of his poem. " Some of my friends," continued he, " differ with me on this plan, and think this depopulation of villages does not exist—but I am myself satisfied of the fact. I remember, in my own country, and have seen it in this." He then read what he had done of it that morning, beginning,

> " Dear lovely bowers of innocence and ease,
> Seats of my youth, when every sport could please,
> How often have I loitered o'er thy green,
> Where humble happiness endear'd each scene.
> How often have I paus'd on every charm,
> The shelter'd cot—the cultivated farm,
> The never-failing brook—the busy mill,
> The decent church, that topt the neighbouring hill,
> The hawthorn bush, with seats beneath the shade,
> For talking age and whispering lovers made."

" Come," says he, " let me tell you this is no bad morning's work ; and now, my dear boy, if you are not better engaged, I should be glad to enjoy a *Shoe-maker's holiday* with you."

The first morning's work was no doubt read also on that occasion ; it had consisted only of the two opening couplets. By the second day, he was well into his stride. If ever he wrote poetry, he was writing it then.

Did he ever write poetry ? I must cite the best authority known to me, Professor Housman's discourse on the " Name and Nature of Poetry." " I think," he says, " that to transfuse emotion—not to transmit thought, but to set up in the reader's sense a vibration corresponding to what was felt by the writer—is the peculiar function of poetry."

Apply that test to the lines which Goldsmith read out to Cooke that May morning in 1768, and do they not set up a vibration? They open, as so often in Goldsmith, with a sudden lift of the voice, as if in song, invoking memory that can evoke: and then comes the detail, fondly recalled.

Yet Mr. Housman holds that in the period lying between Samson Agonistes and the Lyrical Ballads in 1798, what passed for poetry was not poetry at all. Satire, controversy and burlesque throve, " forms of art in which high poetry is not at home. . . . To poets of the eighteenth century high and impassioned poetry did not come spontaneously, because the feelings which foster its birth were not then abundant and urgent in the inner man."

Now, beyond question, Goldsmith's two poems (there are only two which count) are typical of the eighteenth century. In both the " plan " is to set out an argument, and " The Deserted Village " is even a " poem with a purpose," written to enforce a political view. " The Traveller " also, though it is not a theory of government, is a view of governments, and of the effects produced by different types of government. Neither of these themes is logically connected with emotion; and I think myself that those parts of the poems which to my mind are poetry, even by Professor Housman's standard, do not strictly belong to the theme. When I feel such a vibration as he speaks of, it is always in response to the emotion which in both the poems dominates the argument—always the same emotion, a wanderer's longing for home, and his memories of home; his longing for memories of the old familiar faces and the unforgotten love. I feel it in the opening of " The Traveller ":

> Remote, unfriended, melancholy, slow,
> Or by the lazy Scheldt or wandering Po, . . .
> Where'er I roam, whatever realms to see,
> My heart untravell'd fondly turns to thee:
>   .   .   .   .   .
> Eternal blessings crown my earliest friend,
> And round his dwelling guardian saints attend.

Is there not emotion here? is there not in that invocation

what C. E. Montague called " the high vibrant note of great verse ? " Both poems are linked to the same memory, the same name—but a memory and a name of more than one person. The " heart untravelled, Still to my Brother turns "—yet the brother is father as well ; and the kind uncle Contarine may also enter into that composite memory-picture.

" The Traveller " was addressed and was dedicated to Henry Goldsmith. A month had not gone by after " The Deserted Village " began to be composed, before Oliver Goldsmith had news of Henry's death ; and under that impulse the passage must have been written which describes the village preacher, and which thousands from that day to this have known by heart. Yet, if I am faithfully to record my own reactions, according to Professor Housman's method, the effect of this passage does not seem to be really the effect of poetry. It has its value, but another value. There is nothing in it that is not done, and better done, in the prose of the " Vicar of Wakefield " ; yet it sticks in the memory as prose never will or can. But then I read this :

> In all my wanderings round this world of care,
> In all my griefs—and God has given my share—
> I still had hopes, my latest hours to crown,
> Amidst these humble bowers to lay me down ;
> To husband out life's taper at the close,
> And keep the flame from wasting by repose :
> I still had hopes, for pride attends us still,
> Amidst the swains to show my book-learned skill,
> Around my fire an evening group to draw,
> And tell of all I felt, and all I saw ;
> And, as a hare whom hounds and horns pursue
> Pants to the place from whence at first she flew,
> I still had hopes, my long vexations past,
> Here to return—and die at home at last.

What has this to do with the argument against depopulation ? Nothing strictly : or at most it is preluding to the picture of what depopulation has destroyed. But as the voice suddenly lifts into this melancholy moving chant, emotion vibrates through it—even through the gentle self-mockery—and I vibrate too. One could come back to such lines after reading what is best in Virgil and still feel their charm. Like the best in Virgil they retain their freshness after wear and tear in ten thousand schoolrooms.

If " The Deserted Village " has been more of a favourite than its companion—though the earlier has more freshness of feeling—the reason is that here, along with musing emotion, we get touches every now and then of the poet's gentlest humour: not laughter, but a tender memory of laughter.

Let us agree with Professor Housman that we only get what he means by poetry unalloyed from those eighteenth-century writers in whom a touch of the moon's influence deranged the too perfect reasonableness of their age—from Collins, from Smart, from Blake and from Cowper. Still I cannot admit that the eighteenth century was wholly in the wrong about Goldsmith.

A poet almost always gets more generous judgment from his contemporaries than from posterity ; naturally, for he speaks what is, daily, in their minds as well as in his ; he can more easily set up sympathetic responses ; and from the standpoint of biography, it is perhaps more important to realize what he meant to them than what he means to us. The most informed and critical judgment of that day was certainly possessed by another poet, and one certainly not prejudiced in Goldsmith's favour. Gray probably knew that Goldsmith had reviewed his Odes grudgingly : he must have known that in the dedication to " The Traveller " Goldsmith had even gone trailing his coat about " mistaken efforts of the learned to improve the art of poetry."

What criticisms have we not heard of late in favour of blank verse and Pindaric odes, choruses, anapæsts, and iambics, alliterative care and happy negligence ! Every absurdity has now a champion to defend it : and as he is generally much in the wrong, so he has always much to say ; for error is ever talkative.

Yet when Gray's friend Nichols brought down " The

Deserted Village " and read it out from beginning to end, Gray listened attentively and pronounced, " This man is a poet."

Johnson, of course, approved the poem, though he thought it rather too much an echo of " The Traveller " : Burke was enthusiastic. Oddly enough, the man least impressed was Reynolds, who told Northcote that Goldsmith as a poet, " was, he believed, about the degree of Addison." His judgment had not been affected even by the dedication of " The Deserted Village " to him, in terms that were singularly moving :

I can have no expectations, in an address of this kind, either to add to your reputation, or to establish my own. You can gain nothing from my admiration, as I am ignorant of that art in which you are said to excel : and I may lose much by the severity of your judgment, as few have a juster taste in poetry than you. Setting interest therefore aside, to which I never paid much attention, I must be indulged at present in following my affections. The only dedication I ever made was to my brother, because I loved him better than most other men. He is since dead. Permit me to inscribe this Poem to you.

It may be said that Reynolds's reply to Northcote's question proved the truth of Goldsmith's compliment to his judgment. Yet there is something in the saying *securus judicat orbis terrarum*, and the world at large puts Goldsmith much above Addison. Like it or not, one has to face the fact that very few writers of verse have given so much pleasure to posterity. Whether it was truly the pleasure of poetry is another question ; but he has certainly given the pleasure of good writing to many who have little poetic taste. There is always in my mind the memory of a political meeting not far from Goldsmith's home, where much was said against the big grazing farms that once had been closely tilled ; where clearances such as Goldsmith described had happened within living memory. More than one of us had seen a man come back in old age from America, who had earned his passage out by wages paid for pulling down the buildings and walls on his parents' farm and on those of their neighbours. One speaker, a big rough countryman, after recalling instances of this kind, suddenly thundered out :

> Ill fares the land, to hastening ills a prey,
> Where wealth accumulates, and men decay :
> Princes and lords may flourish, or may fade ;
> A breath can make them, as a breath has made :
> But a bold peasantry, their country's pride,
> When once destroyed, can never be supplied.

The words took fierce meaning : from that speaker to that audience, the vibration was powerful : I thought to myself, how unexpectedly a great writer can come to life. The passage is rhetoric, of course ; but there is a case to be made for good rhetoric ; and Goldsmith gives plenty of examples in support of it :

> The man of wealth and pride
> Takes up a space that many poor supplied.
> Space for his lake, his park's extended bounds,
> Space for his horses, equipage and hounds.

Language could not be much simpler, but how it rings !

The writing is not always so simple : Goldsmith, despite his own cult of simplicity, did not escape the Johnsonian infection, and in one instance he has paid for it by being perpetually misunderstood. Forster quotes a letter telling how a certain Miss Clara Brooke, " being once annoyed at a masquerade by the noisy gaiety of Goldsmith, who laughed heartily at the jokes with which he assailed her, was induced in answer to repeat his own line—' And a loud laugh which spoke the vacant mind.' Goldsmith was quite abashed at the application—as if by the word ' vacant ' he rather meant barren than free from care." It appears, then, that his contemporaries understood him rightly, just as they knew what Dr. Primrose meant when he said, " Every morning waked us to a repetition of toil, but the evening repaid us with vacant hilarity." Yet in this case over-addiction to the classics and neglect of the true masters in English literature had spoilt Goldsmith's fine instinct for words : and thousands of people have quoted this line, giving to it in good faith the sense to which Miss Brooke twisted it in witty malice. As a consequence, he who wanted laughter above all things comes down to us through this saying in a sniffish attitude like Horace Walpole's.—If the line be understood as is now habitual, there were a great many " vacant minds " in front when Tony Lumpkin came in cracking his whip, saw and conquered.

Also, in both the poems we find the ungenial word " contiguous." The Swiss peasant—

> Sees no contiguous palace rear its head,
> To shame the meanness of his humble shed.

And in the companion poem—

> Where then, ah! where shall poverty reside,
> To 'scape the pressure of contiguous pride?

" Neighbouring " does not express exactly the same : but the word has not won acceptance—though Johnson would not have objected to it. Johnson, indeed, might have written either of these particular couplets. Yet there is generally a broad difference between his style and Goldsmith's. Goldsmith had finished his poem with an invocation to the Muse, imploring guidance for " erring man " :

> Teach him, that states of native strength possest,
> Though very poor, may still be very blest.

Johnson added—and Goldsmith let him add—

> That trade's proud empire hastes to swift decay,
> As ocean sweeps the laboured mole away ;
> While self-dependent power can time defy,
> As rocks resist the billows and the sky.

These four last lines are a good example of what Mr. Housman calls " sham poetry." But how is one to class this couplet?

> No more the smith his swarthy brow shall clear,
> Relax his ponderous strength and lean to hear.

Not perhaps poetry in Mr. Housman's sense ; but there could hardly be better writing : except indeed in this, that

Goldsmith is writing of men in the tavern, yet here he clearly visualizes the smith beside his forge. "Ponderous strength" brings the sledgehammer into the picture, which, like so much else in Goldsmith, makes one think of Morland's work.

The poems are rich, too, in felicities of expression, often humorous, such as—

> Where village statesmen talked with looks profound,
> And news much older than their ale went round.

and—

> Still the wonder grew
> That one small head could carry all he knew.

Or sometimes the felicity is more sententious :

> Fools who came to scoff remained to pray.

But, above all, from that day to this, "imagination fondly stoops to trace" the portrait of a village tavern :

> The white-washed wall, the nicely sanded floor,
> The varnished clock that clicked behind the door;
> The chest contrived a double debt to pay,
> A bed by night, a chest of drawers by day;
> The pictures placed for ornament and use,
> The twelve good rules, the royal game of goose;
> The hearth, except when winter chilled the day,
> With aspen boughs and flowers and fennel gay;
> While broken tea-cups, wisely kept for show,
> Ranged o'er the chimney, glistened in a row.

It will be noted how the frugal artist has used once again his idea from the early mock heroic description of Scruggen's garret :

> The cap contrived a double debt to pay,
> A cap by night, a stocking all the day.

But, more important, those who know the two countries will recognize how far the imaginary Auburn is distant from the real Ballymahon or Lissoy. It is true that in 1822, when a meeting was held in Ballymahon on Goldsmith's birthday to consider the erection of a memorial to him, one Mr. Hogan, who had acquired the principal house in the parish and given it the name of Auburn, announced that since his coming to the neighbourhood, he had rebuilt the Three Jolly Pigeons, restored the Twelve Good Rules and Royal Game of Goose, enclosed the hawthorn, then almost cut away by the devotion of literary pilgrims, and also planted Goldsmith's favourite hill at Lissoy.

I question greatly whether any of these ornaments was ever seen before in county Longford. A public-house in England may be the Three Pigeons, the Young Volunteer, or the Queen's Head and Artichoke; in Ireland it is Sweeney's, or Boyle's or George Conway's—or, in the hotel class occasionally, somebody's " Arms." The other furniture sounds to me much more English than Irish : Goldsmith wrote with a mind stored during several years of study for this poem with images from England. I cannot agree with the Rev. Mr. Graham from Lifford in county Donegal (chief promoter of this abortive attempt to set up a memorial) that " the love of Ireland was always uppermost in his mind." It was always undermost : it was at the roots of everything. But Ireland for Goldsmith did not mean Ireland, it meant home—home in the quiet country places. He never wanted to write about Ireland as Ireland; he wanted to write about country as distinct from town. The most beautiful object in nature, he says, is " an English farmer's daughter." Yet what lies deepest works through —here or in the " Vicar." The schoolmaster and the parson assuredly lived near Lissoy gate ; the hawthorn hedge which figures in both pictures comes, I am sure, from memory. It is true that the church to which they went from Lissoy is on a hill—though so are, how many churches in England and in Ireland ! One gets better evidence of what he was visualizing as he wrote, when we learn that the Primrose family had a walk of only two miles to morning service, but that it was five miles by carriage road (with consequences which appear in the story). To-day they could drive the two miles ; but the causeway across the bog

beyond the lake which lies between Lissoy house and Kilkenny West church was presumably not built in those
days.

What does that signify? Nothing: except that, in making his picture of idyllic country life, sometimes memory
suggested exact details to him; but more often, details that
memory must have suggested—such as the bog and lake—
were deliberately set aside. What possesses his mind all
through these two poems, and through his far greater prose
poem, is the memory of that life whose poet he peculiarly is
—the life of the small country parsonage, quintessentially
characteristic of England and of the Protestant Ireland to
which Goldsmith belonged. It is that life, not seen from
close quarters as Crabbe saw it, but far away through a
tender mist of memory: seen by one who came from it
but was not of it.—There is, if we choose to press it, an
element of unreality both in the novel and the poems. We
read his letter to Dan Hodson: "If I climb Hampstead hill
than where nature never exhibited a more magnificent prospect, I confess it fine: but then I had rather be placed on the
little mount before Lissoy gate and there take in—to me—
the most pleasing horizon in nature": we read the opening
of "The Traveller": we read that more passionate cry of
the wanderer, mounting to its climax:

> I still had hopes, my long vexations past,
> Here to return—and die at home at last.

We read them, and we say to ourselves, He never saw Lissoy
again, nor any sod of Ireland.—But then we ask, Why not?
The answer is, I think, not merely that the will was wanting,
or the means, but that he knew in his heart how little harmony there could be between what he had become and what
he longed after. It was not the journey that lay between
him and Lissoy; it was all the way between what he had
been and what he was. Yet while his brother lived, the
longing lasted. After that, his only singing impulse was
spent; the close of "The Deserted Village" is an invocation to poetry—and a farewell:

Dear charming nymph, neglected and decried,
My shame in crowds, my solitary pride;
Thou source of all my bliss, and all my woe,
That found'st me poor at first, and keep'st me so;
Thou guide by which the nobler arts excel,
Thou nurse of every virtue, fare thee well!

He wrote verse again, but never poetry. He was forty-two when this poem appeared, and singing time is generally over by then for those writers who only write verse when they have something to say that cannot be said in prose. But these moving lines tell us one thing. Oliver Goldsmith was to himself in his own judgment essentially a poet; yet, I think, he kept that judgment to himself. He was never, like Hans Andersen whom in so many ways he resembles, *recitator acerbus*, the ruthless declaimer spouting his own verse at all times and places. The Goldsmith who wanted to shine, and fretted if he could not, was Goldsmith the philosopher. Some of his literary intimates no doubt heard of the poems from him; Johnson certainly did. But I think Johnson was only concerned with those parts of the poems which he himself could amend or even add to: I doubt if he even guessed at that feeling which Oliver Goldsmith, entrusting to a published verse what his tongue would never utter, called " my solitary pride."

CHAPTER XII

"SHE STOOPS TO CONQUER"

SINCE Goldsmith would not come to Lissoy, once more Lissoy came to Goldsmith—though at first only through the post. His youngest brother Maurice, living at home, as Oliver himself had done, without any employment, and not provided as Oliver had been with a university degree, now wrote to the famous man for assistance. So, it appears, did his sister Jenny, wife of the struggling farmer. They conveyed to him at the same time the information that Mr. Contarine at his death—twelve years earlier—had left Oliver a small sum, fifteen pounds (say fifty to-day), which was in the hands of Mrs. Lawder, Contarine's daughter and her husband.

Goldsmith's reply gives us a better picture of the real man than all the stories in Boswell and the rest; but it is puzzling. Did he really write, as he says? and, if so, why did he get no answer? Frankly, I think we must harden our hearts to disbelieve him. Staring him out of countenance was the fact that his near kindred were in distress while he was buying masquerade suits from Mr. Filby; and he ran away from the confrontation. Neither is there a word about his brother's death which was indeed by this time more than a year gone by.

Then there is more than a dash of Jack Lofty (whose influence with the great was seen in the " Good-natured Man ") in this talk of interest and ability to save.—What follows in the letter may, I think, refer to the piece of news which set them on writing. The Academy of Arts had just been founded, on the suggestion of Reynolds, and royal patronage secured ; Reynolds was chosen its first President by acclamation : and he immediately contrived to associate writers with the institution by naming Johnson Professor of Ancient Literature and Goldsmith Professor of Ancient History. These appointments linked them to the body and entitled them of right to a place at the annual dinner.—Here is the letter, dated January, 1770 :

DEAR BROTHER,—I should have answered your letter sooner, but in truth I am not fond of thinking of the necessities of those I love, when it is so very little in my power to help them. I am sorry to find you are still every way unprovided for ; and what adds to my uneasiness is, that I have received a letter from my sister Johnson, by which I learn that she is pretty much in the same circumstances. As to myself, I believe I could get both you and my poor brother-in-law something like that which you desire, but I am determined never to ask for little things, nor exhaust any little interest I may have until I can serve you, him and myself more effectually. As yet no opportunity has offered, but I believe you are pretty well convinced that I will not be remiss when it arrives. The king has lately been pleased to make me Professor of Ancient History in a royal Academy of Painting, which he has just established, but there is no salary annexed ; and I took it rather as a compliment to the institution than any benefit to myself. Honours to one in my situation are something like ruffles to a man that wants a shirt. You tell me that there are fourteen or fifteen pounds left me in the hands of my cousin Lawder, and you ask me what I would have done with them. My dear brother, I would by no means give any directions to my dear worthy relations at Kilmore, how to dispose of money, which is, properly speaking, more theirs than mine. All that I can say is, that I entirely, and this letter will serve to witness, give up any right and title to it ; and I am sure they will dispose of it to the best advantage. To them I entirely leave it, whether they or you may think the whole necessary to fit you out, or whether our poor sister Johnson may not want the half, I leave entirely to their and your discretion. The kindness of that good couple to our poor shattered family, demands our sincerest gratitude, and though they have almost forgot me, yet, if good things at last arrive, I hope one day to return, and encrease their good humour by adding to my own. I have sent my cousin Jenny a miniature picture of myself, as I believe it is the most acceptable present I can offer. I have ordered it to be left for her at George Faulkener's, folded in a letter. The face, you well know, is ugly enough, but it is finely painted. I will shortly also send my friends over the Shannon[1] some mezzotinto prints of myself, and some more of my friends here, such as Burke, Johnson, Reynolds and Colman. I believe I have written an hundred letters to different friends in your country and never received an answer from any of them. I do not know how to account for this, or why they are unwilling to keep up for me those regards which I must ever retain for them. If then you have a mind to oblige me, you will write often whether I answer you or not. Let me particularly have the news of our family and old acquaintances. For instance, you may begin by telling me about the family where you reside, how they spend their time, and whether they ever make mention of me. Tell me about my mother, my brother Hodson, and his son ; my brother Harry's son and daughter, my sister Johnson, the family of Ballyoughter, what is become of them, where they live, and how they do. You talked of being my only brother, I don't understand you—Where is Charles ? A sheet of paper occasionally filled with news of this kind, would make me very happy, and would keep you nearer my mind. As it is, my dear brother, believe me to be yours, most affectionately,

OLIVER GOLDSMITH.

Maurice Goldsmith finally decided to be bound to a trade (as Oliver had once expected to be bound) and fitted himself to keep a cabinet-maker's shop in Dublin. Charles was lost to sight and sound in Jamaica. But before long, Oliver's nephew, son of his eldest sister and Dan Hodson, arrived in London, a half-fledged medico, and proceeded to live on his uncle, though he set up as apothecary in Newman Street. Mr. William Filby appears to have afforded him the same credit as he extended to the successful author, and lived to be sorry for it.

Meanwhile Goldsmith, who found Lissoy so far off, made an expedition to France. No doubt he would have gone to Ireland gladly in the same company, for he was in a party with Mrs. Horneck and her daughters. He wrote about it to Reynolds, saying how they had reached Calais in three

[1] Kilmore was in Roscommon.

237

hours and twenty minutes, but seasick, " as my machine to prevent seasickness was not completed." (He does not need to explain to Reynolds, " This is my Goak.") He goes on in the very vein of the Vicar. " We were glad to leave Dover, because we hated to be imposed upon ; so were in high spirits at coming to Calais, where we were told that a little money would go a great way." Everybody was agog to help and the " party were well enough pleased with the people's civility," till they came to be paid : " when every creature that had the happiness of but touching our trunks with their fingers, expected sixpence ; and had so pretty, civil a manner of demanding it, that there was no refusing them." Then a valet offered his services for which they had no occasion, " so we gave him a little money, because he spoke English and because he wanted it."— There, for the eye of Joshua Reynolds, is Oliver Goldsmith, etched by himself.—Another letter, nine days later, came from Paris :

With regard to myself I find that travelling at twenty and at forty are very different things. I set out with all my confirmed habits about me, and can find nothing on the Continent so good as when I formerly left it. One of our chief amusements here is scolding at everything we meet with, and praising everything and every person we left at home. You may judge therefore whether your name is not frequently bandied at table among us. To tell you the truth, I never thought I could regret your absence so much as our various mortifications on the road have taught me to do.

It was not only the difference between twenty and forty that made " lying in barns, quarrelling with postillions " and the rest so much harder to put up with ; it was having ladies to look after : I cannot believe that this much-travelled man was ever a good courier.

I have little to tell you more, but that we are at present all well, and expect returning when we have stayed out one month, which I should not care if it were over this very day. I long to hear from you all : how you yourself do, how Johnson, Burke, Dyer,

Chamier, Colman, and every one of the club do. I wish I could send you some amusement in this letter, but I protest I am so stupefied by the air of this country (for I am sure it can never be natural) that I have not a word to say. I have been thinking of the plot of a comedy which shall be entitled "A Journey to Paris," in which a family shall be introduced with a full intention of going to France to save money. You know there is not a place in the world more promising for that purpose.

There had been a project for him to go down with Reynolds into the painter's native Devon, but that had to be abandoned. "I have so outrun the constable, that I must mortify a little to bring it up again."

For God's sake the night you receive this take your pen in your hand and tell me something about yourself, and *my*self, if you know of anything that has happened. About Miss Reynolds, about Mr. Bickerstaff, my nephew, or anybody that you regard. I beg you will send to Griffin the bookseller to know if there be any letters left for me, and be so good as to send them to me at Paris. They may perhaps be left for me at the porter's lodge opposite the pump in Temple-lane. The same messenger will do. I expect one from Lord Clare from Ireland. As for others I am not much uneasy about [them].

Is there anything I can do for you at Paris ? I wish you would tell me. The whole of my purchases here, is one silk coat which I have put on, and which makes me look like a fool. But no more of that. . . . I will soon be among you, better pleased with my situation at home than I ever was before. And yet I must say, that if anything could make France pleasant, the very good women with whom I am at present would certainly do it. I could say more about that, but I intend showing them this letter before I send it away.

So the hack was in harness again, abridging a Roman history, and writing a "Life of Bolingbroke," to be prefixed to a reprint of the "Dissertation on Parties"—not a congenial subject. But earlier in the year, for the same publisher, Davies, he had furnished a "Life of Parnell" which needs close attention : for in it, Goldsmith, now at the height of his reputation, sets out more fully than elsewhere his literary creed. Also, it is a piece of work which gave

Johnson the occasion to speak his mind of Goldsmith definitively, in that language which he disdained to use for the epitaph. Writing the " Lives of the Poets," when it came to Parnell's turn, Johnson began in these words :

The Life of Dr. Parnell is a task which I should very willingly decline, since it has been lately written by Goldsmith, a man of such variety of powers, and such felicity of performance, that he always seemed to do best that which he was doing ; a man who had the art of being minute without tediousness, and general without confusion ; whose language was copious without exuberance, exact without constraint, and easy without weakness. What such an author has told, who would tell again ? I have made an abstract from his larger narrative ; and have this gratification from my attempt, that it gives me an opportunity of paying due tribute to the memory of Goldsmith.

After these sonorities, the opening of Goldsmith's 'Parnell' makes a pleasant contrast :

The life of a scholar seldom abounds with adventure. His fame is acquired in solitude ; and the historian, who only views him at a distance, must be content with a dry detail of actions by which he is scarcely distinguished from the rest of mankind. But we are fond of talking of those who have given us pleasure ; not that we have anything important to say, but because the subject is pleasing.

From the first this study of a poet by a poet is strongly touched by a thought of the writer's own case :

He was admitted a member of the College of Dublin at the age of thirteen, which is much sooner than usual, as at that university they are a great deal stricter in their examination for entrance, than either at Oxford or Cambridge. His progress through the college course of study was probably marked with but little splendour ; his imagination might have been too warm to relish the cold logic of Burgersdicius, or the dreary subtleties of Smiglesius ; but it is certain, that as a classical scholar, few could equal him.

Again, after a brief outline of Parnell's career, he writes :

Such is the very unpoetical detail of the life of a poet. Some dates, and some few facts scarcely more interesting than those that make the ornaments of a country tombstone, are all that remain of one whose labours now begin to excite universal curiosity. A poet, while living, is seldom an object sufficiently great to attract much attention ; his real merits are known but to a few, and these are generally sparing in their praises. When his fame is increased by time, it is then too late to investigate the peculiarities of his disposition.

There is surely a thought here of another poet than Parnell : and still more certainly in what follows :

Parnell, by what I have been able to collect from my father and uncle, who knew him, was the most capable man in the world to make the happiness of those he conversed with, and the least able to secure his own. He wanted that evenness of disposition which bears disappointment with phlegm, and joy with indifference. He was ever very much elated or depressed, and his whole life was spent in agony or rapture. But the turbulence of these passions only affected himself, and never those about him : he knew the ridicule of his own character, and very effectually raised the mirth of his companions, as well at his vexations as at his triumphs.

When we come to the final appraisement of a writer who " in a very few years attained a share of fame equal to what most of his contemporaries were a long life in acquiring," we have a declaration of faith which is also a declaration of war :

He appears to me to be the last of that great school that had modelled itself upon the ancients, and taught English poetry to resemble what the generality of mankind have allowed to excel. A studious and correct observer of antiquity, he set himself to consider nature with the lights it lent him ; and he found that the more aid he borrowed from the one, the more delightfully he resembled the other. To copy nature is a task the most bungling workman is able to execute ; to select such parts as contribute to delight, is reserved only for those whom accident has blest with uncommon talents, or such as have read the ancients with indefatigable industry. Parnell is ever happy in the selection of his images, and scrupulously careful in the choice of his subjects. His productions bear no resemblance to those tawdry things which it has for some time been the fashion to admire ; in writing which the poet sits down without any plan, and heaps up splendid images without any selection ; where the reader grows dizzy with praise and admiration and yet soon grows weary, he can scarcely tell why. . . .

His poetical language is not less correct than his subjects are pleasing. He found it at that period in which it was brought to its highest pitch of refinement ; and ever since his time it has been gradually debasing. It is indeed amazing, after what has been done by Dryden, Addison and Pope, to improve and harmonize our native tongue, that their successors should have taken so much pains to involve it in pristine barbarity. These misguided innovators have not been content with restoring antiquated words and phrases, but have indulged themselves in the most licentious transpositions and the harshest constructions, vainly imagining, that the more their writings are unlike prose, the more they resemble poetry : they have adopted a language of their own, and call upon mankind for admiration. All those who do not understand them are silent, and those who make out their meaning are willing to praise, to show they understand. From these follies and affectations the poems of Parnell are entirely free : he has considered the language of poetry as the language of life, and conveys the warmest thoughts in the simplest expression.

The writer whom Goldsmith is thinking of here is certainly not only Parnell. A later preference of Parnell's " Night Piece on Death " to " all those night pieces and churchyard scenes that have since appeared " makes certain (if it were necessary) the application of his censure to Gray.

Apart from hack-work, good, bad or indifferent (and the " Bolingbroke " was bad), we get in this period one piece from the real Goldsmith—and a thing of a new kind, another proof of his versatility. He had been seeing a great deal of his rich Irish friend : " Goldsmith is at Bath with Lord Clare," Johnson writes to Boswell in March, 1771. How long he was with Clare, at Bath or at his house in the country, we do not know ; but a letter to Bennet Langton written from Brick Court on September 7 tells us something about the whole group, and much about himself :

I see Mr. Beauclerc very often both in town and country. He is now going directly forward to become a second Boyle : deep

in chemistry and physics. Johnson has been down upon a visit
to a country parson, Doctor Taylor : and is returned to his old
haunts at Mrs. Thrale's. Burke is a farmer, *en attendant* a better
place ; but visiting about too. Every soul is a-visiting about and
merry but myself. And that is hard too, as I have been trying
these three months to do something to make people laugh. There
have I been strolling about the hedges, studying jests with a most
tragical countenance. The Natural History is about half finished,
and I will shortly finish the rest. God knows I am tired of this
kind of finishing, which is but bungling work ; and that not so
much my fault as the fault of my scurvy circumstances. They
begin to talk in town of the Opposition's gaining ground ; the
cry of liberty is still as loud as ever. I have published, or Davies
has published for me, an "Abridgement of the History of
England," for which I have been a good deal abused in the newspapers for betraying the liberties of the people. God knows I
had no thought for or against liberty in my head ; my whole aim
being to make up a book of decent size, that, as 'Squire Richard
says, would do no harm to nobody. However, they set me
down as an arrant Tory, and consequently an honest man. When
you come to look at any part of it, you'll say that I am a sour
Whig.

Now, at some time in 1771, Clare sent the poet a haunch of
venison, and Goldsmith acknowledged the compliment by
a composition which to my mind is at least as good as, for
instance, Horace's account of his encounter with a bore : in
other words, it is a minor masterpiece in the art of hitching
an amusing story into witty verse :

The haunch was a picture for painters to study,
The fat was so white, and the lean was so ruddy ;
Though my stomach was sharp, I could scarce help regretting
To spoil such a delicate picture by eating ;
I had thoughts in my chambers to place it in view,
To be shown to my friends as a piece of virtù ;
As in some Irish houses, where things are so so,
One gammon of bacon hangs up for a show :
But, for eating a rasher of what they take pride in,
They'd as soon think of eating the pan it is fried in.

Then he digresses to say, " it is truth I'm telling you and

no lie," and refers Clare back to his nephew Mr. Byrne to confirm the usage of " potatoes and point."   But :

> To go on with my tale : as I gazed on the haunch,
> I thought of a friend that was trusty and staunch ;
> So I cut it, and sent it to Reynolds undrest,
> To paint it, or eat it, just as he liked best.

What was a single man in chambers to do with the rest of it ?

> There's Howard, and Coley, and H——rth, and Hiff,
> I think they love venison—I know they love beef.
> There's my countryman Higgins—oh ! let him alone,
> For making a blunder, or picking a bone.
> But hang it !—to poets who seldom can eat
> Your very good mutton's a very good treat ;
> Such dainties to them their health it might hurt,
> It's like sending them ruffles, when wanting a shirt.

Clare, it will be noted, is presumed to know at least by name and reputation the gentry with whom Goldsmith forgathered at his so much less select Wednesday club.   Still, they also were poets : the story goes on to own up to keeping even worse company ; for in comes " an acquaintance, a friend, as he called himself "—

An under-bred, fine-spoken fellow was he,
And he smiled as he looked at the venison and me.
" What have we got here ?   Why, this is good eating !
Your own, I suppose—or is it in waiting ? "
" Why, whose should it be ? " cried I with a flounce ;
" I get these things often "—but that was a bounce :
" Some lords, my acquaintance, that settle the nation,
Are pleased to be kind—but I hate ostentation."
   " If that be the case then," cried he, very gay,
" I'm glad I have taken this house in my way.
To-morrow you take a poor dinner with me ;
No words—I insist on't—precisely at three ;
We'll have Johnson, and Burke ; all the wits will be there ;
My acquaintance is slight, or I'd ask my Lord Clare.
And now that I think on't, as I am a sinner,
We wanted this venison to make out the dinner.
What say you—a pasty ?   It shall, and it must,
And my wife, little Kitty, is famous for crust.

Here, porter! this venison with me to Mile-end;
No stirring—I beg—my dear friend—my dear friend."
Thus, snatching his hat, he brushed off like the wind,
And the porter and eatables followed behind.

And then comes the sketch of the dinner with tripe and
spinach, liver and bacon. ("Now, my lord, as for tripe,
it's my utter aversion, And your bacon I hate like a Turk or
a Persian.")   But the final catastrophe is—

> terrible news from the baker:
> And so it fell out, for that negligent sloven
> Had shut out the pasty on shutting his oven.

In short, it is a brilliant study of low life where it is vulgar-
est; and, as so very often, Goldsmith tells us how he has
been fooled.   But he is writing for a man who, he knows,
will laugh with him rather than laugh at him; and the piece
ends with one of those disguised compliments for which
Swift had given the model, and then, a final little gay
emphasis on the fact that This is really a good thing, well
brought off.

> At least, it's your temper, as very well known,
> That you think very slightly of all that's your own:
> So, perhaps, in your habits of thinking amiss,
> You may make a mistake, and think slightly of this.

One gets, perhaps, not the whole of Goldsmith in these
verses, but at least Goldsmith as he was with this witty and
good-natured friend.   It is the Bohemian promoted, used
to the best company, having the finest sense of refinement
but without the self-protecting equipment to keep vulgarity
at arm's length; and all the time, keenly sensitive to the
ambiguity of his position; fully aware that to the mass of
mankind he is still down among the anonymous gentry,
who "are authors like you."

The one writes "The Snarler," the other "The Scourge"—
Some think he writes "Cinna": he owns to "Panurge."

In short, the swan knew he was a swan, but was still aware
of the gutters where he was the ugly duckling: and at the

same time was amused by his own rueful recognition of the taint that hung about him.

But at any rate the piece which he warns Clare not to make the mistake of underrating is a bold excursion into the Low.—That word must have been always in his mind while he was " trying these three months to do something to make people laugh—strolling about the hedges, studying jests with a most tragical countenance." The work did not go on quickly—for there was also the Natural History with its eight volumes to be got through. Boswell gives us a glimpse of this country workshop of his, which was not the " Shoemaker's Paradise," but somewhere in the same direction.

Goldsmith told us, that he was now busy in writing a Natural History ; and, that he might have full leisure for it, he had taken lodgings, at a farmer's house, near to the six-mile stone, on the Edgeware-road, and had carried down his books in two returned post-chaises. He said, he believed the farmer's family thought him an odd character, similar to that in which the " Spectator " appeared to his landlady and her children : he was *The Gentleman*. Mr. Mickle, the translator of " The Lusiad," and I, went to visit him at this place a few days afterwards. He was not at home ; but having a curiosity to see his apartment, we went in, and found curious scraps of descriptions of animals, scrawled upon the wall with a black lead pencil.

I must leave till later the consideration of the hack-work whose materials surrounded him, and follow the comedy's fortunes. It seems to have reached Colman's hands early in 1772 ; and if Goldsmith had been slow in writing, Colman was slower still in considering. All the heartbreak about the " Good-natured Man " had to be gone through again : Goldsmith's letter to Colman tells its own story.

DEAR SIR,—I intreat you'll relieve me from that state of suspense in which I have been kept for a long time. Whatever objections you have made, or shall make, to my play, I will endeavour to remove and not argue about them. To bring in any new judges either of its merits or faults I can never submit to. Upon a former occasion, when my other play was before Mr.

Garrick, he offered to bring me before Mr. Whitehead's tribunal, but I refused the proposal with indignation. I hope I shall not experience as hard treatment from you as from him. I have, as you know, a large sum of money to make up shortly; by accepting my play I can readily satisfy my creditor that way; at any rate I must look about to some certainty to be prepared. For God's sake take the play and let us make the best of it, and let me have the same measure at least which you have given as bad plays as mine. I am your friend and servant,

OLIVER GOLDSMITH.

Finally, the despairing author sent a copy of his play to Garrick, begging him to take it: then, "upon more mature deliberation and the advice of a sensible friend," he wrote that it was "indelicate to throw upon him the odium of confirming Mr. Colman's sentence." He asked to have the play back, and said that since he could get it acted at the other theatre, he would not give up his appeal "from Mr. Colman's opinion to the judgment of the town." Anybody who has seen an author kept on tenterhooks by theatrical potentates will be familiar with the symptoms: a dentist's chair is ease compared to these experiences. Johnson's letters take up the story.

Dr. Goldsmith has a new comedy, which is expected in the spring. No name is yet given it. The chief diversion arises from a stratagem by which a lover is made to mistake his future father-in-law's house for an inn. This, you see, borders upon farce. The dialogue is quick and gay, and the incidents are so prepared as not to seem improbable.

This was on February 22, a fortnight after the play was recalled from Garrick. On March 4 Johnson writes to another correspondent:

Dr. Goldsmith has a new comedy in rehearsal at Covent-Garden, to which the manager predicts ill success. I hope he will be mistaken. I think it deserves a very kind reception.

It got one: but he had to fight every inch of the way for what he would have called a comedy of nature. Colman, Johnson said later, "was prevailed on at last by much solicitation, nay, a kind of force, to bring it on." The actors were as bad. Mrs. Abington, for whom Miss Hardcastle's part had been specially written, would not play it ; Goldsmith had to give up a song intended for her, since Mrs. Bulkeley who took the part could not sing ; the leading men refused, except Shuter, who had made the first play, and who advised trying Lee Lewis, a young actor, hitherto the theatre's Harlequin, for the *jeune premier*. Then there was war over the finish : Garrick had written a prologue and nobody dare cavil at that : but there was the epilogue. Goldsmith tells the story to Cradock, a stage-struck parson, who amongst others had tried his hand to produce what would be acceptable :

The story in short is this ; Murphy sent me rather the outline of an epilogue than an epilogue, which was to be sung by Mrs. Catley, and which she approved.

Mrs. Bulkeley, hearing this, insisted on throwing up the part, unless, according to the custom of the theatre, she was permitted to speak the epilogue. In this embarrassment I thought of making a quarrelling epilogue between Catley and her, debating who should speak the epilogue ; but then Mrs. Catley refused after I had taken the trouble of drawing it out. I was then at a loss indeed ; an epilogue was to be made, and for none but Mrs. Bulkeley. I made one, and Colman thought it too bad to be spoken. I was obliged therefore to try a fourth time, and I made a very mawkish thing as you'll shortly see. Such is the history of my stage adventures, and which I have at last done with. I cannot help saying that I am very sick of the stage, and though I believe I shall get three tolerable benefits, yet I shall upon the whole be a loser, even in a pecuniary light ; my ease and comfort I certainly lost while it was in agitation.

There was trouble too about the title : Reynolds said, " You ought to call it ' The Belle's Stratagem,' and if you do not, I will damn it." However, all came to an end, and, as Northcote tells, Sir Joshua and a large party of his friends assembled to dine at a tavern and go on to the show. Goldsmith was there, but so parched with anxiety that he could not swallow a morsel, and slipped away by himself. He

MR. SHUTER, MR. QUICK AND MRS. GREEN

in the characters of Hardcastle, Tony Lumpkin and Mrs. Hardcastle ("She Stoops to Conquer," Act V, Scene 1)

From the "Gabrielle Enthoven" Collection at the Victoria and Albert Museum

was wandering about in St. James's Park when an acquaintance met him and said he ought to be at the theatre in case some sudden alteration was needed. He went there and came into the wings just in time to hear a hiss. (People thought it too improbable that Mrs. Hardcastle, after the drive in the dark under Tony's guidance, could believe herself forty miles from home, when she was just at her own duck-pond.) " What's that ? " said the frightened author. " Pooh, Doctor ! " said Colman, " don't mind squibs when we have been sitting near two hours on a barrel of gunpowder."—Cooke says that " the Doctor never forgave it to Colman to the last hour of his life."

That single hiss was drowned in a torrent of laughter. Contemporary evidence is worth quoting. In Lloyd's " Evening Post " of March 15–17 (on the same page which advertised a new edition of " The Poems of Ossian, Son of Fingal," Translated from the Gaelic by James Macpherson, Esq.), there appeared this " Theatrical Intelligence."

The characters of the new Comedy, called " She Stoops to Conquer, or the Mistakes of a Night," performed on Monday night at Covent Garden Theatre for the first time were as follows :

HARDCASTLE . . .	*Mr. Shuter.*
MR. MARLOW . . .	*Mr. Lewes.*
SQUIRE TONY LUMPKIN .	*Mr. Quick.*
MR. HASTINGS . . .	*Mr. du Bellamy.*
SIR CHARLES MARLOW .	*Mr. Gardner.*
LANDLORD AND DRUNKEN SERVANT . . .	*Mr. Thompson.*
DANCING BEAR-LEADER AND HARDCASTLE'S SERVANT .	*Mr. Saunders.*
COMPANIONS TO THE SQUIRE	*Mr. Bates, Mr. Holtom and Mr. Davis.*
MRS. DOROTHY HARDCASTLE	*Mrs. Green.*
MISS CONSTANTIA HARDCASTLE	*Mrs. Bulkeley.*
MISS NEVILL . . .	*Mrs. Kniveton.*
PIMPER	*Mrs. Willems.*

The Comedy is written by Dr. Goldsmith and it is founded on a plot exceedingly probable and fertile ; each Act contains a great deal of natural business and incident ; the characters are for the most part entirely original ; they are well drawn, highly finished, and admirably supported from the first to the last scene of the piece. It abounds with genuine wit and humour, without the aid of Irish bulls, forced witticisms, or absurd conceits ; the audience is kept in a continual roar ; occasionally a sentiment is delivered, but then it arises naturally from the fable and the character. The dialogue is nervous and spirited ; no attempt is made by the author to avail himself of the vitiated taste of the times ; he has offered the public a true comic picture which pleased though it differed essentially in manner, skill and finishing from those which of late years have been received and encouraged. Hardcastle is a good-natured, particular old fellow, fond of telling a story and ridiculous, without offending—Mr. Marlow, a man of sense, education and breeding ; but, as many men are, exceedingly timid in the presence of modest women of accomplished education, though impudently familiar in company with those of low degree. This character is, as far as we can recollect, an original one and the success with which it was received is a proof that it is by no means an unnatural one.—The Squire is a compound of whim and good-natured mischief, the engine of the plot, the source of infinite mirth, and a variety of very laughable mistakes which arise in a simple, artless manner, of which the Author has taken an admirable advantage and from it produced a very comic effect, without exceeding the line of probability. Mrs. Dorothy Hardcastle, a foolishly fond mother and no bad wife. Miss Constance, a sensible lovely girl, full of spirit and good humour. Miss Nevill and Mr. Hastings, two very affectionate and enterprising lovers.

The Prologue was written by Mr. Garrick and spoken by Mrs. Woodward ; it was very laughable and had a good effect. The speaker enters in mourning, with a handkerchief to his face, lamenting the death of Miss Comedy whose departure would naturally drive Woodward and Shuter from the theatre. However, he acquainted the audience that a Doctor had administered towards the relief of this Comedy, and it rested with them to pronounce whether he was a quack or a regular Physician. Part of it was formed on the hints thrown out by Mr. Foote in his Puppet Show, ridiculing the modern taste for sentimental dialogues. The Prologue had wit and humour and was delivered with great spirit and propriety by Mrs. Bulkeley.

A social incident added piquancy to the evening. George III's brother, the Duke of Gloucester, had secretly married Horace Walpole's beautiful niece, Lady Walde- grave, daughter, but not the legitimate daughter, of Sir Edward Walpole. By March, 1772, it was public know- ledge that the Court refused to countenance this union; and the public was for the Duke and his bride. The Theatrical Intelligence goes on:

The Duke of Gloucester was in the stage box. When he entered the house, he was received with great shouts of appro- bation. In one part of the play Hastings says to Miss Nevill— " We'll go to France, for there even among slaves marriage is respected." This the audience thought applicable to the Duke's marriage, and marked their respect for him by a very particular Plaudit.

Oddly enough, there is no mention of this in Horace Walpole's Letters. He wrote on March 16 to Lady Ossory, on hearsay: " There was a new play by Dr. Goldsmith last night which succeeded prodigiously." But when he had seen it we get the reactions of a critical highbrow. He wrote again on March 27:

What play makes you laugh very much, and yet is a very wretched comedy? Dr. Goldsmith's " She Stoops to Conquer." Stoops indeed!—so she does, that is the Muse; she is draggled up to the knees, and has trudged, I believe, from Southwark fair. The whole view of the piece is low humour, and no humour is in it. All the merit is in the situations, which are comic; the heroine has no more modesty than Lady Bridget, and the author's wit is as much *manqué* as the lady's; but some of the characters are well acted, and Woodward speaks a poor prologue, written by Garrick, admirably.

Later, on May 27, to Mason, another high-sniffer:

Dr. Goldsmith has written a Comedy—no, it is the lowest of all farces. It is not the subject I condemn, though very vulgar, but the execution. The drift tends to no moral, no edification of any kind. The situations, however, are well imagined, and make one laugh, in spite of the grossness of the dialogue, the forced witticisms, and total improbability of the whole plan and conduct. But what disgusts me most is, that though the characters are very low, and aim at low humour, not one of them says a sentence that is natural or marks any character at all. It is set up in opposition to sentimental comedy, and is as bad as the worst of them. Garrick would not act it, but bought himself off by a poor prologue.

This censure contains an admission: one is made to laugh. Northcote says that when he had gone to see the play (on an order from the author) Goldsmith asked what he thought of it. Northcote " could not presume to be a judge of its merits." " Did it make you laugh ? " " Exceedingly." " Then," said the Doctor, " that is all I require." Northcote asked no better than to laugh, but Horace Walpole laughed *invita Minerva*, against his literary conscience. We can all agree that the " drift tends to no moral " : but as to saying that there is no sentence that is natural, Tony Lumpkin is a perfect representation of what in Ireland we call a " buckeen " : the gentleman's son who consorts by preference with stable boys. It is not only an Irish type, Scott drew it in " Waverley " ; but it reached a fuller exuberance among the Irish landlord class. As to the heroine's lack of modesty, again and again the Hornecks were present at rehearsals with Dr. Johnson (whose intimidating presence reduced poor Shuter to speechless decorum) ; and if they had thought Miss Hardcastle unladylike, they would have said so. At that same period, it should be remembered, Lady Susan Fox Strangways and Lady Sarah Lennox slipped out in disguise and sold oranges in the street for an adventure. It was not at all a prim age, in spite of sentimental comedy ; and if, as it seems to me, Miss Hardcastle is much more like a person, and less a puppet, than either lady in " The Good-natured Man," " these very good women," Mrs. Horneck and her daughters, have to be thanked for it.

I have said already that (over and above the reference back to the absurd " mistakes of a night " when Goldsmith was on his way to school) there seems to be more than a touch of Goldsmith in young Marlow.

I'm doom'd to adore the sex, and yet to converse with the only part of it I despise. This stammer in my address, and this awkward prepossessing visage of mine, can never permit me to soar above the reach of a milliner's 'prentice, or one of the duchesses of Drury-lane.

And again, when the pretended barmaid begins to give away the situation and assumes another part, Marlow is mortified and is all for bolting away : Miss Hardcastle pretends to cry : her gallant is overcome : " This is the first mark of tenderness I ever had from a modest woman, and it touches me."

Given all the absurd assumptions of the play, that line has real nature : and as I read it, Goldsmith has thought himself into this fantastic situation which can only be made believable by supposing a hero who had lived cut off from womenfolk of his own breeding—as, in fact, had for many long years been Goldsmith's own case.

But there is another very different strain of characterization. Mrs. Hardcastle is certainly some relation to Mrs. Primrose, and when she is trying to make up affairs between Tony and his cousin she has one of Mrs. Primrose's devices. " Back to back, my pretties, that Mr. Hastings may see you." Again, when she is haranguing her unmanageable Tony, I cannot but think that Oliver Goldsmith remembered somebody else who had a good-for-nothing lump of a son hanging about the house : " Wasn't it all for your good ? "—" I wish you'd let me and my good alone then. Snubbing this way when I'm in spirits. If I'm to have any good, let it come of itself ; not to keep dinging it, dinging it into one so." Those last words seem to come alive and instinctive out of the bottom of memory.

The best authority that I can consult tells me that the humours of " She Stoops to Conquer " are hard to " put across " nowadays. Modern actors do not easily feel them and enter into them. That is not surprising. Nothing, not even a dead novel, is quite so dead as a dead comedy. The surprising thing is that the play should be alive at all. Out of that whole century of wit, only this play and Sheridan's survive without the help of music, which did so much

for the " Beggars' Opera " ; and even that had only a
sudden and occasional revival. But Goldsmith and Sheridan have been played without ceasing over a century and a
half. The same authority holds that the screen scene from
the " School for Scandal " has something in it which keeps
it immune from decay : that no such difficulty exists there
as with " She Stoops to Conquer." And my instinct agrees.
But in the plays you have Sheridan at full stretch of his
amazing wit; all you get from " She Stoops to Conquer "
is Goldsmith's fun. It is fun of the simplest and most
primitive kind ; bucolic comedy, if it can be called comedy
at all ; and the country changes less quickly than the town.
That, I think, is why it has been able to survive ; that and
the extraordinary force of Goldsmith's hilariousness. This
is not the Goldsmith of the " Vicar of Wakefield," the
Goldsmith whose humour is as fresh for us as it was for
Johnson and Burke and Sir Joshua ; this is the Goldsmith
of George Conway's public-house and of the Wednesday
Club at the Globe Tavern, the Goldsmith who had a passion
for laughing and making people laugh. Witnesses such as
the younger Colman, and Lord Clare's daughter, say that
Goldsmith was the best hand ever known at amusing
children. " She Stoops to Conquer " is really written to
persuade grown-up people to be as uncritical as children, to
stop thinking of what is probable and just let themselves be
made to laugh.

Goldsmith's love of fun went with his love of a good
song ; and in this play he showed he could write one. A
month after the play appeared at General Oglethorpe's
house, he dined along with Johnson and there was serious
debate which Goldsmith started, upon the evil of luxury.
Johnson promptly battered him with sentences of very good
sense, and Goldsmith dodged out of argument, raising a
laugh ; Johnson attacked again, turning the laugh on him
even about pickle-shops ; but then they left the table and
" drank tea with the ladies." Goldsmith sang Tony Lumpkin's song about the Three Jolly Pigeons and then " a very
pretty one to an Irish tune which he had designed for Miss

Hardcastle." This song, " Ah me, when shall I marry me ? " goes to the " Humours of Ballymagarry," and it was Boswell who saved the words by getting him to write them down. After Goldsmith's death he sent them to the " London Magazine."

Before this pleasant dinner-party a disagreeable incident had arisen out of the play. Kenrick, Goldsmith's old enemy, had published a general onslaught on the playwright and his works. But apparently Goldsmith's devotion to a well-known beauty had become talk of the town, and after some observations on Miss Hardcastle's determination to make a conquest of young Marlow, the article added : " Was but the lovely H——k as much enamoured, you would not sigh, my gentle swain, in vain." Goldsmith, with a companion, went round to the office of the paper, demanded to see the publisher, a certain Mr. Evans, and complained of " a scurrilous attack " on himself and " an unwarrantable liberty taken with the name of a young lady." Thereupon he struck Evans with a cane ; the blow was returned, Evans was the bigger man, there was an undignified scuffle and Goldsmith went home in a coach, covered with oil from an upset lamp and in general disfigured. Evans took an action for assault, which was settled by Goldsmith's undertaking to pay fifty pounds to a Welsh charity.

That is not how it should have worked out in a story ; but Goldsmith had no gift for the decorative gesture ; he was not cut out for the rôle of a champion ; and the press attacked him, treating his case as if he had merely made undue fuss about criticism of his work. Finally, he replied by a public letter in the " Daily Advertiser." " The press," he said, " has turned from defending public interest, to making inroads upon private life. . . . By recurring to legal redress, we too often expose the weakness of the law, which only serves to increase our mortification by failing to relieve us. In short, every man should singly consider himself as a guardian of the liberty of the press, and, as far as his influence can extend, should endeavour to prevent its licentiousness from becoming at last the grave of its freedom."

How his friends took the incident may be gathered from Boswell, who records seeing Goldsmith's protest in print.

The apology was written so much in Dr. Johnson's manner, that both Mrs. Williams and I supposed it to be his; but when he came home, he soon undeceived us. When he said to Mrs. Williams, " Well, Dr. Goldsmith's *manifesto* has got into your paper "; I asked him if Dr. Goldsmith had written it, with an air that made him see I suspected it was his, though subscribed by Goldsmith. *Johnson.* " Sir, Dr. Goldsmith would no more have asked me to write such a thing as that for him, than he would have asked me to feed him with a spoon, or to do any thing else that denoted his imbecility. I as much believe that he wrote it, as if I had seen him do it. Sir, had he shown it to any one friend, he would not have been allowed to publish it. He has, indeed, done it very well; but it is a foolish thing well done. I suppose he has been so much elated with the success of his new comedy, that he has thought every thing that concerned him must be of importance to the publick." *Boswell.* " I fancy, Sir, this is the first time that he has been engaged in such an adventure." *Johnson.* " Why, Sir, I believe it is the first time he has *beat*; he may have *been beaten* before. This, Sir, is a new plume to him."

That is not a kind comment on a gentleman who had done what he thought a gentleman should do. It is not always easy to like Johnson for his attitude to Goldsmith. Nevertheless, when the play was published it bore this dedication :

To Samuel Johnson, LL.D.

Dear Sir,—By inscribing this slight performance to you, I do not mean so much to compliment you as myself. It may do me some honour to inform the public, that I have lived many years in intimacy with you. It may serve the interests of mankind also to inform them, that the greatest wit may be found in a character, without impairing the most unaffected piety.

Even this could no doubt be construed as a manifestation of vanity, though scarcely of envy. But in truth, if facts are candidly considered, nothing that we know about Oliver Goldsmith is more admirable than his unshakable attachment to Samuel Johnson.

CHAPTER XIII

"ANIMATED NATURE" AND "RETALIATION"

WITH the success of "She Stoops to Conquer" Goldsmith had reached the height of his reputation. The play brought in several hundred pounds; but a financial ebb set in quickly, which he sought to meet by new and vast schemes of compilation. He was to edit a Popular Dictionary of the Arts and Sciences. Of this, however, the booksellers fought shy, and he turned back to the theatre, seeking to persuade Garrick into reviving the "Good-natured Man" with Garrick as Croaker. There are letters about this; Goldsmith agreed to cut out Lofty; he would agree to anything. Finally, Garrick closed with the project, and immediately the knack at hoping revived.

MY DEAR FRIEND,—I thank you! I wish I could do something to serve you. I shall have a comedy for you in a season or two at furthest that I believe will be worth your acceptance, for I fancy it will make a fine thing. You shall have the refusal.

Then follows detail about a bill for sixty pounds, and the end is—"May God preserve my honest little man, for he has my heart."

Nothing came of this, however. Indeed, there was not time. There is little more to chronicle but hack-work and makeshifts; a reprint of the "Enquiry" (for which only five guineas was paid), a Grecian History begun— and the "Animated Nature" completed. All was work which he accepted, and even sought after, for the sake of the money; but clearly he believed that it was no way to employ a poet.

There were, however, differences in the hack-work. Grecian history was probably a true drudgery: but no one can read his " Animated Nature " without discovering passages that have zest and bring us near to the author.

The book has a most friendly and engaging commencement. Admitting in frankly generous terms that he has taken Buffon for his guide, Goldsmith points out that this serves only for the history of quadrupeds:

Thus having made use of M. Buffon's lights in the first part of the work, I may, with some show of confidence, recommend it to the public. But what shall I say to that part where I have been left entirely without his assistance? As I would affect neither modesty nor confidence, it will be sufficient to say that my reading upon this part of the subject has been very extensive ; and that I have taxed my scanty circumstances in procuring books which are on this subject, of all others, the most expensive. . . .

The delight which I found in reading Pliny first inspired me with the idea of a work of this nature. Having a taste rather classical than scientific, and having but little employed myself in turning over the dry labours of modern system-makers, my earliest intention was to translate this agreeable writer and by the help of a commentary to make my work as amusing as I could. Let us dignify natural history ever so much with a grave appellation of a useful science, yet we still must confess that it is the occupation of the idle and the speculative, more than of the busy and ambitious part of mankind. My intention, therefore, was to treat what I then conceived to be an idle subject in an idle manner : and not to hedge round plain and simple narratives with hard words, accumulated distinctions, ostentatious learning, and disquisitions that produce no conviction. . . . It will be my chief pride if this work may be found an innocent amusement for those who have nothing else to employ them, or who require a relaxation from labour.

There follows an outline of the studies which " are requisite to make an expert naturalist who shall be able, even by the help of a system, to find out the name of every object he meets with ":

But when this tedious, though requisite, part of study is attained, nothing but delight and variety attend the rest of his journey. Wherever he travels, like a man in a country where he has many friends, he meets with nothing but acquaintances and allurements in all the stages of his way. The mere uninformed spectator passes on in gloomy solitude ; but the naturalist, in every plant, in every insect, and every pebble, finds something to entertain his curiosity and excite his speculation.

I do not suppose that many nowadays will be tempted to turn back to this work which continued to be reprinted for half a century ; but those who do will find entertainment ; sometimes in the turn of a phrase, like that about " the cockchafer or Maybug, an animal, the noxious qualities of which give it a very distinguished rank in the history of the insect creation " ; sometimes in a story which he repeats but does not vouch for, such as that of Nicholas Pesce who often swam from Sicily to Calabria as a postman carrying letters, and was lost plunging for a second time into Charybdis to retrieve a larger gold cup than that which he had already earned by bringing it up.

Or again it may be in his reference to the belief that swallows " sink into the deepest lakes and find security for the winter season by remaining there in clusters at the bottom." About this Goldsmith is sceptical : Dr. Johnson was not and has told us how it was done. " He seemed pleased to talk of natural philosophy," Boswell says. " ' Swallows certainly sleep all the winter. A number of them conglobulate together, by flying round and round and then all in a heap throw themselves under water and lie in the bed of a river.' " I quote this because of Johnson's recorded remark that if Goldsmith could distinguish a cow from a horse it was the furthest extent of his information. But in fact Goldsmith was country-bred and had a countryman's noticing eye. His Irish memories supply many details. " In decoys when ducks are caught, the men who attend them universally keep a piece of turf burning near their mouths upon which they breathe, lest the fowls should smell them and fly away." " A gentleman whom I knew in Ireland kept two seals, taken very young, in his house for ten years." Another had tamed otters (trained by a process which is described) and these were very valuable, as one could catch fish enough to sustain a whole family.

" Young badgers are easily tamed, play with the dogs and follow their master about the house, but seem of all animals the most fond of fire, so that they often burn themselves trying to get near it." " Carrier pigeons were sent by our princes to their subjects with the tidings of some fortunate event, or from lovers to their mistresses with expressions of their passion. The only use we now see made of them is to be let fly at Tyburn when the cart is drawn away ; pretty much as when some ancient hero was to be interred, an eagle was let off from the funeral pile, to complete his apotheosis."

One could multiply such gleanings : but I turn to passages which tell us more of the man. Here, for instance, is the sentimentalist or social philosopher.

The cow is more especially the poor man's pride, his riches and his support. There are many of our peasantry that have no other possessions but a cow ; and even of the advantages resulting, the poor are but the nominal possessors. In Germany, Poland and Switzerland every peasant keeps two or three cows, not for the benefit of his master, but for himself. The meanest of the peasants there kills one cow at least for his own table, which he salts and hangs up and thus preserves a delicacy all the year round. . . . A piece of beef hung up there is considered as an elegant piece of furniture which though seldom touched at least argues the possession of opulence and ease. But it is very different in our country where, at least for some years past, our lower rustics are utterly unable to purchase meat any part of the year and by them even butter is considered as an article of extravagance.

Elsewhere we have remarks on education, which show that no age has a monopoly of faddists.

When men speculate at liberty upon innate ideas or the abstracted distinctions between will and power, they may be permitted to enjoy their systems at pleasure . . . but when they allege that children are to be kept wet in the feet to prevent them catching cold, and never to be corrected when young for fear of breaking their spirits ; these are such noxious errors that all reasonable men should endeavour to oppose.

I have ever found it a vain task to try to make a child's learning its amusement. . . . The child ought to have its share of play and will be benefited thereby, and for every reason also, it ought to have its share of labour. The child therefore should by times be put to its duty and be taught to know that the task is to be done or the punishment to be endured.

But he is no way blind to the fact that the young often learn most of what is useful to them from other children, and in play. "A child is not idle because it is playing about the fields, or pursuing a butterfly ; it is all the time storing its mind with matter to think about later." Very little system is necessary : "the natural and common course of education is the best."

At times the social philosophy goes deeper.

Men (he held) except at sea, seldom die of absolute hunger ; the decline of those unhappy creatures who are destitute of food on land being more slow and unperceived. Man is unfit for a state of precarious expectation. That share of provident precaution which incites him to lay up stores becomes his torment when totally unprovided. Thus the mind being continually harassed by the situation, it at length influences the constitution and unfits it for all its functions. Some cruel disorder, but in no way like hunger, seizes the unhappy sufferer ; so that all those men who have thus long lived by chance, and whose every day may be considered a happy escape from famine, are known at last to die in reality of a disorder caused by hunger, but which in the common language is called a broken heart. Some of these I have known myself when very little able to relieve them ; and I have been told by a very active and worthy magistrate that the number of such as die in London for want is much greater than one would imagine. I think he talked of two thousand a year. Much greater (he goes on to add) is the number of deaths from repletion.

Such a passage is not far removed from the verse of his poems : a little transposition would make all the change needed. But here is an observation even more closely allied to the central thought of " The Traveller," man's perpetual pursuit of " some superior existence " :

" Even in the womb he begins to feel the want of something he does not possess : a sensation that seems coeval with man's nature and never leaves him till he dies. The embryo even then begins the struggle for a state more marked by pleasure and pain."

We gain also much light on Goldsmith's special disposition and experience ; there is for instance an eloquent and only too well-informed dissertation upon bugs.—He expresses his dislike of the game laws—severe in France but only local : " In England the prohibition is general ; and the peasant has not a right to what even slaves, as he is taught to call them, are found to possess."—Cockfighting is " a mean and ungenerous amusement—declining every day and it is to be hoped will in time become the pastime of the lowest vulgar." Goldsmith adds, no doubt with a characteristic exaggeration of his own powers, that he " could give such instructions with regard to cockfighting and could so arm one of these animals against the other, that it would be almost impossible for the adversary to survive the final onset."

But the most revealing passage that I find is in his dissertation on the human countenance, when he dwells on the special expressiveness of the eye which " not only receives the emotions, but transmits them by sympathy." " Such persons as are shortsighted are in a manner entirely cut off from the language of the eyes, and this gives an air of stupidity to the face which often produces very unfavourable prepossessions. However intelligent we find such persons to be, we can scarcely be brought back from our first prejudice."—When we find this observer going on to emphasize the importance of attention to clothes as an antidote to such prepossessions, we have the reason, or one reason, for Mr. Filby's bills.

But, what principally stays with me from desultory reading of the " Animated Nature " is a sense of Goldsmith's great love for birds. It extended (not so un-

naturally as some may think) to a great interest in all the
methods of birdcatching, of which he gives details. I
have noted earlier his special familiarity with the water-
fowl that abounded about the Shannon and its tributaries ;
and his description of the bittern's booming is well known.
But I had rather dwell on his loving attention to what is
familiar to everyone : the robin's song,—not so strong or
varied as that of other birds, but " soft, tender and well-
supported and the more to be valued as we enjoy it the
greatest part of the winter." Rooks and their " plans of
policy " he watched with patient amusement " from my
window in the Temple " and described all their operations.
But simply as pieces of writing, I had rather quote his
account of what no doubt was daily before his eyes at the
farmer's house in the Edgware Road, though it had been
familiar to him from the beginning of memory : the life
of the ordinary fowl-yard. He is eloquent upon the hen
when she has a family about her. " Her affection and her
pride then seem to alter her very nature "—unselfish and
valiant as she was " voracious and cowardly." " When
marching at the head of her little troop, she acts the
commander, and has a variety of notes to call her numerous
train to their food or to warn them of approaching danger."
And he tells how he had once seen such a commander send
her brood to cover in a hedge while she herself boldly
faced a fox that came to plunder, " till the lookers-on
and a good mastiff routed him."

Much less sympathetic is his study of a creature from
whom all country-bred children have suffered.

The turkey-cock with the insolence of a bully pursues anything
that seems to fear him, particularly lap-dogs and children, against
both of which he seems to have a particular aversion. On such
occasions after he has made them scamper, he returns to his
female train, displays his plumage around, struts about the yard,
and gobbles out a note of self-approbation.

But of all birds in the farmyard, none was so dear to
Oliver Goldsmith as the goose. It is true that in the

"Citizen of the World" he had given an unsympathetic picture of this fowl, "always extremely proud and excessively punctilious. The pond, she said, was hers, and she would maintain a right in it, and support her honour, while she had a bill to hiss or a wing to flutter." Yet in "Animated Nature" full amends is made for these slighting observations, though the tribute is addressed not to the goose but to her lord protector.

The gander visits his female twice or thrice a day, and sometimes drives her off to take her place, where he sits with great state and composure. But beyond that of all animals is his pride when the young are excluded; he seems then to consider himself as a champion, not only obliged to defend his young, but also to keep off the suspicion of danger; he pursues dogs and men that never attempt to molest him; and though the most harmless thing alive, is then the most petulant and provoking. When in this manner he has pursued the calf, or the mastiff, to whose contempt alone he is indebted for safety, he returns to his female and her brood in triumph, clapping his wings, screaming and shewing all the marks of a conscious superiority. It is probable, however, these arts succeed in raising his importance among the tribe when they are displayed; and it is probable that there is not a more respectable animal on earth to a goose than a gander.

That is perfect Goldsmith. He goes on, feelingly:

A young goose is generally accounted very good eating; yet the feathers of this bird still farther increase its value. I feel my obligations to this animal every word I write, for however deficient a man's head may be, his pen is nimble enough upon every occasion; it is happy for us that it requires no great effort to put it in motion.

All these results of careful observation touched with quiet humour have the charm of a Morland picture; and they make his lovers regret that he never acted on the idea which he suggested one day in a conversation that ended in a famous repartee—the only instance when Boswell admits that his hero got the worst of it in such a contest.

Sir Joshua Reynolds was in company with them one day, when

Goldsmith said, that he thought he could write a good fable, mentioned the simplicity which that kind of composition requires, and observed, that in most fables the animals introduced seldom talk in character. " For instance (said he), the fable of the little fishes, who saw birds fly over their heads, and envying them, petitioned Jupiter to be changed into birds. The skill (continued he,) consists in making them talk like little fishes." While he indulged himself in this fanciful reverie, he observed Johnson shaking his sides and laughing. Upon which he smartly proceeded, " Why, Dr. Johnson, this is not so easy as you seem to think ; for if you were to make little fishes talk, they would talk like WHALES."

In fact, I have little doubt but that Goldsmith, given more years, would have attempted a thing that lay so handy to him. The novel he had clearly put aside—and, I think, poetry also. Cooke believed that he would have devoted himself increasingly to the stage, and certainly everything would pull that way. Yet I doubt if a man so curiously limited in the power to invent a plot or a story would have added anything of value to the British repertory. He had won his fight for the Low, and we may be well content to leave it at that. But in fables of birds there was good reason to hope for at least a masterpiece—especially as his thoughts were now turning to a quieter life in some country lodging.

Yet from now on, we have to write of what might have been ; though no one guessed that his days were counted. Boswell, calling on him early in May, 1773, to take leave before his departure for Scotland, little thought that it would be their last meeting. He chronicled assiduously examples of Goldsmith's " jealousy and envy " of the greater man disclosed in that conversation. Johnson was to join Boswell for their projected tour, and Goldsmith said " he would be a dead weight for me to carry, and that I should never be able to lug him along through the Highlands and Hebrides. Nor would he patiently allow me to enlarge upon Johnson's wonderful abilities ; but exclaimed, ' Is he like Burke, who winds into a subject like a serpent ? ' ' But, (said I,) Johnson is the Hercules who strangled serpents in his cradle.' "

Still, it was on this occasion that Boswell saved for us the song designed to be sung by Miss Hardcastle ; and since Macaulay has " dusted his jacket " about this silly repartee, let him depart in peace to his lairdship.

There is one other pleasant thing to write about in this last year of Goldsmith's life.   The rest is unhappily a very sad story.

According to Cumberland (reported by Northcote in his " Life of Reynolds "), after one of the perpetually recurring dinners at Sir Joshua's house, Burke proposed an adjournment to the St. James's Coffee-House, which was afterwards " occasionally repeated with much festivity and good fellowship."

Dr. Barnard, Dean of Derry, Dr. Douglas, afterwards Bishop of Salisbury, Johnson, Garrick, Sir Joshua, Goldsmith, Edmund and Richard Burke, Hickey, an attorney, an Irishman, and a friend of the Burkes, commemorated by Goldsmith, and two or three others, constituted the party.

What happened on one of these occasions is recorded by a principal actor—no less a man than Garrick.

At a meeting of a company of gentlemen, who were well known to each other, and diverting themselves, among many other things, with the peculiar oddities of Dr. Goldsmith, who never would allow a superior in any art, from writing poetry down to dancing a hornpipe, the Doctor with great eagerness insisted upon trying his epigrammatic powers with Mr. Garrick, and each of them was to write the other's epitaph.   Mr. Garrick immediately said that his epitaph was finished, and spoke the following distich extempore :

> Here lies Nolly Goldsmith, for shortness call'd Noll,
> Who wrote like an angel, but talk'd like poor Poll.

Goldsmith, upon the company's laughing very heartily, grew very thoughtful, and either would not, or could not, write anything at that time : however, he went to work, and some weeks later produced the following printed poem called " Retaliation," which has been much admired, and gone through several editions.

The publick in general have been mistaken in imagining that this poem was written in anger by the Doctor; it was just the contrary; the whole on all sides was done with the greatest good humour; and the following poems in manuscript were written by several of the gentlemen on purpose to provoke the Doctor to an answer, which came forth at last with great credit to him in " Retaliation."

Thus the company sketched in a series of portraits by Goldsmith in the poem is not " The Club," but a less select assembly; it includes not only the two lesser Burkes, but Ridge and Hickey, Irish lawyers of no special distinction—who in all probability owed their admission to Goldsmith. The poem opens with an introductory passage, having one or two touches of the retaliating foil:

Of old, when Scarron his companions invited,
Each guest brought his dish, and the feast was united;
If our landlord supplies us with beef, and with fish,
Let each guest bring himself—and he brings the best dish;
Our Dean shall be venison, just fresh from the plains;
Our Burke shall be tongue, with the garnish of brains.

Dropping one or two others, we come to more pointed lines.

Our Garrick's a salad; for in him we see
Oil, vinegar, sugar, and saltness agree:
To make out the dinner, full certain I am,
That Ridge is anchovy, and Reynolds is lamb;
That Hickey's a capon, and, by the same rule,
Magnanimous Goldsmith a gooseberry fool.

As usual, the last laugh and the loudest is kept to be raised against " the Good-natured Man." But retaliation proper begins with the " epitaphs." Dean Barnard gets pride of place and lenient handling, as an honoured visitor, not one of the *habitués*.

If he had any faults, he has left us in doubt,
At least, in six weeks I could not find 'em out.

Then comes Burke, and the lines on him are too well known

to need quotation; yet one circumstance is not often noted concerning the couplet—

> Though fraught with all learning, yet straining his throat,
> To persuade Tommy Townshend to lend him a vote.

Boswell tells us that Goldsmith had used another name here; but when Townshend made unpleasant remarks in Parliament about Johnson's pension, Goldsmith hitched him in for this contemptuous reference: and the shaft has stuck.

The two other Burkes follow and then a dozen couplets are devoted to Cumberland—between whom and Goldsmith there was no love lost. Northcote tells how one day while they sat at dinner in Sir Joshua's house a presentation copy of a poem by Cumberland was brought in. "Goldsmith immediately laid hold of it, and began to read it, and at every line cut almost through the paper with his finger-nail, crying out, 'What d——d nonsense is this?' for the Doctor could not bear to hear of another's fame; when Sir Joshua caught it out of his hands, saying, 'No, no, don't do so; you shall not spoil my book, neither.'" But what Goldsmith detested worst was Cumberland's success in sentimental comedy; these lines are a satire disguised as compliment.

> Here Cumberland lies, having acted his parts,
> The Terence of England, the mender of hearts;
> A flattering painter, who made it his care
> To draw men as they ought to be, not as they are.
> His gallants are all faultless, his women divine
> And comedy wonders at being so fine;
> Like a tragedy queen he has dizen'd her out,
> Or rather like tragedy giving a rout.
> His fools have their follies so lost in a crowd
> Of virtues and feelings, that folly grows proud;
> And coxcombs, alike in their failings alone,
> Adopting his portraits, are pleas'd with their own.
> Say, where has our poet this malady caught,
> Or, wherefore his characters thus without fault?
> Say, was it that vainly directing his view
> To find out men's virtues, and finding them few,

> Quite sick of pursuing each troublesome elf,
> He grew lazy at last, and drew from himself?

After some good-humoured lines on Douglas the critic, we
come to the central effort—the retort to Garrick's pert
little epigram :

> Here lies David Garrick, describe me who can,
> An abridgment of all that was pleasant in man ;
> As an actor, confest without rival to shine ;
> As a wit, if not first, in the very first line :
> Yet, with talents like these, and an excellent heart,
> The man had his failings, a dupe to his art.
> Like an ill-judging beauty, his colours he spread,
> And beplaster'd with rouge his own natural red.
> On the stage he was natural, simple, affecting ;
> 'Twas only that when he was off, he was acting.
> With no reason on earth to go out of his way,
> He turn'd and he varied full ten times a day :
> Though secure of our hearts, yet confoundedly sick,
> If they were not his own by finessing and trick ;
> He cast off his friends, as a huntsman his pack,
> For he knew when he pleas'd he could whistle them back.
> Of praise a mere glutton, he swallow'd what came,
> And the puff of a dunce, he mistook it for fame ;
> 'Till his relish grown callous, almost to disease,
> Who pepper'd the highest was surest to please.
> But let us be candid, and speak out our mind,
> If dunces applauded, he paid them in kind.
> Ye Kenricks, ye Kellys, and Woodfalls so grave,
> What a commerce was yours, while you got and you gave !
> How did Grub-street re-echo the shouts that you rais'd,
> While he was be-Roscius'd, and you were be-prais'd !
> But peace to his spirit, wherever it flies,
> To act as an angel and mix with the skies :
> Those poets, who owe their best fame to his skill,
> Shall still be his flatterers, go where he will,
> Old Shakespeare receive him with praise and with love,
> And Beaumonts and Bens be his Kellys above.

There are incidental kicks, it will be seen, bestowed
here on Goldsmith's special aversions ; but the main

portrait stands out a masterpiece in its kind. It is no doubt a minor kind. Boswell said once, with the usual touch of condescension, that he "liked to hear honest Goldsmith rattle away." Well, here he is, to all appearance rattling away, in a metre that no artist would choose for serious expression. Compare this with Pope's portrait of Addison and the difference of quality is manifest : Pope's masterpiece is charged with passion, a passion often admirably effective in literature, the passion of hate.

Vindictive writing is of all kinds the easiest to succeed with, but it is rare indeed to find satire lasting which has no anger in it. Pope accumulates eloquent praise on his victim only to prepare a contrast that shall give deadly emphasis and added venom to the final stab, when the voice pauses an instant before the blow is delivered :

> Who would not laugh if such a man there be ?
> Who would not weep if Atticus were he ?

But Goldsmith puts his satire first, to close on the affectionate courtesy of a superb compliment.

Yet, and this is characteristic of the man, he must have known that Garrick, swamped with applause, was not likely to be propitiated even by such a tribute when it came mixed with satire ; and we have the evidence of Davies that Garrick was displeased. Now, Goldsmith may have possibly been foolish enough not to foresee this ; but courage is an endearing quality, especially in the weak. The playwright, distressed and dunned never more than at this period, found himself challenged to a bout at repartee by the Lord Paramount of the stage ; and Garrick's good will meant more to him than that of any man in England. Yet, so challenged, he hit back with perfect good-nature but with all the force and dexterity that he could command. Who would not like him the better for this lack of caution ?

Then came another of the lesser sketches, Hickey, the " special attorney," and last of all, a study of the man to whom he had written :

The only dedication I ever made was to my brother because I loved him better than most men. He is since dead. Permit me to inscribe this poem to you.

But Reynolds is not finished: the writer only got so far as to put in a touch of the gentle ironic mockery which he used in drawing the Vicar. We may be certain that here also there would have been some final tribute.

Cunningham says, I do not know on what ground, that Goldsmith intended to have concluded with his own character. It may be. But I wonder if Johnson was deliberately omitted. It seems indeed that he was not at the dinner when the challenge was issued; yet he was so often of the same company that he could easily have been included: and in some of the other effusions to which this gave rise, he appears. My own feeling is that Goldsmith was deterred by a feeling of reverence; that in his own way, which was certainly not Boswell's way, he thought of " the big man " as sacrosanct.

" Retaliation " was not published by its author in print. But Cooke lets us know that Goldsmith was too pleased with it to keep it to himself, and showed it to Burke, pledging him to secrecy. Burke answered that, before he would promise, he must know if it had been shown to anyone else. Goldsmith confessed that he had given a copy to Mrs. Cholmondeley; and very soon Burke by inquiring found that copies had been copied and were in circulation: so that finally the author had to read it at the Club, " where, though *some* praised it, and others *seemed* highly delighted with it," there was a general sense that publication would be " not altogether so proper."

And according to Cooke, the word went round that Goldsmith was not just " the Good-natured Man," a safe mark for any usage; he was treated with a new respect. Observing this, he left " Retaliation," " so he expressed himself to a friend, as a rod in pickle for any future occasion."

CHAPTER XIV

FUNERAL HONOURS

THE rod in pickle was not kept long. Back at Edgware Goldsmith was busy quill-driving, and racking his brains how to raise the wind; then in March, 1774, he moved to the Temple Chambers of which he was trying to sell the lease. Overwork and lack of exercise had brought on a strangury, which was painful, and by the 25th he thought he was in a fever, and against a doctor's advice insisted on taking the famous James's powders, of which there is endless mention in Horace Walpole and other letter-writers of that time. Another doctor, Fordyce, newly elected to the Club, was fetched in, actually from Gerrard Street, and the next week, still another. It was this last consultant, Dr. Turton, who said to him: " Your pulse is in greater disorder than it should be from that degree of fever. Is your mind at ease ? " and got the answer : " No, it is not."

The end came, after convulsions, on April 4.

Walpole writing to Mason, of the death, begins by saying, of course, that the powders would have saved him, but the physicians interfered. " His numerous friends," he goes on, " neglected him shamefully at last as if they had no business with him when it was too serious to laugh " : and he suggests that the epitaphs in " Retaliation " " had perhaps made them not sorry that his own was the first necessary." I see no reason to believe this. Northcote in his own Memoir wrote that Reynolds took charge of the dead man's affairs, and acted as a self-appointed executor. It is good at least to know that what skill could do then was done for him. Howes, one of the several doctors engaged, published an account of the case ; and Dr. Kirkpatrick concludes that the treatment was reasonable, given the resources of the time. He adds also the comforting observation that Goldsmith's unhappy state of mind may have been the effect of his physical condition rather than its cause. We need not believe that his death was due to that fever of the mind produced by anxiety which he himself so feelingly described in the passage concerning destitution which I have quoted elsewhere.[1]

Moreover, if unskilled help—the help of the helpless— could have availed, he had it. The staircase at Brick Court is said to have been filled, while he lay dying, with the poorest of the city, unhappy ones who had known his kindness : very likely among them, the poor sempstresses who begged Cradock to urge that, paid for or unpaid, his work should be sent to them. Cooke does not make any complaint of lack of attention during his illness, but is discontented about the funeral attendance—to which mark of respect he as an Irishman attached great importance.

On the death of Goldsmith (he says), which happened on the 4th of April, 1774, his friends suggested to have him buried in Westminster Abbey, and his pall was to have been supported by the present Marquis of Lansdowne, Lord Louth, Sir Joshua Reynolds, the Hon. Topham Beauclerc, Mr. Edmund Burke, and Mr. Garrick ; but though poets are often caressed during their life-time, it is not uncommon for them to be neglected at their deaths. Like the invited guests in Scripture, most of these gentlemen sent excuses, and a few coffee-house acquaintances of the Doctor's, rather suddenly collected together, attended his remains to the Temple burial-ground, where they were deposited on Saturday evening, the 9th of the same month.

Among these mourners of whom Cooke speaks slightingly, one was Mr. Robert Day, an Irish barrister ; and it is possible that the friend who shared his room and often saw Goldsmith there with him, attended also. This friend was Henry Grattan.

P. 261.

273

There was one tribute paid which probably Goldsmith would have valued beyond any ceremony with the most distinguished pall-bearers. When news of their friend's death reached the Hornecks, they sent instantly to ask a remembrance of him and, Northcote told Hazlitt, " though the coffin was nailed up, it was opened again at their request, such was the regard which Goldsmith was known to have for them, and a lock of his hair cut off." In the next century, perhaps fifty years after Goldsmith's death, it was still in the possession of the Jessamy Bride.

Hazlitt describes in his Seventh " Conversation " an interruption caused " by the entry of the beautiful Mrs. Gwyn, beautiful even in years. After she was gone, I remarked how handsome she still was. In her the Graces had triumphed over time,—she was one of the Ninon de l'Enclos people, of the list of the immortals. I could fancy the shade of Goldsmith in the room looking round with complacency. ' Yes,' said Northcote, ' that is what Sir Joshua used to mention as the severest test of beauty ; it was not skin-deep only. She had gone through all the stages and had lent a grace to each.'"

Let it be remembered of Goldsmith that he was so remembered by such a lady.

The friends of his circle too did not leave him without honour. It was Reynolds, Northcote tells us, who suppressed the idea of a costly public funeral, preferring to apply what money could be procured to a more lasting memorial ; it was Reynolds who went himself to Westminster Abbey and fixed upon the place where the monument now stands over a door in the Poets' Corner. Nollekens was chosen to execute the sculpture, Johnson to compose the epitaph. To my eye it looks as if Reynolds had at least some hand in designing the ornamentation in which the portrait bas-relief is set. At all events the two artists then foremost in painting and sculpture combined with the acknowledged head of letters to produce a worthy monument.

Reynolds chose the site well ; the monument is one

OLIVARII GOLDSMITH
Poetæ, Physici, Historici,
qui nullum fere scribendi genus
non tetigit,
nullum quod tetigit non ornavit;
sive risus essent movendi,
sive lacrimæ,
affectuum potens, at lenis dominator;
ingenio sublimis, vividus, versatilis;
oratione grandis, nitidus, venustus:

Hoc monumento memoriam coluit
Sodalium amor,
Amicorum fides,
Lectorum veneratio.
Natus Hibernia, Forneiæ Lonfordiensis
in loco cui nomen Pallas,
Nov. XXIX, MDCCXXXI.
Eblanæ literis institutus,
Objit Londini.
Apr. IV. MDCCLXXIV.

MEMORIAL TO GOLDSMITH
in the Poets' Corner, Westminster Abbey
By courtesy of the Dean and Chapter

of the few that do not encumber the natural lines of the building : it falls well into its place. Boswell tells how once Johnson and Goldsmith visited Poets' Corner and Johnson quoted Virgil : *Forsitan et nostrum nomen miscebitur istis.*[1] In Poets' Corner the names are indeed together among the elect : Johnson's inscribed on the stone floor, over the place of his actual burial. He has no epitaph, but the name and date. No one, I suppose, felt equal to writing it. When he had written Goldsmith's, the Club would have preferred to have it in English ; and since no one dared to beard the dictator, they wrote a petition in the shape of a Round Robin so that no man's name stood first. Burke presented it : but Johnson snorted out that he would not disgrace the Abbey walls with anything so common.

The Club was right. All that is remembered of the epitaph is the phrase that signifies : " There was hardly any form of literature that he did not put his hand to, and whatever he touched he made elegant." It is the praise of a hack of genius ; and in the opening description, " *poetae*, *physici*, *historici*," Goldsmith is made to figure equally under significant and insignificant attributes. Who wants to remember that he was an historian, or student of medicine and natural history ? There is no doubt as to his versatility ; but, using the word poet as he used it, to cover all work of invention whether in prose or verse, it was as a poet that he was so amazingly versatile. We know exactly what Johnson really meant, from this recorded dialogue.

Johnson. " Take him as a poet, his ' Traveller ' is a very fine performance ; ay, and so is his ' Deserted Village,' were it not sometimes too much the echo of his ' Traveller.' Whether, indeed, we take him as a poet,—as a comick writer,—or as an historian, he stands in the first class." *Boswell.* " An his-

---

[1] The story goes on to say that as they walked back to Fleet Street, passing under Temple Bar, Goldsmith chuckled as he quoted, " *Forsitan et nostrum nomen miscebitur istis,*" and pointed to the Jacobite skulls still mouldering on top.

torian! My dear Sir, you surely will not rank his compilation of the Roman History with the works of other historians of this age?" *Johnson.* "Why, who are before him? *Boswell.* "Hume—Robertson,—Lord Lyttelton." *Johnson.* (His antipathy to the Scotch beginning to rise.) "I have not read Hume; but, doubtless, Goldsmith's History is better than the verbiage of Robertson, or the foppery of Dalrymple." *Boswell.* "Will you not permit the superiority of Robertson, in whose history we find such penetration—such painting?" *Johnson.* "Sir, you must consider how that penetration and that painting are employed. It is not history, it is imagination. . . . Besides, Sir, it is the great excellence of a writer to put into his book as much as his book will hold. Goldsmith has done this in his History. Now Robertson might have put twice as much into his book. . . . Goldsmith tells you shortly all you want to know: Robertson detains you a great deal too long. No man will read Robertson's cumbrous detail a second time; but Goldsmith's plain narrative will please again and again. . . . Sir, he has the art of compiling, and of saying everything he has to say in a pleasing manner. He is now writing a Natural History, and will make it as entertaining as a Persian Tale."

This well-known passage should be taken in conjunction with some observations of Johnson's on his own work.

Upon his mentioning that when he came to College he wrote his first exercise twice over, but never did so afterwards: *Miss Adams.* "I suppose, Sir, you could not make them better? *Johnson.* "Yes, Madam, to be sure I could make them better. Thought is better than no thought." *Miss Adams.* "Do you think, Sir, you could make your Ramblers better?" *Johnson.* "Certainly, I could." *Boswell.* "I'll lay a bet, Sir, you cannot." *Johnson.* "But I will, Sir, if I choose. I shall make the best of them you shall pick out, better." *Boswell.* "But you may add to them. I will not allow of that." *Johnson.* "Nay, Sir, there are three ways of making them better;—putting out,—adding,—or correcting."

Now, my quarrel with Johnson is that he lumps together those parts of Goldsmith's works which could often have been improved (generally by excisions) and those others, like the "Vicar of Wakefield" and many of the essays—

to say nothing of the poems—where it is evident that the highest degree of finish has been attained without sacrifice of ease. In short, Johnson misunderstood Goldsmith as a writer; and the only part of his epitaph which has life in it, praises dexterous versatility. The eulogistic epithets of the close are as dead as old sermons—and not because they are in Latin: witness Swift's epitaphs: witness the part of this in which Johnson expressed what he really felt strongly. And in spite of ourselves we must always be affected by Johnson's judgment of Goldsmith. We cannot think of one man without calling up an image of the other. Foote, we all know, was going to mimic Johnson on the stage, and was prevented by Johnson's intimation that he would buy an oak stick—not such as were commonly sold for sixpence, but a shilling's worth of oak stick. But Cradock lets us know that Foote's project was to mimic Johnson and Goldsmith together in a " double turn."

Doctor Major and Doctor Minor, they come down to us together, and we must look to Johnson for help in a final appraisement. Here is his announcement to Boswell of their friend's death:

Of poor dear Dr. Goldsmith there is little to be told, more than the papers have made publick. He died of a fever, made, I am afraid, more violent by uneasiness of mind. His debts began to be heavy, and all his resources were exhausted. Sir Joshua is of opinion that he owed not less than two thousand pounds. Was ever poet so trusted before?

What he wrote next day to Bennet Langton is even more significant.

Chambers, you find, is gone far, and poor Goldsmith is gone much further. He died of a fever, exasperated, as I believe, by the fear of distress. He had raised money and squandered it, by every artifice of acquisition and folly of expense. But let not his frailties be remembered; he was a very great man.

Every word in that, as was said of Bright's speeches, seems to weigh a pound: and not least the last one. We are bound to ask what it implies. A great man must have courage. Goldsmith showed that in his independence, his refusal of work that he considered to be unworthy, his disdain of interested dedications ; but most of all he showed literary courage in disregard of current false standards in taste. Yet I do not think that Johnson was aware of this value in his friend : at least, if he was, we find no expression of it. He meant by greatness some intellectual quality ; and we know that he thought meanly of Goldsmith's knowledge. There is no doubt of his admiration for the literary craftsman : but would that have made him use a phrase so emphatic as " a very great man " ? I think that in reality we have here an impressive tribute to that quality in Goldsmith which was least apparent in ordinary life : Johnson realized his wisdom. " No man was wiser when he had a pen in his hand." The " very great man " was, to Johnson, the moral teacher.

As such, Goethe praised Goldsmith ; as such the world at large has accepted him so completely that even the hint of frailties in him will be resented by many. But as such his contemporaries found it difficult to consider him : and the better they knew him, the greater the incongruity appeared. It is emphasized in the character sketch which Garrick produced after " Retaliation " had been passed from hand to hand.

Here, Hermes ! says Jove, who with nectar was mellow,
Go fetch me some clay—I will make an odd fellow.
Right and wrong shall be jumbled,—much gold and some
    dross ;
Without cause be he pleas'd, without cause be he cross ;
Be sure, as I work, to throw in contradictions,
A great lover of truth, yet a mind turn'd to fictions ;
Now mix these ingredients, which, warm'd in the baking,
Turn to learning and gaming, religion and raking.
With the love of a wench, let his writings be chaste ;
Tip his tongue with strange matter, his pen with fine taste ;
That the rake and the poet o'er all may prevail,
Set fire to his head, and set fire to his tail ;
For the joy of each sex, on the world I'll bestow it,
This scholar, rake, Christian, dupe, gamester, and poet.

It is not possible to say with certainty which of these were the "frailties" that Johnson desired to have forgotten. He was not over-censorious : "Steele, I believe," he said to Boswell, "practised the lighter vices." This probably included occasional tipsiness, a lighter vice from which Goldsmith was free and Boswell was not. It may include gaming, and probably some sexual irregularities. Concerning play, Goldsmith, if pressed, would have said that he never played high ; nor did he, by the standards of his time. But Cradock says that whenever he got a matter of thirty pounds he would go to certain companions in the country hoping to double it—and come back empty. Even at the Bunburys' house, play was the fashion, and we have an amusing epistle from him, part verse and part prose, which describes a game of cards at the end of which—"Why, the Doctor is looed." And no doubt he often lost five pounds in an hour when five pounds meant a week's work to him.

His addiction to women must have been notorious, to judge by Garrick's skit ; and even if Johnson had set that down among the "lighter vices," it would have ranked high in the "follies of expense." Broadly, I think, what angered Johnson to the heart was the thought that his friend had squandered health and happiness in squandering money, until the torment of worry made an end of life itself.

It is right to recall that the spending was often in response to pity. Glover has a story how Goldsmith was once at cards in a friend's house and suddenly rushed from the table and disappeared. His host, thinking he had been taken ill, went to look for him but found him returning, and asked what had been the matter. "It was the voice of that ballad-singer outside the window," he said. "She sounded so miserable I could not bear it any longer." So he ran out with his largess.—But we have to say to ourselves that if he earned a blessing with half a crown, he very probably dropped as much money at the cards as made a serious matter for his tailor.

At all events we may be reasonably sure that Johnson did not judge his conduct too severely ; and it seems that in those last months, weeks and days, he paid the price, with increasing torment.

What was it, then, that caused so much disquiet on that sick-bed ? Money troubles ? They were no new thing. Yet Goldsmith had always been able to believe that he could somehow or other work off the booksellers' advances, but now doubtless the thought was present that the opportunity might not be his. He may have known indeed (though he could hardly have guessed the full extent of their future profitableness) that the trade had works of his, bought for a lump sum, which would bring in returns through the years, handsomely cancelling out all indebtedness. But there was Mr. William Filby, tailor : there were probably a score of petty creditors whose needs, as he could never forget, were like his own. Cradock tells in his Memoirs of two little women, sempstresses or laundresses, who begged that he would make Goldsmith continue to come to them for what he required. " We would work for him for nothing," they said, " and we know he would pay us if he could." The sick man as he lay tossing may have been tormented by the certainty that these kind souls must go short of their due, since the day would never come when he could pay them.

But I doubt if to one who had been all his adult life a debtor many such scruples were left. Death itself was the trouble. It was hard for any man to live much with Johnson and not be somewhat affected by a morbid dwelling on the fear of death. Yet the normal average enjoying man, and Goldsmith was such a man, is not normally beset by terror of " dumb forgetfulness," or by any clinging to " the warm precincts of the pleasant day." Even when death is most abnormally close in a hundred chances, he does, as we all learnt, go about his business enduring and enjoying, in a very normal state of mind ; and I do not believe that the thought of death was much present to Goldsmith while he was able to run about.

But on a sick-bed it was another matter. " Be a good man, my dear," the dying Sir Walter said to Lockhart, " be a religious man ; nothing else will be of any use to you when you come to lie here." He did not say anything about avoiding debt. Goldsmith was, it is clear, a simple believing Christian, just as Sir Walter was ; but when he came to " lie there," I do not think he could find in his conscience the consolations which Sir Walter had—and which, it seems, were of great comfort to Mr. Pitt. When it came to dying, Mr. Pitt was able to reflect on " the innocency of his life." Now Mr. Pitt's financial affairs were just as badly involved as Oliver Goldsmith's ; but that did not trouble him. He remembered that he had observed his religious duties, and especially that he kept the commandment which to the English race means " morality." Goldsmith, I fear, held himself sadly a sinner in these respects, and suffered because he had not done those things which in his sincere faith a good man should do, and had done those things which a good man should not.

Well, of late, another Oliver, very different from Oliver Goldsmith, having in common nothing but the gift of humour, has been picturing Mr. Pitt face to face with the Recording Angel and putting up this plea of " innocency " —only to find that the judge is solely concerned to know what he did in his special and proper business, the service of his country. Mr. Pitt's answer on that matter gives entire satisfaction to the court.

For my own part, I cannot imagine a recording angel— provided the angel was a Christian—who would be severe on Oliver Goldsmith. If, however, he were an angel in the likeness of Thomas Carlyle (which is very much as many have pictured that august officer), we know that he would have had a cordial welcome for the big overbearing Englishman and his big dictionary : but we may well believe that the spendthrift, dissolute, blundering little Irishman would have found small grace. Industry, he might have pleaded ; but then he would be told that he should be ashamed to look back on a life of transplanting knowledge which better men had sweated to amass. What facts had he discovered, established or ascertained? And if Goldsmith had stammered out something about carrying on "my father's business," he would have been knocked down with an iron-bound volume of the Old Testament.

I fear we have to admit that in his last hours Goldsmith was tortured by fear of the Recording Angel; and that he found no consolation in the prospect of a lift in the Fame Machine.

There, however, we can be sure of ourselves. The coachman would have said to his anxious passenger— "What is all this baggage? I have no room for works in many volumes. But I notice under your other arm, where the load is not so heavy, two books of verse which take up very little space; two plays also, and plays, if they be good, are a sure passport. And from your left breast-pocket I see the corner of a romance peeping out. Something tells me that I can carry that work to any destination you may be pleased to name. These Essays too and some pleasant trifles may go along with us. You can leave the rest behind; they may serve to satisfy those persons whom I see approaching, as if they wished to detain you for their own purposes. Pray step in at once, Sir."

Assuredly, the Fame Machine carried Goldsmith's name and works to many lands. Yet the tribute of his admirers is most conspicuous, where it should be, at the centre of Dublin, where all the strains that make up Ireland meet and mingle. Goldsmith was never, like Swift, Ireland's champion; but—unlike Swift—he never wrote a line that sharpened Irish divisions or added to bitterness between England and Ireland. He has therefore been accepted without partisanship as one of Ireland's glories; and whatever dreams of commemoration he may have cher-

Photo: T. H. Mason, Dublin.

STATUE OF GOLDSMITH
by Foley at the gate of Trinity College, Dublin

ished were surely more than fulfilled when his statue was set up facing College Green beside that of Edmund Burke. These were the men chosen to represent the pride of Dublin University, out of a list that included also, to name two only, Swift and Berkeley. And in that splendid association Goldsmith came first; from 1864 onwards he had his place on the right hand of the gate; five years later, Burke balanced him on the left. Both statues, provided from public subscription, were the work of a great Irish sculptor. Yet I have always thought that Foley succeeded better with the homely downlooking student than with the august orator.

If there is irony in the thought that Goldsmith should be so honoured in the place where he had his first and bitterest experience of humiliation, what was his life but one long series of incongruities? and there is a grace about his memory which can rob irony of its sting.

Yet the same mocking contrast lurks about the latest and most touching monument to his memory. Forty years ago, Sir Walter Besant and other men of letters raised funds for a memorial window to be placed in Forgney Church where Oliver Goldsmith's father and his brother had each in his turn the cure of bodies and souls. There was public competition for designs. In the one chosen, an Irish designer, Mr. Watson, of Youghal, suggests Sweet Auburn and its church in the background, but shows in front the good clergyman exhorting his flock. Over this main design is inset a medallion with the poet's head in profile.[1] But the clergyman himself, whether we take him to stand for Charles Goldsmith, Henry Gold-

---

[1] The inscription on the window reads:

" To the Glory of God and in memory of Oliver Goldsmith born in this Parish Nov. 29th, 1728."

There is also a brass tablet beside the window with the following inscription:

" To the Glory of God and in memory of Oliver Goldsmith, Poet, Novelist, Playwright, born in this parish, of which his father was for 12 years curate. This window is erected by lovers of the man and of his genius. 21 August 1897."

smith, or the Vicar of Wakefield, has assuredly the likeness of Oliver, the disorderly Bohemian prodigal son, who never returned. Yet to the home and the altar, to all that this church window represents, no one was ever so constant as this incorrigible vagabond. In the Alps, in London slums, in his chambers in the Temple or his farm-house by the Edgware Road, his memory ceaselessly framed images of the simple pieties and pleasures in which he was nurtured, and used them to illustrate his homebred philosophy. While he lived, life itself was too hard for the philosopher; he never had the best of the argument. But once death cleared away that superficial jumble of frailties, the essential man stood out; a teacher with the finest sense of values, whose wisdom commended itself by gentle yet searching laughter, but a teacher just as fully convinced of his right and duty to teach as any vicar that ever stood in the pulpit of Forgney—or of Wakefield.

INDEX

Printed in Great Britain by Butler & Tanner Ltd., Frome and London